If human beings are not simply rational ar but storytelling animals, what are the imp ogetics? In our post-Christian society, the l "the greatest story ever told," if it is told at a... ...ay, various stories pit one community's identity and interests against others. Accordingly, those who wish to defend gospel truth must learn how to recover the plausibility, goodness, and beauty of the Bible's account of what God is doing through Jesus Christ to make things right. *Telling a* Better *Story* proceeds with proper confidence to do just that. Josh Chatraw is faithfully attuned to the biblical text while listening with one ear cocked to the various cultural texts (including films) that compete for the attention and allegiance of our hearts and minds. The way forward, he rightly argues, is to show that the Christian story answers our burning questions and leads to flourishing communities. By telling a better story, and embodying it, we "take captive every thought to make it obedient to Christ."

KEVIN J. VANHOOZER, research professor of systematic theology, Trinity Evangelical Divinity School

The gospel is, first of all, a *true* story, but it is a story after all. With intellectual verve and winsome charm, *Telling a* Better *Story* not only tells but shows how the gospel outnarrates all the other plots offered. Only when our apologetics reaches the imagination of our story-starved age will it be compelling. This book does just that. Definitely a must-read!

MICHAEL HORTON, J. Gresham Machen professor of systematic theology and apologetics, Westminster Seminary

If we are to be compelling witnesses for Jesus, we can't offer answers to questions people are no longer asking. Apologetics, then, is never a static endeavor. It requires listening as well as talking—which makes *Telling a* Better *Story* an essential book for equipping the church. Using a broad array of sources, Joshua Chatraw has incisively explored the reigning cultural scripts and illuminated the beauty and coherence of the gospel by contrast. This is a book to underline, to study, and to discuss in groups. I look forward to recommending it widely.

JEN POLLOCK MICHEL, award-winning author of *Surprised by Paradox* and *Keeping Place*

Joshua Chatraw issues a call to maturity in this remarkable and stirring book, which tells the "better story" of Jesus Christ. Much as many may want to ignore or dismiss Jesus, he does not give us that option, even nearly two thousand years later. I can't wait to share this book with friends and family who do not yet believe. And I will teach this book in my church too, so we never forget that the Christian story is not only true but also beautiful.

COLLIN HANSEN, author of *Blind Spots: Becoming a Courageous, Compassionate, and Commissioned Church*

Josh Chatraw points to a better way to do apologetics in our increasingly fragmented world—a way that is more sensitive to beauty, more winsome, and more comprehensively related to human experience. This book will help believers share their faith in a way that actually makes sense to secular people around them—and not only logical sense, but cultural and emotional sense too. All Christians who want to share the gospel more effectively in our current cultural setting should read this book!

GAVIN ORTLUND, senior pastor,
First Baptist Church of Ojai

An extraordinary exegete of both Scripture and society, Joshua Chatraw has become a leading thinker and writer about what a powerful and penetrating apologetic strategy requires in our late-modern age. Mining insights from the likes of C. S. Lewis, Charles Taylor, Augustine, and many others, he shows readers inspiring and innovative ways to generate substantive conversations about God—starting with more intentional listening. Dialogical and engaging, irenic and relational, his "inside out" approach highlights how the cross of Christ can best meet our most compelling existential needs—for meaning and morality, beauty and hope, love and worship—and satisfy our deepest human hungers and highest aspirations. The wild truth of Christianity makes it eminently worthwhile to learn how best to tear down barriers and build bridges of trust and understanding. This book will help you do just that.

DAVID BAGGETT, professor of philosophy and
director of the Center for Moral Apologetics,
Houston Baptist University

Telling a *Better* Story

Telling a *Better* Story

How to Talk About God in a Skeptical Age

Joshua D. Chatraw

ZONDERVAN REFLECTIVE

Telling a Better *Story*

Requests for information should be addressed to:
Zondervan, *3900 Sparks Dr. SE, Grand Rapids, Michigan 49546*

ISBN 978-0-310-10863-4 (softcover)

ISBN 978-0-310-10865-8 (audio)

ISBN 978-0-310-10864-1 (ebook)

Cover design: Emily Weigel
Cover image: © banyumilistudio / shutterstock
Interior design: Kait Lamphere

Printed in the United States of America

HB 03.12.2024

To my brother Ben,
who lives the Better Story

"I looked for something to love, lover of loving that I was."

SAINT AUGUSTINE, *CONFESSIONS*

"But the little sticky leaves, and the precious tombs, and the blue sky, and the woman you love! How will you live, how will you love them?"

ALYOSHA, *THE BROTHERS KARAMAZOV*

"For who knows what is good for a person in life, during the few and meaningless days they pass through like a shadow? Who can tell them what will happen under the sun after they are gone?"

TEACHER, ECCLESIASTES 6:12

"Oh, how I wish this could last forever. And yet change mocks us with her beauty."

OLAF, *FROZEN 2*

"It is for this reason that the present age is better than Christendom. In the old Christendom, everyone was a Christian and hardly anyone thought twice about it. But in the present age the survivor of theory and consumption becomes a wayfarer in the desert, like St. Anthony; which is to say, open to signs."

WALKER PERCY, *SIGNPOSTS IN A STRANGE LAND*

Contents

Foreword

On October 22, 2014, Josh Chatraw invited me to meet with him at the Starbucks on the campus where we both taught. He had an ambitious agenda for us: design a book proposal for a reimagined apologetic. Between sips of coffee, he shared with great clarity vital aspects of his vision for apologetics. Perhaps most importantly, along with being cross-shaped and cross-centered, it would be an "integrative, relevant, and culturally engaging" approach. We pitched the idea to Zondervan—they liked it, and away we went.

For nearly three years, we met every Friday for breakfast to talk about how to help people have better apologetic conversations. Besides that, our offices were right next to each other—fertile ground for his creative juices. I remember distinctly the day Josh walked into my office (okay, it may have been more like a sprint) and optimistically unpacked his construal of the "inside out" structure. I realized he was on to something innovative yet very basic to doing apologetics in our late-modern context. It was a simple, user-friendly apologetic tool for our times, yet grounded in a theology as ancient as Jesus Christ's incarnation and as epic as Augustine's *The City of God*. Since the release of *Apologetics at the Cross: An Introduction for Christian Witness* in the spring of 2018, the "inside out" method has been received and used enthusiastically.

Today, Josh serves as an apologetic practitioner in Raleigh, North Carolina, where he daily works out his apologetic approach at a street level. Yet, while serving as the theologian in residence at Holy Trinity Church, directing the New City Fellows, and creating the newly launched Center for Public Christianity, Josh has not lost pace on his literary output. He has coauthored and coedited two more texts with Zondervan: *Cultural Engagement: A Crash Course in Contemporary Issues* and *The History of Apologetics: A Biographical and Methodological Introduction.*

As is evident in his practitioner and publishing life, Josh continues to develop his vision for a reimagined apologetics. In this most recent book, *Telling a Better Story*, he broadens the appeal and use of the "inside out" method by integrating it more clearly and helpfully with gospel storytelling. Through a narrative approach, he demonstrates for the reader how to situate life's biggest questions within God's big story. He locates our quest for meaning, a true self, happiness, inclusion, and reason within the unfolding drama of God's better story of redemption in Jesus Christ.

Telling a Better Story is the result of Josh's creativity and his persistent cultivation of a fresh vision for apologetics. It is the next step in a storied approach that equips believers for fruitful apologetic conversations. Read it and reap.

Mark D. Allen

Introduction

At one time in the West, Christianity seemed plausible because elements of the Christian story were intentionally woven into the fabric of everyday life. Leading institutions, daily practices, and common communication assumed realities such as a heavenly realm, a transcendent moral code, sin, divine judgment, and the possibility of ultimate redemption. These formed the tacit background of much of the culture's everyday stories, the tapestry of meaning by which people lived. At the very least, the belief in God—and more specifically the God of the Bible—seemed a viable option for most and was generally viewed as a positive influence on society. For many believers, Christianity had an assumed credibility that allayed doubts. The critiques were still there, but they didn't feel as weighty.

Now the cultural narratives that seep into our psyches have changed, and with this shift, what people view as "common sense" has changed as well. The basic categories assumed in the Christian story are no longer taken for granted. And in many cases, this gospel story is presumed to not only be false, but an oppressive leftover from the past.

Living in this increasingly post-Christian context means believers should no longer expect the ministry strategies of a bygone friendlier context to be as effective. In more secular contexts (in major cities or with just about anyone under the age of around forty), the need to have a practical apologetic—a way to make a defense and appeal for Christianity—is as vital as ever.

Part 1 of this book answers the questions of ***what*** has changed, ***why*** this matters, and ***how*** apologetics can be applied in everyday life. Part 2 provides trajectories for engaging others with the gospel using a framework called "inside out." Because, as the philosopher Charles Taylor has written, "we are in fact all acting, thinking, and feeling out of backgrounds and frameworks which we do not fully understand,"[1] it is these frameworks or, as we will refer to them, stories that we must learn to interact with. The challenge is that most of these stories loom in the background of people's lives, framing what is good, true, and beautiful without them being fully aware of the script. "Inside out" offers a way to interact with these shifting plausibility structures and with our culture's most popular story lines, while keeping the gospel at the center. The aim of these chapters is not to improve your storytelling in general, but rather to model a way to tell God's story as a ***better*** story than its rival stories. Part 3 explores three general challenges posed to the Christian story itself: (1) Is the Christian story oppressive? (2) Is it an unloving story? (3) Is it simply not true? We will see that while these challenges aren't to be taken lightly, they also serve as opportunities to contrast secular scripts with God's story and to speak with the faith, hope, and love that emanates from the One who entered into our story.

NOTES

1. Charles Taylor, *A Secular Age* (Cambridge, MA: Harvard University Press, 2007), 387.

PART
1

A Better Story about Apologetics

chapter

1

In Search of a Better Way

Once upon a time, our descendants gathered around campfires and told stories to explain the world. By passing down primitive tales, they gave each other myths to provide meaning and direction in life. That was then. But now we've come of age. Science, reason, and technology have freed us from the captivity of such enchanted fairy tales. We now have our computers, algorithms, and common-sense reason as our guides to live better lives and to make a better world.[1]

Or so we're told.

The problem with this "anti-story" tale is that no one escapes the need for stories. We may invent new technology, but we aren't doing away with them. We are just inventing new mediums by which to pass them down. The likes of Netflix, Amazon, and YouTube have replaced our sage elders around the campfire, but the stories are still being told. Our big, life-explaining stories (often called metanarratives) are communicated through a myriad of smaller stories we hear and tell each day, and they frame how we live and answer the big questions of life. Who are we? What is the meaning of life? What is the fundamental problem, and how can it be fixed? Is there reason to have hope?

THE NEED TO LISTEN CLOSELY

Christians should pay close attention to how, even in the most "enlightened" modern cultures, our novels and movies remind us of the human hunger for something beyond this world. Tim Keller recounts how prior to the release of the first *Lord of the Rings* movie, "there was a host of articles by literary critics and other cultural elites lamenting the popular appeal of fantasies, myths, and legends, so many of which (in their thinking) promoted regressive views. Modern people are supposed to be more realistic. We should realize that things are not black and white but gray, that happy endings are cruel because life is not like that."[2]

He cites an article in *The New Yorker* that chides fans of Tolkien's novel: "It is a book that bristles with bravado, and yet to give in to it—to cave in to it [to really enjoy it] as most of us did on a first reading—betrays . . . a reluctance to face the finer shades of life, that verges on the cowardly."[3] Yet despite such calls for "realism," we can't seem to help ourselves. The popularity of *Stranger Things* and *Marvel* superhero movies, as well as the intergenerational *Star Wars* craze, reveals that it is not just "realistic" narratives we crave. As Alan Jacobs observes, the love of such fantastical stories and a fascination with the paranormal aren't signs that this story of enlightened disenchantment has failed to color the lenses by which we view the world, but that it generally has—"and sometimes we hate it."[4] It's as if we have inherited glasses that screen out the vision of an otherworldly hope to supposedly give us a view of "how it really is," and yet something deep inside us can't help but long to continue the search.

We live in an age where people imagine they have cast off ancient but erroneous wisdom for the wisdom of modern ideals. Our world is now one where "what you see is what you get," and thus personal freedom and self-expression have become salvific ends. Consumerism and pop psychotherapy are the means. And yet, as we will see later, our modern scripts have often not worked out so well for us. The pursuit of individual freedom has meant losing true love. Consumerism has led to despair. And our pop psychology has removed neither our guilt nor our anger. And with the loss of a traditional understanding of sin, we've also lost the resources needed to truly forgive and find peace with one another. The cultural narratives that promised heaven on earth have instead led us to a very different place.

Something's missing. There is a shallowness that gnaws away at the fleeting happiness these narratives offer. The realities of life have a way of applying such pressure that at times even the cynic can't help but peer into the secular crevasses beneath his feet. People can't help but feel the existential angst when the script they've assumed begins to break down. "But what other story is there?"

Don't assume that those who begin to look for a better story or even resist modernity's disenchanted version of the world—peeking over the edge and wondering, *Maybe there is another story that makes better sense?*—will automatically turn to Christianity. They might dabble in new spiritual quests out of curiosity in the search for something more, or maybe just for the novelty of it.[5] At times, people unsatisfied with the loss of transcendence reach for a vague "invent it yourself" spirituality that calls for little to no sacrifice, no final judgment, and no real inconvenience to modern sensibilities, all the while promising your best life now. (They might even mistakenly think this is Christianity!) No matter which option is selected, to remain in a reductionistic mechanical world or one of the reactionary cafeteria-style "spiritual" choices, Christianity often still seems implausible.

While the perspective of our Christian ancestors and their common-sense, "can't imagine it otherwise" belief in an enchanted world and divine accountability seems a long way from today, one piece of good news is that stories haven't gone out of style. For all our cultural distance, we're still gathering to tell stories and to be shaped by them. We attempt to explain the world through story. And the stories we tell turn around and explain us.[6] Consequently, even when a culture seems to have abandoned the gospel, they haven't abandoned story. They can't. Stories, both big worldview stories that remain unarticulated by many and the small micro-stories we interact with in our daily lives, provide a way into their world—and a bridge into sharing God's story.

This book is about engaging the deepest aspirations of our secular friends and asking them to consider how the story of the gospel, as strange as it may seem to them at first, just may lead them to what their heart has been looking for all along. This, of course, will mean asking them to do some thinking (and us doing some thinking and rethinking of our own), as well as challenging them to be as critical with their unbelief as they are with the possibility of belief. This also will mean coming alongside others, not with a posture of opposition, but rather with a posture of invitation: "Come, taste and see."

IN DESPERATE NEED OF HOPE

As I was completing this book, a friend's younger brother died unexpectedly. By the time I caught up with my friend by phone, a week had passed. He was still grieving, but I was also surprised by how he was processing the tragedy. I could hear a hopeful confidence in his voice. I knew that for the last five or six years, he had been maturing in his faith. And in talking with him, my own spirit was lifted as we reflected on the love of God, the resurrection of our Savior, and the life to come.

His brother's death pressed home a sense of urgency about the salvation of his loved ones. While the brother who had passed away was a believer, another brother remained a skeptic. Over the past week, he had watched his brother grieve without any hope. My friend had invited his brother to accompany him to church numerous times over the past years with little success. He had shared the gospel with him, but had seen no response.

This brother had grown up attending church but had grown increasingly cynical in graduate school, and Christianity seemed far-fetched. My friend had given him a popular apologetic book that made traditional arguments in support of Christianity in the hope that they could discuss the book together, but it didn't get any traction. It quickly became clear that the popular apologetic "moves" that had been suggested for reaching his brother just weren't going to work.

As he described his frustration to me, my friend confessed that he didn't want to argue with his brother; he simply wanted to talk, to have conversations that might lead him out of his skepticism. As I listened, I couldn't help but smile at the Lord's timing, realizing that this book was written for the need my friend had shared. Like many believers today, he needed a way to winsomely communicate the gospel to people shaped by a culture that is in desperate need of hope, yet skeptical of religious faith.

A CHALLENGE FOR EVANGELISM

Until recently, most outreach strategies have focused on verbally sharing the gospel, getting unbelievers to attend an evangelistic event, being able to answer basic intellectual questions, yet still assuming that unbelievers understood and shared a common framework for considering religious claims. This approach worked when we lived in a culturally Christian society—the context in which most of our past outreach strategies were developed. Christianity was seen as a cultural good, something that helped society flourish and function well. "Good" people went to church. Attending religious events such as revivals or church services—the primary vehicles for the Christian message—was both implicitly and explicitly encouraged. Our society had a general respect for religion, so you could stick to inviting people to church, passing down our faith to our own kids by teaching them the Bible, and occasionally sending someone to the "experts" when a hard question arose.

If you haven't noticed, things have changed. Today, there is a growing social sentiment that discourages people from attending "churchy" events or even seriously considering the Christian message. But why is this so?

A shift has occurred in Western culture. Not only is God absent from the fabric of our most important institutions and cultural centers, but an array of competing views about life's most important questions are available to the public. Religious belief is simply one option among many—and an increasing number see it as a strange one at that.[7] More than just disagreements over minor details, it increasingly feels like we aren't even in the same ballpark on our thinking about the most important questions of life. One only needs to spend a few minutes on social media to see that what seems like "common sense" to one group may sound like lunacy to another. We may use similar vocabulary, but buried beneath our disagreements are different assumptions about life and its meaning and purpose, about reason and morality. People have so many misunderstandings, critiques, and fears about Christianity, it's hard to even know where to begin.

In addition to the challenge of effective communication within this context, the attempt itself to convert is often seen as morally questionable because it requires telling people that their very identities must change (and, of course, in an important sense, they are right!). It's fine to say that Christianity works for you personally, but claiming that Christianity is the *only* way is exclusive and intolerant. A private faith may be a good thing for you personally (as long as you're not too extreme about it), but calling for someone else to change their religious views is intolerant, if not dehumanizing ("This is who I am!"). Such a cultural climate can lead to strange looks when we invite our secular friends to church and awkward conversations when we share Christ. If we're honest, we can easily be tempted to keep our faith to ourselves.

As we find ourselves in an increasingly post-Christian culture, approaches that assume people will come to hear a famous speaker (for example, traditional revivals) will be largely ineffective in this environment. People aren't waiting around for a relationship with God or for their "sins" to be divinely forgiven—something that most of the standard evangelistic programs of the last fifty years assumed.

Yet we need to keep things in perspective. This is not the first time the church has faced such challenges. Larry Hurtado, who specialized in early Christianity, provided a helpful summary on the early church's place within culture:

> Early Christianity of the first three centuries was a different, even distinctive, kind of religious movement in the cafeteria of religious options of the time . . . In the eyes of many in the Roman era, Christianity was very odd, even objectionably so . . . Even among those who took the time to acquaint themselves more accurately with Christian beliefs, practices, and text, the response was often intensely negative.[8]

It's striking how similar their situation was to ours today. In order to meet the challenges of modern pluralism, we would do well to learn from our beginnings. The church was born in a pluralistic society with little to no access to cultural power and was ridiculed, when it was not just ignored. At the same time, however, we can't directly translate their approach to our context as if nothing has changed. Much has.

One difference is that Christians are no longer the "new kids on the block." In the early church, Christians were seen as strange and even as a potential threat (not unlike today), but we had yet to wield power . . . or abuse it. In the West today, Christianity is increasingly viewed as authoritarian and coercive, both because of its dark chapters of violence and forced conversion (e.g., the imperial era, the Crusades) and because of its exclusivity and moral demands. Opponents of Christianity are no longer simply arguing that it is untrue or illogical, but also that it's dangerously oppressive. Many of the ethical commands of Christianity and the concept of divine judgment fly in the face of the prevailing norms of our culture. These kinds of moral issues are *the* chief apologetic challenge of our age. More than anything else, they make non-Christians deeply question the beauty and goodness of our faith. Central to our task, then, is learning how to help others see the splendor of God and his purposes by reimagining the world through the Christian story.

A CHALLENGE FOR DISCIPLESHIP

Living in a secular age also means that the way people believe has changed. Faith has become far more fragile. Christians now face a dizzying array of religious and nonreligious options for belief, many of which are held by intelligent and admirable people. Many feel the constant pressure of the skeptical currents they swim against daily and confess that swimming against their own personal doubts can be exhausting. A favorite passage of many of my Christian university students has been Mark 9:24—"I do believe; help me overcome my unbelief!"—because it epitomizes their regular struggle with faith. And it isn't just young people who feel this pressure. *New York Times* columnist and Yale professor David Brooks, who recently converted to Christianity, has described how much he has needed "persistence to faith through doubts . . . persistence in faith through suffering and anxiety . . . persistence in faith through struggle."[9] J. K. Rowling, the author of the international bestselling *Harry Potter* series, makes a similar confession about her faith in the Christian promise of an afterlife: "The truth is that . . . my faith is sometimes that my faith will return. It's something I struggle with a lot . . . On any given moment if you asked me [if] I believe in life after death, I think if you polled me regularly through the week, I think I would come down on the side of yes—that

I do believe in life after death. [But] it's something that I wrestle with a lot."[10] While Brooks and Rowling are committed to their faith, they both admit that belief in certain core tenets comes and goes. In admitting this, they may be more honest than most, but they are not unique.

Belief, in ways different from the past, now feels the pressures of unbelief. Christians are not immune from doubts, and even the most devout need others to help them believe. As Brooks explains, "I find that as long as there are five or ten people in your life whose faith seems gritty and real and like your own, that keeps the whole thing compelling."[11] Being "gritty" and "real," of course, means more than saying "hello" on Sunday mornings and chatting about the weather and sports. It means cultivating communities in which members genuinely care for each other. Local churches should serve as a living and breathing apologetic—an embodiment of faith, hope, and love. Yet helping each other believe also means being able to answer tough intellectual questions. Part of the authenticity of compelling communities is a regular digging into the questions behind the doubts we all struggle with. Often people just need to know that someone cares—a hug or a shoulder to cry on. But there are times when people need others to take their intellectual questions seriously.

A CHALLENGE FOR PREACHING

Though I've argued we can't rely on traditional revival-like events, this shouldn't be taken to mean we should give up on our weekly services as apologetic opportunities. Yet it will often take more relational investment and conversations on the front end before many will be willing to join us. First, our church services are an opportunity to invite outsiders to peek over to the other side and wonder, *What if?* If church members know the preacher will respectfully engage their unbelieving friend's secular stories, they are more likely to invite them, and if they come, their friends are more likely to listen. Second, the reality is that Christians now feel the pull of the other side. Like it or not, secular narratives put pressure on believers and in various ways take us captive. Our plausibility structures have shifted. We find ourselves asking, *What if I'm wrong?* In engaging with objections to the gospel in preaching, we encourage the faith of the faithful and help them deal with their doubts. Third, the church will learn how to speak about faith from what they hear coming from the pulpit each week. Sermons can become, among other things, a model for apologetic conversations.

We can no longer act like we're living in Christendom. The more "post"-Christian a society becomes, the more we will need to think carefully about our approaches to evangelism, discipleship, and preaching. Given the massive shift in culture and the tendency to talk past each other, and given that our baseline assumptions about the world are so varied, we need a way forward for having productive conversations with unbelievers and for helping believers learn to doubt their own doubts. We need not only an approach that allows us to get on the mental register of our unbelieving friends, but a way to go even deeper—to tap into their hearts and point them to a better way. To a *better* story.

NOTES

1. I'm paraphrasing a passage from Christian Smith, *Moral, Believing Animals: Human Personhood and Culture* (Oxford: Oxford University Press, 2003), 63–64.
2. Timothy Keller, *Hidden Christmas: The Surprising Truth Behind the Birth of Christ* (New York: Viking, 2016), 25.
3. Keller, *Hidden Christmas*, 25.
4. Alan Jacobs, "On the Myth of Disenchantment," *The New Atlantis*, May 9, 2018, http://text-patterns.thenewatlantis.com/2018/05/on-myth-of-disenchantment.html.
5. See, for instance, Christine Smallwood, "Starstruck: In Uncertain Times, Astrology Makes a Comeback," *New Yorker*, October 28, 2019, www.newyorker.com/magazine/2019/10/28/astrology-in-the-age-of-uncertainty.
6. In support of secular ideology being expressed as modern myths, see Eric Csapo, *Theories of Mythology* (Oxford: Blackwell, 2005), 9, 276–301; Mary Midgley, *The Myths We Live By* (New York: Routledge, 2003); John Milbank, *Theology and Social Theory*, 2nd ed. (Oxford: Blackwell, 2006), 267–72.
7. See Charles Taylor, *A Secular Age* (Cambridge, MA: Harvard University Press, 2007), 3.
8. Larry W. Hurtado, *Destroyer of the Gods: Early Christian Distinctiveness in the Roman World* (Waco, TX: Baylor Press, 2016), 183.
9. David Brooks, *The Second Mountain: The Quest for a Moral Life* (New York: Random House, 2019), 251.
10. Quoted in Shawn Adler, "'Harry Potter' Author J. K. Rowling Opens Up about Books' Christian Imagery," October 17, 2007, www.mtv.com/news/1572107/harry-potter-author-jk-rowling-opens-up-about-books-christian-imagery.
11. Brooks, *Second Mountain*, 247.

chapter

2

The Story Lives On

The incredible success of the *Harry Potter* franchise is illustrative of the enduring appeal of stories—and how echoes of the gospel persist in many of our cultures most beloved stories. In an article titled "How Harry Potter Changed the World," the authors gush over the books' success in the more than twenty years since the first book was published: "*Harry Potter* has since become such an all-encompassing phenomenon that from this vantage point, it's hard to see the full scope of what it accomplished."[1] Although many factors contributed to making the series a worldwide phenomenon, Constance Grady and Aja Romano observe that the driving force of the series' success is straightforward: "The *Harry Potter* series is a phenomenon because it tells a story that millions of people loved, and it introduced the world to an enormous and magical world that millions of people have dreamed of escaping into."[2] But it is not just magic spells and quidditch matches that make this story so enticing. As author J. K. Rowling explains about her series, "To me [the religious parallels have] always been obvious." She comments on two biblical citations—"The last enemy that shall be destroyed is death" (1 Corinthians 15:26) and "Where your treasure is, there will your heart be also" (Matthew 6:21)—found in the final book on the tombstones of Harry's parents and Dumbledore's mother and sister: "I think those two particular quotations he finds on the tombstones at Godric's Hollow, they sum up—they almost epitomize the whole series."[3]

The story is framed by two acts of sacrificial love—a mother who gave her life to save her son, and the son who willingly goes to his death so that all those he loves would live. The savior of the story is, of course, Harry Potter, the young wizard whose life had always been leading to the moment he would allow himself to be struck by evil unto death, only to live and return to defeat evil. Ironically, despite some of the fierce critiques the books and movies received from some Christians (for its elements of sorcery and witchcraft), it does not take a literary critic to realize the story significantly mirrors the story of Christ.

It's not just that our storying nature, as we suggested in the last chapter, provides a seed for engaging unbelievers. Another piece of good news is that as nonbelievers tell their stories—to explain the world, to hope for a better day, to warn of evils—somewhere in the distance, God's story looms.[4]

AN OPPORTUNITY IN POST-CHRISTENDOM

Even in—or better yet, especially in—societies where Christianity has been relegated to an out-of-date relic of yesteryear, people are surprised to find that what they love about their favorite stories is that in them they encounter traces of the gospel story. In fact, once the gospel has entered the bloodstream of a culture, even skeptics and doubters can't help but at times be struck by the sublime, and even inescapable, features of *the* story. Some are honest enough to confess that the Christian story has a haunting allure.[5] As the atheist Julian Barnes once admitted, "I don't believe in God, but I miss Him."[6] What does that mean?

Barnes is not talking about a Christian faith he once had. He never did. Instead Barnes is gesturing at the sense of the moving aesthetic pull of its narrative. James K. A. Smith explains the temptation for Barnes:

> "The Christian religion didn't last so long merely because everyone believed it" (p. 53), Barnes observes. It lasted because it makes for a helluva novel—which is pretty close to Tolkien's claim that the gospel is true because it is the most fantastic fantasy, the greatest fairy story ever told. And Barnes, a great lover of both music and painting, knows that much of what he enjoys owes its

> existence to Christianity . . . Thus he finds himself asking, "What if it were true?" . . . What would it be like, he asks, to listen to Mozart's *Requiem* and take it as nonfiction?[7]

Others are much more antagonistic, yet still can't help but mirror, often unwittingly, the Christian story in significant ways. For all the talk of repressive Christian ethics and the confidence in our ability to reason and use common sense to guide how we should live, the reality is the Western world's moral sensibilities are still living off the fumes of the Christian story. The nineteenth-century founder of liberal humanism, John Stuart Mill, is an example of how the Christian story reverberates even in secular accounts today:

> Mill was unusual in not having been reared in any traditional faith. But, like everyone else in mid-Victorian England, he was shaped in his thinking and feelings by Christianity. When he insisted that morality did not depend on religion, he invoked an idea of morality that was borrowed from Christian religion. When he affirmed that humankind was improving, he was relying on the belief that the human animal is a collective moral agent—an idea that also derives from Christianity.[8]

This is why Friedrich Nietzsche, the scathing critic of Christianity who wrote at the end of the nineteenth century, also turned his sights on the atheists of his day. For he realized that even these "secular" men weren't free from *the* story.[9] Still today, fully escaping it proves elusive.

The historian Tom Holland, a longtime secular progressive, recently wrote that despite his faith in God fading during his teen years, he now realizes his most fundamental instincts about life only make sense as an inheritance from the Christian story. Holland's book, *Dominion*, is a journey through Western history to narrate how our culture's moral ideals derive "ultimately from claims made in the Bible: that humans are made in God's image; that his Son died equally for everyone; that there is neither Jew nor Greek, slave nor free, male nor female."[10] Human rights, a universal concern for the vulnerable, human equality, sexual restraint, the reverence for humility, and the notion of moral progress itself are just a few of our common ideals that have developed in light of the Christian story. Holland can't get past the irony: "The West, increasingly empty though the pews may be, remains firmly moored to its Christian past."[11]

In the last chapter, we noted that the track record of Christian misdeeds makes for a powerful objection in a post-Christian era, different from the challenges the early church faced before it wielded power. The good news, however, is that the Christian story has been deeply ingrained into the moral ideals and longings of our secular age. This means that while a *post*-Christian culture presents new challenges, it also presents new opportunities—for your unbelieving friends are probably more "Christian" than they realize. That is, they embrace certain Christian ideals and beliefs, but as we will see, these assumptions don't always make much sense within their current script. They need a *better* story.

Holland himself recognizes how much the Western civilization's future depends on our coming to grips with the history of our shared ideals. As he puts it, since our modern moral aspirations are "not from reason or from science, but from the distinctive course of Christianity's evolution—a course that, in the opinion of growing numbers in Europe and America, has left God dead—then how are its values anything more than the shadow of a corpse? What are the foundations of its morality, if not a myth?"[12] This is the right question. Yet as Holland goes on to suggest, not all myths are untrue. What if the "myth became fact"?[13]

A BETTER STORY ABOUT STORIES

We've seen that the problem with the "thin" rationalistic story introduced at the beginning of chapter 1 is at least threefold. First, stories are unavoidable for us humans. As Ursula Le Guin observes, "There have been great societies that did not use the wheel, but there have been no societies that did not tell stories."[14] Despite the cries of those who claim that we as modern enlightened people should come of age and simply logic-chop our way to truth, story still remains our *lingua franca*. Second, our culture continues to be captured by imaginative stories that point to our inherent longing for another world. Third, through the stories we love to tell and hear—from Mozart's *Requiem* to liberal humanism's moral tale of universal love to J. K. Rowling's story of sacrificial death and resurrection—we're reminded that even in post-Christian cultures, we can't seem to escape the echoes and, at times, the allure of the gospel story.

We need a *better* story about stories. Why do humans of all cultures in all times insist on telling stories? Why do otherworldly tales continue to capture our imagination, even in a disenchanted age? Why do themes of guilt, sacrifice, redemption, and resurrection remain palpable in even the most secular corners of our contemporary world?

C. S. Lewis and J. R. R. Tolkien help us answer these questions. Humans continually tell, think about, and define ourselves by stories because that's exactly what we were designed to do. Alister McGrath explains how both Lewis and Tolkien saw human beings as "created by God with an innate capacity to create myths as echoes of a greater story or 'story of a larger kind.'"[15] As Tolkien says, we are "sub-creators" subconsciously mirroring our creator and even echoing the "supreme" story that "entered History."[16] For Lewis, there is "a narrative embedded within the deeper structures of the created order, which enables, shapes and moulds the construction and narration of human stories."[17] The Christian story gives us a better story about stories; "the structures and themes of the divine narrative are found within the created order, especially the human imagination."[18]

Human potentiality is reached not by giving up on stories, which we can't really do, but by embracing the true story of the world—the story that elucidates all other stories. The good news is that there is something in the human heart, even amid the culture shifts and our disordered fallen condition, that longs for the better story.

A BETTER STORY FOR APOLOGETICS

Since this book is about how the Christian story is *the* better story, it falls into the category of what has traditionally been labeled "apologetics." Recently, some have felt apologetics to be out of style, deeming it a relic from an overly rationalistic, Enlightenment age—a power play that has lost its persuasive potency. But this cynicism is fueled by a narrative that is, among other problems, too simple to be true.

Making persuasive appeals for and answering objections to Christianity is not only modeled and commanded in the Scriptures (Colossians 4:6; 1 Peter 3:15), but it is on display as a key feature in the writings of early church leaders (long before the Enlightenment).[19]

Yet even though critics go too far when they dismissively reject apologetics, we shouldn't dismiss their concerns. Apologetics has at times been practiced in ways that ignore complexity in favor of easy answers, assume an outdated understanding of how people arrive at their beliefs (that it is basically just by "reason"), and encourage excessive combativeness.

The need of the hour is a mature apologetics that is historically informed and theologically rooted in the gospel itself. This will require not only knowing how to give reasons for our faith, but also knowing how to stoke imaginations, model cruciform lives, and publicly confess both our own personal shortcomings and the failures of the church throughout history. (We do, after all, have some planks to remove from our own eyes.) This isn't typically what many people think when they hear the word *apologetics*, but that is only because we as the church have not fully come to grips with our past—both the wisdom it has to offer us and the mistakes we've made along the way.[20] The good news is that recent developments have sought to recover a contextual and holistic self-consciousness, as well as the Christian virtues essential for reviving an apologetics for everyday life.

Once viewed as a tool to win debates, apologetics is now becoming more focused on generating productive conversations that open doors for people to consider the gospel. Rather than encouraging others to use what Charles Taylor refers to as "conversation-stoppers" (e.g., "I have a three-line argument which shows that your position is absurd or impossible or totally immoral") or what Alan Jacobs refers to as the habit of "militarizing discussion and debate,"[21] many apologists are emphasizing the need for Christians to become better listeners who seek to understand the person they are speaking with before making appeals. This enables us to meet people where they are and find points to affirm before finding points to challenge.

This more conversational, back-and-forth approach is well suited to the fragmented era we live in because it recognizes the powerful impact that intellectual and cultural frameworks have on the way we (and the person we are speaking with) craft and perceive arguments. Even if you live in what used to be a culturally Christian area, like the Midwest or the Bible Belt, you don't have to walk very far beyond your front door or your home page to realize that people with the "facts" come to very different conclusions about life. Certainly most people with whom you interact will agree that 2 + 1 = 3 and that you can't have a married bachelor. Basic math and basic logic broken into its simplest forms can pretty much find universal agreement. Scholars recognize this kind of basic logic to be an aspect of rationality, "which [is] generally thought to be independent of a given individual's cultural location."[22]

However, development within the social sciences has pointed out that another decisive feature for determining the rationality of a belief is bound up in the "prevailing cultural metanarrative, which influences our judgements about what is to be deemed 'reasonable' or corresponding to 'common sense.'"[23] This helps us understand why two intelligent people using the same basic logic and looking at the same question can come to drastically different positions. It is not because one is dumb and the other is smart. IQ has little to do with it. Rather, their foundational frameworks for rationality are different, which leads to distinct conclusions on life's biggest questions.

This observation should have a profound impact on our approach to our unbelieving neighbor because it means we can't assume that people, if given the right "facts" and logic, will agree with us on rational grounds. This is simply not the world we live in, and it's time we respond well by practicing patience, learning how to have productive conversations, and interacting with our unbelieving friends' underlying metanarratives.[24]

Christian thinkers from a variety of different traditions and academic specialties, each in their own way, have followed this path, calling for and modeling an approach of persuasion that interacts with competing intellectual and cultural frameworks while remaining attentive to the historical context.[25] Throughout this book, I leverage these insights and seek to offer a practical approach that capitalizes on the storytelling nature of humans in what I describe as "inside out" apologetics.

We need apologetics. But not just any apologetics will do. Above all, what we need is an apologetics approach that is intentionally shaped by the cross. Cruciform apologists listen to and care for others; their goal is not simply to "win" an argument but to truly help those they speak with—to demonstrate Christ's love for them and invite them to try on the gospel. One important aspect of an apologetics tone that is often neglected is our communal apologetics as the church—the tone of our lives together as we serve others in word and deed. This is an apologetics that depends as much on being the right *type* of person as it does on having the right arguments.[26] The goal is to embody the truth and beauty of the gospel—the ultimate aim of any truly *Christian* apologetics.

NOTES

1. Constance Grady and Aja Romano, "How Harry Potter Changed the World," *Vox*, September 1, 2018, www.vox.com/culture/2017/6/26/15856668/harry-potter-20th-anniversary-explained; see Matthew McCreary, "The Billion-Dollar Business behind the 'Harry Potter' Franchise," *Entrepreneur*, November 18, 2018, www.entrepreneur.com/article/323363.
2. Grady and Romano, "How Harry Potter Changed the World."
3. Quoted in Shawn Adler, "'Harry Potter' Author J. K. Rowling Opens Up about Books' Christian Imagery," October 17, 2007, www.mtv.com/news/1572107/harry-potter-author-jk-rowling-opens-up-about-books-christian-imagery.
4. This point is in line with C. S. Lewis's essay "Myth Became Fact," in *God in the Dock: Essays on Theology and Ethics* (1970; repr., Grand Rapids: Eerdmans, 2014), 54–60, and J. R. R. Tolkien, *Tree and Leaf* (1964; repr., London: HarperCollins, 2001), 70–73.
5. Here I have in mind the mid-twentieth-century American novelist Flannery O'Connor, who referred to the South as "hardly-Christ-centered" but "most certainly Christ-haunted" because it still largely assumed a Christian conception of human beings. As she put it, "The Southerner, who isn't convinced of it, is very much afraid that he may have been formed in the image and likeness of God. Ghosts can be very fierce and instructive. They cast strange shadows, particularly in our literature" (*Mystery and Manners: Occasional Prose* [New York: Farrar, Straus and Giroux, 1969], 44–45).
6. Julian Barnes, *Nothing to Be Frightened Of* (New York: Vintage, 2009), 3.
7. James K. A. Smith, *How (Not) to Be Secular: Reading Charles Taylor* (Grand Rapids: Eerdmans, 2014), 9.
8. John Gray, *Seven Types of Atheism* (New York: Farrar, Strauss and Giroux, 2018), 36.
9. See R. R. Reno, "Nietzsche's Deeper Truth," *First Things* (January 2008), www.firstthings.com/article/2008/01/nietzsches-deeper-truth. Reno interprets Nietzsche to be against Christianity while maintaining a form of Christian anthropology. He summarizes Nietzsche's thought at this point: "Our impulse toward self-denying moral effort arises out of our instinctual lives. Our hearts are restless. Our lives are not governed by the need for survival; instead, human personality is most deeply formed by a creative desire to be and do something *more*. We cannot honestly know ourselves unless we acknowledge that we live as creatures

of ambition." He goes on later to add, "Nietzsche was a strange and complicated man. He clearly despised Christianity and yearned for a form of human life that is creative, free, and fully developed. Yet his most lucid and disciplined investigation into the dynamics of faith ends with a mockery of modern alternatives and a grudging affirmation that the human animal was made to worship, serve, and obey. For if we leave our lives simply as we find them, he suggests, then we are doomed to live a nihilism deeper and more threatening than the most unworldly and aggressive asceticism—life without will. Nietzsche's almost unwilling final affirmation of the ascetic impulse echoes St. Augustine's basic insight into the human condition. Our hearts are restless. The human animal wishes to give itself to something higher. It is a need more basic than our instinctual urges. It is a nature more fundamental than everything our age wishes us to affirm as natural." John Gray, an opponent of Christianity himself, agrees that Nietzsche's work not only critiques Christianity but also at times echoes its story: "Like the Christians he despised, he regarded the human animal as a species in need of redemption" (*Seven Types of Atheism* [New York: Farrar, Strauss and Giroux, 2018], 47).

10. Tom Holland, *Dominion: How the Christian Revolution Remade the World* (New York: Basic, 2019), 523.
11. Holland, *Dominion*, xxv. Or as he writes in his final chapter, "Even in Europe—a continent with churches far emptier than those in the United States—the trace elements of Christianity continued to infuse people's moral and presumptions so utterly that many failed even to detect their presence. Like dust particles so fine as to be invisible to the naked eye, they were breathed in equally by everyone: believers, atheists, and those who never paused so much as to think about religion" (p. 517). We might say today people are breathing in various assumptions from the cultural air—many of which originated by way of the Christian story, but they have now been put within a different plotline in a way that either doesn't fit, contaminates the original ideal, or both.
12. Holland, *Dominion*, 524.
13. See Lewis, "Myth Became Fact," in *God in the Dock*.
14. Ursula K. Le Guin, *The Language of the Night: Essays on Fantasy and Science Fiction* (London: Women's Press, 1989), 25.
15. Alister E. McGrath, *The Intellectual World of C. S. Lewis* (Malden, MA: Wiley-Blackwell, 2014), 64.
16. Tolkien, *Tree and Leaf*, 72–73.
17. McGrath, *Intellectual World of C. S. Lewis*, 65.
18. McGrath, *Intellectual World of C. S. Lewis*, 65.
19. Avery Dulles summarizes this well: "After the first quarter of the second century . . . apologetics became the most characteristic form of Christian writing" (*A History of Apologetics* [San Francisco: Ignatius, 2005], 27). Unsurprisingly, then, there are few leaders in the early church whose body of work did not include contributions in apologetics. Most significant, particularly for this book, is Saint Augustine, the late fourth/early fifth-century bishop of Hippo and the most influential theologian in the Western tradition. For instance, in his *Confessions*, Augustine exposes the idols of his own heart, laying bare his restless desire for God and taking his readers on a journey to God in which the intellect and the heart are intricately woven. And in

The City of God, Augustine uses apologetics to critique Roman culture's idolatrous worship by analyzing their false beliefs and disordered affections in order to make a targeted appeal for the superior beauty and reason of the Christian faith. One way to read this book is as an entry-level retrieval of the apologetic insights of the later Augustine, who was ministering before the advent of Christendom, within his own "cross-pressured" culture that included many different belief options.

20. See Joshua D. Chatraw and Mark D. Allen, "Apologetics within the Great Tradition," in *Apologetics at the Cross: An Introduction for Christian Witness* (Grand Rapids: Zondervan, 2018), 62–101; Benjamin Forrest, Joshua Chatraw, and Alister McGrath, *The History of Apologetics: A Biographical and Methodological Introduction* (Grand Rapids: Zondervan, 2020).
21. Charles Taylor, "Afterword: *Apologia pro Libro suo*," in *Varieties of Secularism in a Secular Age*, ed. Michael Warner, Jonathan VanAntwerpen, and Craig Calhoun (Cambridge, MA: Harvard University Press, 2010), 318; Alan Jacobs, *How to Think: A Survival Guide for a World at Odds* (New York: Currency, 2017), 98.
22. Alister E. McGrath, *The Territories of Human Reason: Science and Theology in an Age of Multiple Rationalities* (Oxford: Oxford University Press, 2019), 25.
23. McGrath, *Territories of Human Reason*, 25.
24. In this book, I will use both meta- and mega- to describe the Christian story, while not implying that Enlightenment metanarratives are the same exact types of stories as the Christian narrative; see Michael Horton, *The Christian Faith: A Systematic Theology for Pilgrims on the Way* (Grand Rapids: Zondervan, 2011), 16–17; Merold Westphal, *Overcoming Onto-Theology: Toward a Postmodern Christian Faith* (New York: Fordham University Press, 2001), xiii–xv. Both authors prefer "mega-" to "meta-" in describing the biblical story because they want to distinguish the Christian story from modernistic metanarratives that are grounded in an alleged autonomous reasoning and spur on coercive ideologies. Others, such as Richard Bauckham, N. T. Wright, and Tim Keller, use the term *metanarrative* as a label for the biblical story but distinguish it as a different kind of meta-story, describing the Christian metanarrative as noncoercive and nontotalizing.
25. See, for example, Alasdair MacIntyre, *After Virtue*, 3rd ed. (Notre Dame, IN: University of Notre Dame Press, 2007), xii–xiv; Taylor, *A Secular Age*, 539–727; Alister McGrath, *Narrative Apologetics: Sharing the Relevance, Joy, and Wonder of the Christian Faith* (Grand Rapids: Baker, 2019); N. T. Wright, *Simply Christian: Why Christianity Makes Sense* (New York: HarperCollins, 2006); N. T. Wright, *History and Eschatology: Jesus and the Promise of Natural Theology* (Waco, TX: Baylor University Press, 2019), 187–277; James K. A. Smith, *How (Not) to Be Secular: Reading Charles Taylor* (Grand Rapids: Eerdmans, 2014); James K. A. Smith, *On the Road with Saint Augustine: A Real-World Spirituality for Restless Hearts* (Grand Rapids: Brazos, 2019), 148–50, 158–76; Christian Smith, *Moral, Believing Animals: Human Personhood and Culture* (Oxford: Oxford University Press, 2003), 88–92; Christian Smith, *Atheist Overreach: What Atheism Can't Deliver* (Oxford: Oxford University Press, 2018); Timothy Keller, *Making Sense of God: An Invitation to the Skeptical* (New York: Viking, 2016), 53–54.
26. See Kevin J. Vanhoozer, *Pictures at a Theological Exhibition: Scenes of the Church's Worship, Witness, and Wisdom* (Downers Grove, IL: InterVarsity, 2016), 232–33.

chapter

3

What Time Is It?

"What time is it?" Staring at my mother with a vacant expression, I asked her once again, "Mom, just tell me—one last time—what time is it?" She told me the time. Thirty seconds passed. I turned to my brother: "Ben, quick question . . . What time is it?"

This was a bizarre exchange I had with my brother and mom as we drove to the hospital. I was seventeen, and earlier that day, I had been at the lake, wakeboarding with my older brother, Ben. During one of my runs, I crashed headfirst into the water—hard. As I got back into the boat, I began asking, "What time is it?" At first it was funny, then scary. I was persistent and earnest enough that Ben realized I wasn't kidding. He took me home as I pestered him, repeatedly, for the time. We picked up our mom and headed straight to the doctor. The entire car ride, I wouldn't let the question go: "Ben, Mom—what time is it?" As you may have guessed, and as the doctor informed my brother, mother, and her confused, time-obsessed son, I had a concussion. As a result I had been thrown into a mental fog. Utterly disoriented, my question was a sincere but tangled attempt to get my bearings. I was reaching for something, anything, to hold on to—like the time—in the hope that it might give me a firm handle on reality.

All's well that ends well, however, and we were all grateful when the doctor assured us that I would recover from my unfortunate state in about twenty-four hours. Sure enough, it wasn't long before my family—including myself—could laugh at the incident. Today, of course, the effects of my concussion are long gone, but the experience has stayed with me. It presents an interesting contrast. With my concussion I was completely disoriented from the world, unable to interpret my surroundings and connect with my brother, mom, or anyone else. Once I had healed, however, not only could I make sense of reality, but I could also see my concussion for what it was, and just how confused I had been.

Thankfully in my case, within twenty-four hours I was back to normal. Unfortunately for most Christians, our "cultural concussion" only seems to become *more* disorienting as time passes. We find ourselves asking fundamental questions about faith and the world around us. *How did we end up here? When did people start thinking like this? My friends believe in completely different things—how do I relate? My coworkers can't stand Christians—where do I even begin?* It's as if we've lost our bearings, and with it our ability to navigate the culture around us. Worse yet, there's no doctor to tell us we need only give it two or three days and our minds will clear up and all will be well. Far from it. We're seemingly stuck in a continual, intensifying contemporary concussion. It's only natural, then, that we would feel overwhelmed, confused, and intimidated.

When someone has a concussion, they're seeing and experiencing the world differently, preventing them from understanding or truly connecting with others. For instance, when I had a concussion, I was frustrated with my brother and mom because they stopped taking my "What time is it?" question seriously. They were frustrated because I kept asking the same question!

One of the first steps in getting our bearings is to seek to understand the context we now find ourselves in. If other people's way of thinking remains completely foreign to us, we will inevitably become overly defensive, angry, or discouraged when trying to speak to them about our faith. Frustrated by an inability to communicate our beliefs effectively, we may experience self-doubt ("Is Christianity even true?"), fear ("I don't want to be hateful or intolerant, so I'll just keep quiet"), resentment ("People are insane and are ruining culture"), or apathy ("People won't listen, so why bother?"). Trading in the humble boldness that Christ has called us to, the Christian chooses to either live out a private faith or an angry faith. And our witness is rarely effective when we're fearful of and angry at the people we're supposed to be reaching.

In order to get our bearings, "What time is it?" is the question we must be asking again and again. Unfortunately, because of the way apologetics or evangelism has so often been taught, focusing on formulaic presentations or logic abstracted from framing cultural narratives, this question rarely gets the attention it deserves. But it needs to be asked. Considering context is essential because we are attempting to reach people who are born into a story at a particular time, in a particular place, into a particular family—all which define much of who we are and how we think. And while there are, of course, certain commonalities that humans share, there is no such thing as an abstract "everyman" completely divorced from culture.

Even in a monocultural society, every person in that society possesses a complex story that shapes behavior and thinking. When considering the deeply pluralistic societies of the West, we must be even more attuned to the seemingly limitless narratives and assumptions by which people's lives are shaped. It's not just our interaction with the world writ large that requires us to ask the time. Our interactions with every *person* must move us to inquire, again and again, "What time is it?"

Complicating things even further is the fact that we are rarely conscious of the way our personal and cultural backgrounds impact our thinking. Many people's assumptions about the world (such as morality, purpose, and personal identity) are just that—*assumptions*. They are taken for granted as "obvious" to any "reasonable" person. Human rights, for instance, may seem to be an obvious moral conviction to people today, but this has not been "common sense" to most people in human history. And as strange as a world of good and evil spirits seems to the modern Westerner, this has been (and remains) "common sense" in much of the non-Western world. We don't so much reason our way to these assumptions as inherit them, and we're hard-pressed to imagine things otherwise. In order to truly understand what is driving someone's unbelief, we must go beneath the surface and identify these assumptions. Some of these assumptions will be personal—unique to each individual—but many of the most powerful assumptions are pervasive and shared by most who live in a modern-day Western culture.

TELLING TIME

In order to understand where Western culture stands today, it is essential to consider and—to the best of our ability—understand where it's been. One way to think about and organize history, and in this case the history of our culture, is to identify shifts in definitions of foundational concepts like reason, tradition, authority, and belief (or lack of belief) in the divine. For Western culture, historians and philosophers often cite two major shifts resulting in three distinct periods: the premodern, modern, and postmodern eras. History, of course, is never as clean-cut as short summaries like the ones I'm about to offer suggest, but the patterns are nonetheless useful.

The Premodern Era

During the premodern era, which lasted until roughly the 1500–1600s, most people assumed an enchanted world. They lived with an awareness that some kind of transcendent being or beings existed, as did a realm beyond or above nature. It was also assumed that there was a higher meaning to life—an order to the universe that one could go with or go against.

Traditional and religious institutions provided the ultimate frameworks through which people reasoned and experienced life, and they were also the center of community. The idea of the "individual" as we know it today did not exist. People were instead defined by their family, their community, their ruler, and their religion. There was a general sense of "we are all in this together." If someone stepped out of line, God or the gods could judge the whole community. The gap between personal and public was negligible; one's private conduct was a public issue. The civil was understood to be inseparable from the sacred.

Much of this mind-set, not surprisingly, aligns well with Christianity—particularly the recognition of the divine and the transcendent, the emphasis on community, and the appreciation for tradition and religious institutions. Yet from the standpoint of the gospel, we should have a nuanced take on this period. The premodern era was filled with many different ideas about transcendence, the world, and human flourishing. False gods abounded. Many fanciful myths and superstitions were often left unchecked without enough critical examination. Traditional institutions far too often were oppressive.

When evaluated by twenty-first-century standards, even the greatest thinkers of the ancient world held degrading views of entire swaths of people. Women were marginalized. The poor were kept in their place. Religion coerced. So while it is foolish to nostalgically look back, wishing we could return to those ancient times, we should look back in order to move forward, for doing so not only gives us perspective for our own time, but it reminds us that we would never be fully at home in any stage in world history. Christians will always need to be ready to give an answer, both challenging and affirming the spirit of any age.

The Modern Era

Around the middle of the second millennium, people began to question whether traditional religious authorities could be trusted. Rejecting the truth propagated by these traditional authorities, individuals attempted to discover truth by believing only what could be logically deduced from what was self-evident. But naturally, the question became, *What is self-evident? How can anyone know whether what they see is reality?*

René Descartes, a defining figure of modernism, set out on a quest to distinguish reality by rejecting everything he *thought* he knew from traditional authorities and starting from his individual, logical reflections. Descartes reasoned that he could doubt everything he thought he believed to be true, as well as everything he perceived with his senses. The one thing he could not doubt, however, was that he was doubting, which meant he was thinking, which meant that, at the very least, he surely existed in some form. (He might only be a brain in a vat, but "I think, therefore I am.") Descartes's conclusion reflects modernism's turn from traditional, external institutions to the individual's own reasoning as the ultimate authority. Widely referred to as "the turn to the subject" (or "the turn to the self"), this was the spirit undergirding the search for truth through reason.[1]

Immanuel Kant, another key figure of this period, declared his current age to have marked "man's emergence from his self-imposed immaturity," and he urged humankind: "*Sapere aude!*" to dare to know, to have courage to use their own reason.[2] The ancient sources of wisdom were dethroned, and in their place was crowned a new source of ultimate authority: individual reason. Mankind, the modern asserted, had come of age. Growing numbers now felt obligated to prove the beliefs they held.

Running parallel to the ideas of Descartes, Kant, and other intellectuals, scientific methods were developed in the modern era and became a defining means of obtaining truth. Under the scientific paradigm, after an individual carefully analyzed and tested the raw data within a prescribed system, the result they obtained constituted verifiable truth. This produced incredible innovation, as evidenced by the myriad of new scientific discoveries and technological advancements that marked this period. These breakthroughs engendered a confidence in this new enlightened rationality and spread to other areas of society, such as politics and ethics. For instance, some began to think that violent wars—often grounded in real or perceived religious squabbles—could now be avoided. While previous eras lacked the necessary mechanisms to seek peaceful resolution in the face of religious wars, the modern era, so the thinking went, would leverage "neutral" universal reason to mitigate and end bloodshed.

And these shifts, of course, impacted religious assumptions. Guided by supposedly autonomous reason and confidently equipped with new methods for discovery, many people, especially leading intellectuals, turned to deism—the belief in a God who built a self-sustaining universe and is now largely absent from it. Since they would only believe what they thought they could "prove," they conceded there was a God (they needed him to ground their morality), but that he didn't intervene in life (miracles could not be proved) or reveal himself in any particular religion (no Bible or holy book could be proven to be inspired). This is a picture of God boxed in by Enlightenment reason rather than revealed through special revelation (e.g., the gospel, Scripture, and Jesus Christ). Eventually, for many, belief in a deistic God could not stand up to the "Reason" that made it, and deism served as a stepping-stone to other more radical options, namely, atheism.

Modernity's eventual acceptance of atheism as a viable option would have been unthinkable for most people in previous generations.[3] What once was implausible, now became plausible: *Maybe there just isn't a God?* The individual, increasingly detached from the thick, sacred communities that characterized premodernism, turned to the "self" to figure things out, while still living in a society with many of the moral and intellectual trappings of Christianity. Universal and autonomous reason was the great hope as the foundation for the individual and for society, but soon enough, a disorienting fog would set in as this pillar of modernity was challenged.

The Late Modern (or Postmodern) Era

The efforts of modernity's standard-bearers to universalize scientific principles and leverage scientific methods and "reason" to solve life's problems and mysteries proved woefully insufficient. There are many reasons for this, and two are worth pointing out here. First, there is little in our experience that can be described with "raw facts." We may be able to speak of math problems and basic logic in terms of "raw facts," but this designation breaks down when considering life's biggest questions. Humans are not computer processors, and our most important questions cannot be solved by running them through an algorithm. This is not a new discovery. Hundreds of years ago, people recognized this point about human nature and pushed back against Enlightenment rationalism, questioning its basic axioms. Most notably, adherents of Romanticism responded by critiquing the Enlightenment's mechanistic flattening out of life, choosing instead to emphasize emotion, nature, and aesthetics (though still alongside the individual's primacy).

Second, one of the hopes of the Enlightenment—that this new kind of knowledge rooted in universal reason and observation would lead to an orderly and peaceful society—was dashed as it became clear that human reason alone was unable to curb violence or provide a universal system of morality. Those who "dared to reason" believed themselves to be liberating society from competing and unprovable religious myths. Yet eventually people began to accuse Enlightenment thinkers of advancing their own unprovable and totalizing myth that bulldozed over others. Modernity's emphasis on "progress" was viewed from the perspective of those in power, who were using what turns out to be their own parochial expressions of "Reason" to oppress the weak and "uncivilized." The modern story of "progress" thus became viewed by some as a story of "domination."[4]

The very notion of Enlightenment progress was often reduced to economic advancement operated by purely instrumental reasoning. What was "good" equaled "what works." And "what works" was often at the expense of the lower class and less wealthy nations. In other words, "progress" was the justifying tool of the powerful, on display in colonialization and the ethnocentric suppression of different cultures. Those pushing back against modernist thought argued that such reductionistic and "totalizing" stories about the world deserved to be challenged. And so they were.

The most widely used term for the period of time extending from the middle of the twentieth century to the present is *postmodernism*. You can see how even in the name, this period is fashioned as a reaction to modernism, and this is partly accurate. But we shouldn't get the impression that our current age is the total opposite of modernism. While postmodern society has challenged important tenets of modernism, it has continued and intensified other assumptions of the Enlightenment. In particular, the individual "self" still rules. For this reason, in this book I will often refer to our current period as *late modernism*.[5]

The rapid shifts taking place from the premodern to modern to late modern eras show our culture today to have been profoundly shaped by an intense turn to the individual. Like moderns, late moderns still set the autonomy of the individual and personal freedom above the claims of tradition, religion, family, and community, but late modernism has exposed alleged "neutrality" as a fiction.

Some late moderns went to an extreme in rejecting the Enlightenment search for *Truth*. They've reasoned that since everyone approaches the external world with a preconceived interpretative framework developed from inherited biology and the biases of the social environment (i.e., nature and nurture), then individual perspectives are all that exist. There is no universal *Truth* (with a capital "*T*") that we can know; we can only know what the *truth* (little "*t*") is for ourselves. At worst, this view leads to arbitrary relativism (truth is totally dependent on the individual person) or hopeless skepticism (truth cannot be found). Thus, ironically, as James Hunter puts it, "The Enlightenment's own quest for certainty resulted not in the discovery of new certainties but rather in a pervasive astringent skepticism that questions all, suspects all, distrusts and disbelieves all."[6]

Taken to an extreme, radical skepticism leads to the belief that there is no meaning. Beyond being a difficult pill for humans to swallow, radical skepticism is completely impractical. Some brave souls have attempted to swallow the pill of meaninglessness, yet the way they live their lives—as if they had purpose—suggests otherwise. In short, their claim of ultimate meaninglessness ignores the realities of basic human experience. No one can be an absolute relativist. No one denies all meaning or morality in practice.

SOME GOOD NEWS ABOUT LATE MODERNISM

While some Christians have sought to retreat from postmodernism back to modernism in order to offer an apologetic, a less reactionary posture toward "postmodern" thinkers can lead to more nuanced and productive interactions. For instance, Jean-François Lyotard approved of the turn against modernism and famously described postmodernism as "incredulity toward metanarratives."[7] However, he didn't have all overarching explanatory stories in his sights but rather a certain type of what most mean by "metanarrative" today. His objection was that modernity had used its own myth—based on the precarious idea that autonomous and universal reason was available to *prove* the answers to life's most important questions—to discredit other story lines that did not live up to this standard.[8] In other words, rationalists created a standard that their own story couldn't live up to. How does this help us?

Practically, this means if you enter into a conversation with a skeptic who demands "proof" in contrast to "faith," don't rush in to line up your "proofs" too quickly. This is not to say you shouldn't reason with them. You should! But as we will see in more detail later, even today's most rationalistic narratives, despite what some loudly claim, aren't accepted because they have been proven as one would prove that 1 + 1 = 2.

Both the believer and the unbeliever are thinking and living within a framing narrative that can't be proven by reason alone. Neither our highest moral ideals, our vision of the good life, the resurrection, nor foundational assumptions like the existence of other minds can be proven or disproven according to a universal reason. What we find as reasonable, virtuous, and beautiful, no matter if someone is an atheist or a Christian, requires faith of some kind. Postmodernism reminds us that there is no metanarrative held by reason alone. This means, at times, we will need to work to level the playing field. Neither belief in God nor disbelief in God can be proven. It is not about faith (belief in God) versus reason (disbelief in God), but about rival types of faith seeking understanding.

So in answering the big questions of life, absolute proof is unavailable, and in some respect the story line we live by has to be accepted in part by faith of some kind. But it would be wrong to conclude that this leaves us all forced to believe blindly. Meta-stories can't be absolutely proven, but they can be compared. We can ask, Which story is most coherent on its own terms? Which story is able to incorporate the insights from other stories in a way that makes sense? Which story is most livable? Which story corresponds with our observations, experiences, and history?

THE STRANGE PRAGMATIC CONTRADICTION

Nevertheless, despite what we can learn from these developments, a real contradiction exists within the typical thinking of many today. A prototypical picture of the ethos of our age can be seen in what philosopher Charles Taylor refers to as the "strange pragmatic contradiction."[9] Our present culture has largely embraced a mentality that says, "You can do whatever you want, as long as it is being done by consenting adults and it doesn't 'hurt' anyone." According to this view, there is no way to know the capital "*T*" truths in life, so "you do you." At the same time, however, people believe strongly in certain values and act as if those values are universal. This is evidenced in the various ways people publicly engage in "virtue signaling" and then shame those who don't live up to the cultural standards of the day (just take a quick look at Twitter this afternoon to see what I mean).

A few years ago (and to a lesser degree today), it was popular for some Christians to triumphantly mock the culture's simple moral relativism. What we see here, however, is a more complicated picture of morality. The fact that our common moral order assumes we should advance human rights and care about the universal welfare of humanity represents perhaps the highest moral ideals for any society in human history. Until recently, there has never been a society embedded with the assumption that all humans are endowed with inalienable rights and that we should treat all people, regardless of age, race, or ethnicity, with benevolence.

These ideals, however, haven't developed from a secularism devoid of religious influence. To the contrary, these secular values, as we saw in the last chapter, were developed from and make clearest sense as *part* of the Christian story. Thus, not only is the late modern framework more complicated than it has often been presented by Christian apologists, but it possesses ideas Christians can and should affirm precisely because it's rooted in Christian thought and tradition. Christians, then, cannot simply critique secular assumptions but must learn to interact with them and show how the biblical story makes far better sense of these noble, moral longings.

But for now, don't miss the deep irony of the "you do you" attitude existing alongside these extraordinarily high moral expectations. Taylor provides a helpful explanation of the "strange pragmatic contradiction" when he writes, "It seems that they [secularists] are motivated by the strongest moral ideals, such as freedom, altruism, and universalism. These are among the central moral aspirations of modern culture."[10] But without a story that situates these moral ideals in something beyond culture or individual preference, these *absolute* ideals are undermined.

How, then, should Christians respond to these shifts? First, Christians should feel relieved by the late modern response to modernity's attempt to obtain certainty through reason alone. When someone claims they are just using "reason" as opposed to "faith," we should help them see that this is not how life works. We all believe deeply in things we can't prove—from basic assumptions about our mind's ability to perceive truth to our highest ideals and aspirations. Later we'll discover how by helping people see that they are already believing and living in a narrative that can't be proven, we can level the playing field in order to invite them to compare their current script with the Christian story.[11]

Second, and as we've discussed, Christians should affirm certain high ideals of our present moral order. After all, human rights and universal benevolence are good things, and they've been injected into Western culture not in spite of but because of Christianity's development. And yet, even though Christians can draw important lessons from and affirm aspects of any cultural period, we're not fully at home during any period, including our current one. The prevailing cultural narratives of the West, then, must be critiqued. With this in mind, part 2 of this book surveys how Christians ought to interact with salient features of late modernism.

LIVING IN A ONE-LEVEL WORLD

An important concept to understand in the shift from the premodern to the modern and late modern eras is what Charles Taylor calls the rise of the "*immanent frame.*"[12] Today the secular narratives teach us to live and operate within the immanent frame, viewing everything in terms of the material world. The modern imagination, which is deeply embedded within our culture, works from the assumption that while people can find significance or meaning in life (immanence), there is no higher, divinely given purpose assigned to them (transcendence).[13]

A helpful way to understand the immanent frame is to picture a two-story building. Our ancestors lived in a two-story world. Humans inhabited the first floor, but this overlapped with a higher realm on the second floor. Theirs was an enchanted world where higher beings were assumed to be active in and relevant to the affairs of everyday life. This higher realm held significance beyond this life while also giving meaning and purpose to our present lives on the first floor. In contrast, we live in a disenchanted, one-story world today that denies the existence of the divine.

Now the commonly shared habits, goals, and symbols of day-to-day life and the meaning ascribed to them point us solely to the physical world around us. Thus, as people, including Christians, inherit the habits, goals, and symbols that undergird our culture, we consciously and mostly subconsciously absorb a desire to live for and long for things only on the first level of our disenchanted world.

And yet even within this one-story frame, some have reacted against the moral order of modernism, which seeks to offer meaning, significance, and morality without ultimate, transcendent meaning or an ultimate, transcendent God. Although some have found the disenchanted new moral order freeing, many others have found it uninspiring and lacking "fullness" and therefore have opted for some type of spirituality—traditional or otherwise.[14] These diverse attitudes have led to what Taylor refers to as the "'nova' effect,"[15] which describes how, even within the immanent frame, there has been a "multiplication of a greater and greater variety of different spiritual options."[16]

But even sincerely religious people live in a *secular age*, an environment that continually exposes the contestability of any kind of belief, and especially religious ones. In this present age, it seems there is no position that cannot and should not be called into question from a variety of angles.

While this may appear discouraging, the "nova effect" should bring some encouragement to Christians who desire to have conversations about Christianity with others. It is true that since our society is built on the assumption of the immanent frame, gospel persuasion can be more difficult. However, the growing "nova effect" among secularists suggests there are cracks in the frame. People are sensing that something is missing, that there must be more to life. We've been asking, "What time is it"—well, *this* is the time we live in, a time when many *secular* people consider the assumptions of a completely immanent framework—with no higher level—to be unsatisfying in some deeper sense. By knowing our culture's time, the mental fog will begin to clear, putting us in a position to empathetically engage our neighbors with the gospel.

WHAT THIS MEANS FOR EVERYDAY CONVERSATIONS

What history has shown time and time again is that ideas and—perhaps even more pertinent—*assumptions* have serious and far-reaching consequences. The existing social structures and frameworks of belief that shape late modernism have led to a distrust of traditional religion and a disdain for anything that might suppress personal desires.

Several years ago, when I was serving as a pastor in a rural church, a small group leader told me about a conversation she had just had with a high school student in her group. She had confronted the girl about the guys she had been hooking up with. She had asked the student, "Why do you even go out with those sort of guys? They're clearly no good." The girl snapped back, "Who are you to tell me what the Bible says? Doesn't the Bible teach us not to judge others? You have no right to say whether they're good or bad, or whether or not I should hang out with them. I'm doing what I feel is right."

That response would sound strange to premodern or modern ears, yet today it's unsurprising, if not expected. It's a near perfect reflection of the West's prevailing and pervasive assumptions. How pervasive? Well, one might expect this attitude from a teen in a big city in New England, but this teen grew up and spent all of her life in a small town in the Bible Belt. It's safe to say she had never read an academic treatise on postmodernism or late modernism, nor was her response the outpouring of conclusions reached through deep reflection. In fact, she had not thought through her response at all but simply regurgitated the cultural influences and social structures of the day. She had breathed in the air of late modernism and exhaled its values.

To interact only with the symptoms—surface-level objections—while ignoring the cultural air and assumptions people have inhaled since birth would be tantamount to treating cancer with Band-Aids. Unfortunately, too many approaches have taught us to do just that. When the cultural air is friendly to Christianity, treating the symptoms and arguing for straightforward belief in God or the historicity of Jesus and his resurrection might work. But when people have inherited assumptions that are increasingly different from those assumed by the Christian story, we must learn not only how to understand our context, but also how to diagnose the disease, warn of the contaminants we have all become accustomed to inhaling, and treat the cancer. In chapter 5, we'll turn to a framework that will provide mental scaffolding for doing just that.

However, the young woman mentioned earlier needed something else, something all people need when journeying through life. Rather than a sparring partner who masterfully presents syllogisms and embarrasses her by simply pointing out her inconsistencies, she needed a spiritual doctor with a bedside manner. She needed a hospital for her soul, a community willing to show her their own wounds while introducing her to the Physician who can mend hers.

NOTES

1. This period is often associated with the Enlightenment, though scholars have recently noted that this is more of a family of movements with different regional manifestations, some more conducive to religion than others; see, e.g., Gertrude Himmelfarb, *The Roads to Modernity: The British, French, and American Enlightenments* (New York: Knopf, 2004).
2. See Immanuel Kant, *An Answer to the Question: "What Is Enlightenment?"* (London: Penguin, 2013), 1.
3. Of course, this doesn't mean there weren't atheists before this period. Just that it did not feel like a viable option for most of the public (see N. T. Wright, *History and Eschatology*, 3–39).
4. Richard Bauckham, *Bible and Mission: Christian Witness in a Postmodern World* (Grand Rapids: Baker, 2003), 5.
5. See Taylor, *A Secular Age*, 716–17.
6. James Davison Hunter, *To Change the World: The Irony, Tragedy, and Possibility of Christianity in the Late Modern World* (New York: Oxford University Press, 2010), 206–7.
7. Jean-François Lyotard, *The Postmodern Condition: A Report on Knowledge* (Minneapolis: University of Minnesota Press, 1984), xxiv.
8. See James K. A. Smith, *Who's Afraid of Postmodernism? Taking Derrida, Lyotard, and Foucault to Church* (Grand Rapids: Baker, 2006), 59–79.
9. Charles Taylor, *Sources of the Self: The Making of the Modern Identity* (Cambridge, MA: Harvard University Press, 1989), 88.
10. Taylor, *Sources of the Self*, 88; for a similar description from someone who is not a Christian, see the "liberal ironist" in Richard Rorty, *Contingency, Irony, and Solidarity* (Cambridge: Cambridge University Press, 1989), xv.
11. At the end of his survey of the history of Western philosophy, C. Stephen Evans makes a similar point about how Christians can appropriate certain gains from postmodernism (*The History of Western Philosophy: From the Pre-Socratics to Postmodernism* [Downers Grove, IL: InterVarsity, 2018], 577–85).
12. Taylor, *A Secular Age*, 542. "Immanent" is an antonym of "transcendent." It may be helpful to remember that God is both immanent (present in this world and operating in it) and transcendent (existing and operating outside of, above, or beyond this world).

13. See Charles Taylor, "Afterword: *Apologia pro Libro suo*," in *Varieties of Secularism in a Secular Age*, ed. Michael Warner, Jonathan VanAntwerpen, and Craig Calhoun (Cambridge, MA: Harvard University Press, 2010), 307.
14. See Taylor, *A Secular Age*, 5; James K. A. Smith provides a helpful gloss for Taylor's usage of *fullness*: "A term meant to capture the human impulsion to find significance, meaning, and value—even if entirely within the immanent frame" (*How (Not) to Be Secular: Reading Charles Taylor* [Grand Rapids: Eerdmans, 2014], 141).
15. Taylor, *A Secular Age*, 300.
16. Taylor, "Afterword: *Apologia pro Libro suo*," 306.

chapter
4
When Talking to Humans

"What is your best argument for Christianity?" the student asked me. We were meeting for the first time in my office, and he was determined to get an answer. "Well, that depends," I responded. "It depends on who I'm talking to and what the situation is." This was not the answer he wanted. The student was clearly devoted to apologetics and also well-informed—he had taken several apologetics classes at his Christian high school and enjoyed them. Now at college and in the office of the apologetics professor, he was eager to cut to the chase (and probably to size me up). And I must hand it to him, he was persistent. "But seriously, if you just had one argument and you didn't know me, what would you *use*?" It was like he was talking about a video game, desperate to unlock the special knockout move of the newest avatar, Dr. Chatraw. He may as well have asked, "What's your go-to punch?" To his disappointment, I explained that I essentially don't have a "knockout blow" or a universal best argument I always use. Far from it, I said, this is not at all how we should think about apologetics.

After a lengthy conversation, the student left frustrated and unconvinced. He wanted me to give him my "go-to move," and I wanted to teach him a *way* to approach conversations. He was like Daniel from *Karate Kid*, wanting to know how to kick and punch because he was tired of being bullied, and I was attempting to teach something more foundational. To his frustration, however, all he heard was, "Wax on!

Wax off!" For those deprived of classic 80s movies, I'm quoting Daniel's karate mentor, Mr. Miyagi, who sought to teach Daniel by having him wax his car. What seemed like a waste of time to Daniel was actually an approach for habituating him into the discipline and movements of karate.

So it is, I'm convinced, with apologetics. We must habituate ourselves to understand foundational questions and assumptions of life and the human experience not *before* but *instead of* jumping into "winner take all" arguments. And though wrestling with foundational issues of theology and anthropology may feel like veering off from the stated goal of apologetics, it in actuality prepares us to effectively and sincerely engage people who think and believe differently. Put simply, usually, apologetics prudence means bypassing the attempt to deliver an easy and early knockout punch; after all, to the other person, it can often just feel like a sucker punch.

Perhaps, however, you're feeling the same way as Daniel, or the student in my office—that we really are spending too much time philosophizing, so maybe it's best, you say, to "cut to the chase." For the sake of argument, then, let's take the "go-to move" approach to apologetics and consider a classic knockout punch—apologetics from cosmology. How effective would this be in everyday conversation?

At its core, the cosmological argument reasons that things come into existence from a creator. There's more to it, of course, and if we were truly looking to take down our unbelieving friend with foolproof thought, then we'd also unpack the importance of causation, contingencies, finitude, and more. How many people would respond to this argument with a sincere and decisive change of heart?

The point is not that the cosmological argument is unsound or impractical. In fact, I suggest later that with the right person at the right time, this and similar arguments can be helpful. But most people on any given day don't walk around thinking about infinite regress or the universe's origins. (If your response is to say, "I do!" then just admit that, in this particular way, you are not in the majority.) This is because these cosmological musings aren't essential to our personhood. People can take them or leave them without much effect on their day-to-day lives.

If an argument abstracted from our essential personhood is your first move, most people will simply disengage. Life is happening. There are things to do—and cosmological causation doesn't alter this fact. Again, this doesn't mean you don't need apologetics in general or cosmological arguments in particular. But making these arguments primary and treating them as applicable in all situations is like a surgeon who always uses a saw, even when a scalpel is in order. Saws can be useful. But we must realize that most situations—most conversations—require a tool with a finer point.

Chapter 3 provided context to effectively "tell the time." The difficulties we face in apologetics today are not the result of people *simply* missing one piece of evidence or one logical step. Instead, the problem is not *just* that they find Christianity unreasonable; they also find it irrelevant—or worse, distasteful. This is the most significant challenge for a Christian witness in a post-Christian society. In this climate, it's important for us to consider who we are as humans and why we make the commitments we do. To do so, we need to start by understanding who we are in relation to our Creator.

WHAT'S LOVE GOT TO DO WITH IT?

God has always existed as three persons in a relationship of mutual self-giving love. He created humans as an overflow of this love, to love and worship him. This is one of the reasons theologians have emphasized that humans at their core are designed to love something greater than themselves. We are fundamentally doxological beings. This is not just a theological truth, however, divorced from human experience. People across time and culture have lived with an inclination to give themselves to something and make it their overriding priority. Even some secular social scientists are sounding rather "theological" in making this point. For example, Jonathan Haidt, an atheist who serves as a professor of social psychology at New York University, has stressed that his own research suggests that "human beings evolved to be religious. It's in our nature . . . There is a God-shaped hole in the heart of each man."[1] Our nature is to instinctually make something god-like, devoting ourselves to it with ultimate allegiance.

God, who is love, designed us to love. Made to love and be loved, each person is on an existential search for a fullness they were created for. As Christian philosopher James K. A. Smith explains, whatever it is that captures our hearts and imaginations inevitably "pushes (or pulls) us to act in certain ways, develop certain relationships, pursue certain goods, make certain sacrifices, enjoy certain things," as we search for the fullness for which we were designed.[2]

Smith, pulling the thread of Augustinian thought, captures a significant point about humans that is pivotal for any discussion about persuasion. Thinking and believing are essential aspects of human nature, and both play a crucial role in discussion, persuasion, decision making, and—by extension—apologetics. However, these human attributes do not by themselves reflect the deep currents of our soul by which our lives are shaped and guided. As discussed, we are not computers, calculating our way through life, and we are not merely "thinking things" as rationalists wrongly imagined—this is a false reduction of what it is to be human.[3] Our reason is actually dependent on our emotions. As Haidt explains, "Human rationality depends critically on sophisticated emotionality. It is only because our emotional brains work so well that our reasoning can work at all."[4]

Placing trust in the personal God of the Bible and having knowledge of his truth are essential to Christianity. Our appeals, then, must include explaining why someone should take truths about God seriously, providing reasons for faith, and showing why this covenantal God—who has entered into history and in love bound himself to the world—should be trusted. But as in our most important relationships,[5] it is not simply a list of facts and evidences that drives people to turn from the powerful allure of the modern gods of our age and worship Christ. A healthy apologetics uses logic and provides evidences, but it also grounds logic and evidence in genuine human connection that gives credence to and resonates with people's deeply held aspirations and affections.[6]

If we view people as one-dimensional thinking beings, our tendency will be to use conversations as a means to offer five-step analytical road maps to God. These mechanisms may contain excellent information and biblical truth, but they're often also in danger of being cold and impersonal, making it easy for people to shrug off our facts and our truth. They are left unconvinced by our arguments, uninterested in our truth, and irritated by our appeals, for their imaginations have been taken captive. For our *sense* of the good and the beautiful can either open or close our eyes to the truth.

IMAGINATION AND THE HEART

Our hearts are closely connected to our imaginations. In biblical usage, the word *heart* usually refers to the *integrative* control center of our lives—including our reason, emotions, and beliefs.[7] And likewise, as theologian Kevin Vanhoozer explains, the imagination engages not only our intellectual faculties but also our beliefs and emotions. The imagination is "a faculty for making or discovering connections and meaningful forms. Analytic reason takes things apart; the synthetic imagination puts things together."[8] A well-formed imagination, then, far from being something that leads to irrationalism, is a form of reasoning that enables someone "to create or perceive meaningful wholes and coherent forms."[9] It allows a person to see how life and the world around us fit together in a meaningful and true whole.

This ability to see how things fit together is a deeply compelling feature of the Christian vision. This is what prompted the Oxford professor C. S. Lewis to write, "I believe in Christianity as I believe that the Sun has risen, not only because I see it, but because by it I see everything else."[10] But not everyone is in the same place as Lewis was when he made this statement, so this raises the question: How do we address people's imagination deficit problems? How do we help people see how Christianity illuminates everything?

The idea of successfully helping others see and believe in the beauty of Christian imagination is intimidating—where do we begin? Thankfully we have real-life examples before us, including Lewis's own journey, that provide helpful guidance. Before Lewis's prominence as a public Christian apologist, he was an atheist who found Christianity unappealing, despite his intellectual prowess and awareness of the typical Christian arguments for faith. And yet even while he was a skeptic, many of his favorite poems and stories began to make him wonder,

Just what if? They enticed him with a vision of a deeper reality that kept nagging at his heart. Certain stories, as he would later say, "baptized . . . [his] imagination."[11] The poems that he grew to love didn't so much as "persuade Lewis to believe in God" as "led him to think that such a belief offered a rich and robust vision of the human life, making him wonder whether there might, after all, be something to be said for their way of thinking."[12] Often a person's heart must be captured before the mind can follow. This rarely happens through a list of "proofs" or logical syllogisms. Lewis's heart was captured through compelling *stories*. As we already saw in chapter 1, Lewis was not alone. "The human mind is a story processor, not a logic processor."[13]

God made us to love—few Christians would dispute this. But we must also recognize how God made us to connect with and through stories. It should be no surprise, then, how the Bible, inspired by a creative God, so frequently makes its appeals through its dramatic narratives and grand narrative.

Persuasion through narrative is a profoundly biblical pattern that finds precedent in Jesus himself. Jesus entered a first-century Jewish context with its own cultural stories.[14] And Jesus knew that many of his fellow Jews had the story partly right—and partly wrong. They correctly believed God created the world as good but that sin had brought death and disorder, and both the world and the human experience were no longer as they should be. They also told the true story of God working in miraculous ways to bless them as a nation, and their expectation that he would one day usher in his superior kingdom—a reign of justice, peace, and joy. Yet for all they got right, they misunderstood how the final chapters would unfold. Many thought this story would conclude with the Messiah coming to judge the Romans and most other Gentiles, while raising up only the outwardly religiously observant Jews to participate in the kingdom.

As Jesus walked the streets of Galilee at the beginning of his ministry, he proclaimed, "The time has come . . . The kingdom of God has come near" (Mark 1:15). Given first-century Jews' understanding of the messianic story, Jesus' contemporaries would have taken his words to signal his initiation of the story's final chapter, whereby he would expel the Romans and launch the kingdom (or at least their interpretation of the kingdom). Jesus, however, entered their cultural story and said both yes and no. He offered a "subversive fulfillment."[15]

In essence Jesus said, "Yes, I am the fulfillment of this old story that you've clung to. I am the King who has been promised to you and who you've been looking for. I am the fulfillment of your deepest longings, but at key points you have the story wrong. You are living out the wrong script. I haven't come to simply save you from the Romans; I've come to save *the Romans* as well. I haven't come to affirm your self-righteousness; I've come to save *you* from yourself. *I* am what you've always been longing for—you just didn't know it."

Jesus challenged and subversively fulfilled the false stories, not mainly through abstract statements or logical syllogisms, but by reorienting his listeners to the true kingdom through metaphors, narrative, and *parables*. For Mark tells us that Jesus' typical approach was to use stories: "With many similar parables Jesus spoke the word to them, as much as they could understand. He did not say anything to them without using a parable" (Mark 4:33–34).[16] The point is not that Jesus *only* told parables, but rather that this was the central way he taught. Jesus would indeed challenge the internal logic of his opponents' claims, such as when he told his opponents it didn't make sense if he exorcised demons by the power of Satan. He also gave evidence for his ministry through miracles. Yet even in these cases, the story Jesus was narrating—with himself as the fulfillment of the Hebrew Scriptures—provided the larger context that made sense of his actions that challenged the expectations of his proponents.

Jesus' use of story finds rich precedent in the narratives that fill the Hebrew scriptures. The prophet Nathan, for instance, could have confronted King David by plainly listing David's offenses and their consequences. He might have said, "King David, you are a liar, an adulterer, and a murderer, and you will reap what you have sown!" Instead, Nathan appealed to David's heart by telling him a story (2 Samuel 12:1–13).

Scholars have increasingly recognized that Genesis 1 and 2 were written, in their ancient context, in part to out-narrate rival Near Eastern creation stories. In contrast to the popular creation myths of the day, the biblical account is not a story of dueling gods and the physical creation as the bad result. The biblical story is presented as more meaningful and beautiful, revealing a creation that is good, fertile, and productive. Rather than portraying human beings as created to do the dirty work of the gods, Genesis assigns to humankind a higher function: to serve as divine image bearers by ruling over the earth and flourishing with life and creativity. Just as God creates, shapes, names, and rules, so do people receive the divine task of performing life-giving work.

In the New Testament, Paul, undergirded with the theology of Genesis 1–2, offers a better metanarrative than the pagan philosophers in Acts 17. Despite being provoked and mocked, Paul doesn't simply dismiss the Athenian culture. He instead builds a bridge, even quoting the Athenians' own pagan philosophers and poets before challenging the inner coherence of their view and proclaiming the true story of Jesus and his resurrection.

The gospel of John introduces Jesus as the *logos* (Word), choosing this popular philosophical word to both resonate with and challenge the Greek conceptions of transcendence. John recasts the *logos* in terms of the Old Testament's conception of the Word and goes further; the *logos* is a person! Jesus is the divine *logos* who gave his life to save the world.

John also tells a better story in his apocalypse, unmasking the reigning political powers to cast a vision of the coming new creation. And most importantly, the Bible, in all its diversity as well as its twist and turns, tells the grand story of God's rescue mission of the world.[17] It is hardly an overstatement to suggest that the most common way the Bible appeals to us is through story. Which makes sense, for the same God who made us storying creatures inspired the storying nature of Scripture. As Kevin Vanhoozer puts it, "Scripture summons the intellect to accept its propositions, but it also [often by way of story] summons the imagination to *see*, *feel*, and *taste* them as well."[18]

OUT-NARRATING RIVAL STORIES: BETTER SMALL STORIES, A BETTER BIG STORY

Beyond just telling stories, we are creatures who are *formed* by our stories.[19] The stories we tell and retell shape our lives. Ask someone a universal question like, "Why are we here?" or "What should we be doing?" and you'll hear them tell a story.[20] And the big stories we assume and live out are attached to all the little small stories we hear, tell, and embrace every day. Take, for instance, how from a young age we are told a story that says, "If you work hard, you'll make it, and life will be good." The tale of the American meritocracy beckons us: "The world is awaiting you. Go achieve, and then you will be satisfied." Even more powerful is the relentless story of consumerism, sold to us through all mediums and channels of life, assuring us, "If you buy *this*, you'll certainly find joy." The right car, the right neighborhood, the right clothes, are said to lead to the good life.

These cultural narratives form our collective imaginations, not because we receive them as a big, comprehensive philosophical package, but because we catch them as the little stories we hear and share every day. When we watch a car commercial, we aren't simply told which one gets good gas mileage; we see pictorial stories of the good life—comfort, prestige, confidence. When we listen to songs on the radio, we hear stories that promise joy through the kingdom of romance. Our modern parables are spread across Netflix and Spotify, aiming our hearts at the false idols of money, sex, and power. The big pervasive stories that answer essential human questions are all the more powerful when buried in social imaginations.[21] We, as C. S. Lewis has stressed, are in need of a better story, with the "strongest spell that can be found to wake us from the evil enchantment of worldliness which has been laid upon us."[22]

While the everyday stories we hear, tell, read, and watch may point us in the wrong direction, they still reflect the intuitive and abiding features of personhood—the pursuit of love, a morality that seems to press itself on us from beyond, the sense of good and evil, the reality of injustice and the longing for vindication, the guilt we can't escape and the redemption we seek, the need for meaning that death will not destroy, and the quest for purpose. Stories both ask existential questions and seek to answer them. We are storytelling animals because stories speak to innate human needs and desires. Every culture speaks in story. Every culture explains in story.

Charles Taylor stresses the importance of story, explaining that everyone believes a story about their life and about history itself: "We can't avoid . . . [master] narratives. The attempt to escape them only means that we operate by an unacknowledged, hence unexamined and uncriticized, narrative. That's because we (modern Westerners) can't help understanding ourselves in these terms . . . Our narratives deal with how we have become what we are; how we have put aside and moved away from earlier ways of being."[23]

Taylor explains that when people say things like, "That approach is medieval" or "that's a progressive thought" or "she is ahead of her time," and so on, they are speaking from a narrative—a coming-of-age story about humankind developing from a corrupt and barbaric way of life into one that is sophisticated and enlightened.[24] Likewise, when people bemoan that things "aren't like they used to be," or that people lack the moral fiber and clear sense of meaning that used to be commonplace, they are buying into the existence of historical narratives and thus forming a "reactionary" narrative of their own. But how does one counter master narratives such as these?

Taylor points us to an answer. Because "various tellings of the story of how we have become carry this sense of secularity as an inevitable consequence," we must challenge these narratives with "another story."[25] C. S. Lewis, not surprisingly considering what we've already observed about his own conversion earlier in this chapter, preceded Taylor in seeing the need for a narrative approach to persuasion. Alister McGrath, a leading Lewis scholar, summarizes Lewis's apologetics approach, as one of "commending and offering counter-narrations rather than counter-arguments against the naturalism and secularism of our age."[26] In other words, "For Lewis, Christian apologetics . . . is thus at its best when it *out-narrates* the ideologies of the world, by showing that the Christian story and its retellings, having captivated our imaginations, also enlighten our minds, and shape our moral vision."[27]

Telling smaller stories that reflect a larger worldview story can shake people out of their culture's false narratives and help them see the beauty and goodness that leads to truth.[28] By telling stories—both macro- and micro-stories, we can invite an unbeliever to drop their weapons, come in, and listen with an open mind and heart. In this way, viewing apologetics through a narrative lens provides an opportunity to challenge an unbeliever's basic assumptions about life and offer a better, more rational, existentially satisfying, practical, and complete vision of the world.[29]

So far, we've laid the groundwork for an approach to persuasion by way of out-narrating the culture's rival stories. In the next chapter, we'll learn a practical way to actually do this. The good news is that we don't have to muster up our own story. We've been given a story that is more than just true; it is the *best story ever told.* It is the story that makes sense of all other stories humans tell about the world. Jesus' story provides the answers to the questions that echo in but can't finally be answered from within these other stories. It tells the story of evil being conquered by good. It tells the story of a Hero who dies for his enemies. It tells the story of a Ruler who loves his feeble subjects so much that he enters into their plight and suffers to save them. This is the story of grace upon grace—the story of a King who gave his only Son, so we could become his sons and daughters. It is the story that leads to the home for which every human heart was made. And quite astonishingly, he has called us to become his storytellers.

NOTES

1. Quoted in Sarah Eekhoff Zylstra, "'An Unlikely Ally': What a Secular Atheist Is Teaching Christian Leaders," February 28, 2019, www.thegospelcoalition.org/article/what-a-secular-atheist-is-teaching-christian-leaders.
2. James K. A. Smith, *Desiring the Kingdom: Worship, Worldview, and Cultural Formation* (Grand Rapids: Baker Academic, 2009), 52. Smith, however, acknowledges, "This isn't to say that the cognitive or propositional is a completely foreign register for us . . . however, it doesn't get into our (noncognitive) bones in the same way or with the same effect" (p. 53).
3. James K. A. Smith, *You Are What You Love: The Spiritual Power of Habit* (Grand Rapids: Brazos, 2016), 3.
4. Jonathan Haidt, *The Happiness Hypothesis: Finding Modern Truth in Ancient Wisdom* (New York: Basic, 2006), 13.
5. David Brooks stresses that we shouldn't see making a commitment to another person as too distant from how we navigate life in general: "Deciding whom to love is not a strange alien form of decision making, a romantic interlude in the midst of normal life. Instead, decisions about whom to love are more intense versions of the sorts of decisions we make throughout the course of life, from what food to order to what career to pursue. Decision making is an inherently emotional business"

(*The Social Animal: The Hidden Sources of Love, Character, and Achievement* [New York: Random House, 2011], 17).

6. A forerunner in a more holistic approach was Blaise Pascal, who sadly did not finish his magnum opus on apologetics before his untimely death. He did, however, leave behind a collection of notes on the subject, where he famously wrote, "The heart has its reasons, which reason itself does not know" (Pascal, *Pensées* [Mineola, NY: Dover, 2003], 78). T. S. Eliot pointed out in the Dover edition's introduction to *Pensées* that Pascal is by no means offering "a defence of unreason"; instead, "the heart, in Pascal's terminology, is itself truly rational if it is truly the heart. For him, in theological matters . . . the whole personality is involved" (p. xviii).
7. The Greek word *kardia* is often used in the New Testament as the "center and source of the whole inner life, with its thinking, feeling, and volition" (see Frederick William Danker, ed., *A Greek-English Lexicon of the New Testament and Other Early Christian Literature*, 3rd. ed. [Chicago: University of Chicago Press, 2000], 508).
8. Kevin Vanhoozer, *Pictures at a Theological Exhibition: Scenes of the Church's Worship, Witness and Wisdom* (Downers Grove, IL: InterVarsity, 2016), 24. Rankin Wilbourne explains how imagination is integral for remembering anything, conducting science, and knowing God: "Any invisible force, anything conceptual, requires us to use our imagination to engage with and understand. This might be why Albert Einstein said, 'Imagination is more important than knowledge.' More than merely seeing what is unreal or fantastic, imagination is used to *image* anything that is real but not visible . . . More important, imagination is necessary to know and enjoy God. How else can we relate to the true God, 'whom no one has ever seen or can see' (1 Tim. 6:16), than by using our God-given imaging capacities—our imaginations? We must use our imaginations if we want to fully inhabit and experience the Christian life" (*Union with Christ: The Way to Know and Enjoy God* [Colorado Springs: Cook, 2016], 18).
9. Vanhoozer, *Pictures at a Theological Exhibition*, 24.
10. C. S. Lewis, *The Weight of Glory* (1949; repr., San Francisco: HarperSanFrancisco, 2001), 140.
11. Lewis uses this phrase in describing the impact that George MacDonald's book *Phantastes* had on him (C. S. Lewis, ed., *George MacDonald: An Anthology* [1946; repr., New York: HarperOne, 2001], xxxviii).
12. Alister McGrath, *C. S. Lewis, A Life: Eccentric Genius. Reluctant Prophet.* (Carol Stream, IL: Tyndale, 2013), 134.
13. Jonathan Haidt, *The Righteous Mind: Why Good People are Divided by Politics and Religion* (New York: Vintage, 2012), 328.
14. See N. T. Wright, *The New Testament and the People of God: Christian Origins and the Question of God* (Minneapolis: Fortress, 1992), 215–43.
15. For more on "subversive fulfillment" and its modern applications, see Daniel Strange, *Plugged In: Connecting Your Faith with What You Watch, Read, and Play* (London: The Good Book Company, 2019).
16. The passage indicates that Jesus spoke more explicitly when he was alone with his disciples. Rather than being intentionally obscure, the parables served as a

dividing line. As Ben Witherington III pointed out, "We must keep steadily in view that there was not an impermeable boundary between outsiders and insiders, but rather, the outsiders who heard and heeded the word would become insiders. Indeed, this was the goal, and the purpose of the parables was not obfuscation but revelation. But part of what the parables revealed was something about the audience" (*The Gospel of Mark: A Socio-Rhetorical Commentary* [Grand Rapids: Eerdmans, 2001], 173). Though at times the parables were misunderstood at a basic level, at other times outsiders understood the basic meaning but were too absorbed in their own idols to see the treasure Jesus was offering in himself and the kingdom. But their negative response in these cases—e.g., "sneering at Jesus" (Luke 16:14)—is an indication that the parable was in some sense understood (though not in the deepest sense of "understanding") and that Jesus' parables were effective in piercing through their complacency, though they responded incorrectly in becoming angry instead of repentant.

17. To see how story plays a central role in the apologetics appeals, often alongside and even framing other types of appeals within the Scriptures, see Joshua D. Chatraw and Mark D. Allen, *Apologetics at the Cross* (Grand Rapids: Zondervan, 2018), 27–61.
18. Kevin J. Vanhoozer, *The Drama of Doctrine: A Canonical-Linguistic Approach to Christian Theology* (Louisville: Westminster John Knox, 2005), 291, emphasis in original.
19. See Christian Smith, *Moral, Believing Animals* (Oxford: Oxford University Press, 2003), 64.
20. Alasdair MacIntyre makes a similar point in his seminal book *After Virtue: A Study in Moral Theory*, 3rd ed. (Notre Dame, IN: University of Notre Dame Press, 2008), 216: "Man is in his actions and practice, as well as in his fictions, essentially a story-telling animal . . . I can only answer the question 'What am I to do' if I can answer the prior question 'Of what story or stories do I find myself a part?'"
21. Charles Taylor stresses that story and imagination are tied together: "I adopt the term imaginary (i) because my focus in on the way ordinary people 'imagine' their social surroundings, and this often not expressed in theoretical terms, but is carried in *images, stories, and legends*" (*Modern Social Imaginaries* [Durham, NC: Duke University Press, 2003], 23, emphasis mine).
22. C. S. Lewis, *The Weight of Glory* (1949; repr., San Francisco: HarperSanFrancisco, 2001), 31.
23. Charles Taylor, "Afterword: *Apologia pro Libro suo*," in *Varieties of Secularism in a Secular Age*, ed. Michael Warner, Jonathan VanAntwerpen, and Craig Calhoun (Cambridge, MA: Harvard University Press, 2010), 300.
24. See Taylor, "Afterword," 300–301.
25. Taylor, "Afterword," 301.
26. Alister E. McGrath, *The Intellectual World of C. S. Lewis* (Oxford: Wiley-Blackwell, 2014), 73.
27. McGrath, *Intellectual World of C. S. Lewis*, 74, emphasis mine. Though Lewis's collective works offer a sweeping paragon of a multidimensional apologetics,

people sometimes assume that he as an apologist was primarily concerned to prove God's existence through offering linear chains of reasoning and evidence. But his widely successful fiction books, such as The Chronicles of Narnia series and *The Screwtape Letters*, were not forays into imaginative stories disconnected from his work as an apologist. Instead, his fiction was an expression of his overall approach. McGrath's careful work on Lewis's apologetics has brought needed clarity to understanding his appeal: "One of the central themes of Lewis's apologetics is that Christianity offers a narrative which is capable of generating a 'big picture' of reality, capable of allowing us to make sense of our subjective experiences and our observation of the world. Lewis does not try to prove the existence of God on *a priori* grounds, but rather invites us to appreciate how what we observe in the world around us and experience within us fits the Christian way of seeing things. Lewis often articulates this way of 'seeing things' in terms of a 'myth' [which he emphasizes in the case of Christianity, happened in history]—that is to say, a story about reality that both invites 'imaginative embrace' and communicates a conceptual framework, by which other things are to be seen. The imagination embraces the Christian narrative; reason consequently reflects on its contents" (*Narrative Apologetics: Sharing the Relevance, Joy, and Wonder of the Christian Faith* [Grand Rapids: Baker, 2019], 25).

28. For a more detailed argument for how narrative is central to all of life and cannot be simply translated into other forms without losing something, see Charles Taylor, "How Narrative Makes Meaning," in *The Language Animal: The Full Shape of the Human Linguistic Capacity* (Cambridge, MA: Harvard University Press, 2016), 291–319.
29. See Wright, *New Testament and the People of God*, 40; James K. A. Smith, *Imagining the Kingdom: How Worship Works* (Grand Rapids: Baker Academic, 2013), 58.

chapter

5

Inside Out

Recall my friend who wanted to help his brother escape from his skepticism. While he had no interest in spending their time together in heated debates, he loved his brother too much to passively avoid conversation about God. He couldn't stand the thought of settling for passing their days watching football and talking sports, numbing himself to what he confessed to believe in order to make for more comfortable Saturdays together. The challenge was that they were working out of different frameworks, living and thinking within distinct stories.

My bet is that if you have made it this far in the book, you can relate to what my friend was experiencing. How might we persuasively communicate *the* story to someone who has been taken captive by a very different (secular) story? First, we need to learn to listen carefully and understand the popular secular story lines. Second, we need a plan. In this chapter, we'll discuss each in turn.

MAPPING THE SECULAR STORY LINES: LISTENING FOR THE PLOT HOLES

I've found that we need to learn to listen closely to people who live within the secular terrain who are honest enough to admit the points at which they feel the pull of religion. Salman Rushdie, a world-renowned novelist and self-proclaimed "hardline atheist" fits the bill.

Even as a committed unbeliever, Rushdie admits religion's ability to satisfy certain human needs better than secular scripts:

> It is important that we understand how profoundly we all felt the needs that religion, down the ages, has satisfied. I would suggest that these needs are of three types; firstly, the need to be given an articulation of our half-glimpsed knowledge of exaltation, of awe, of wonder; life is an awesome experience, and religion helps us understand why life so often makes us feel small, by telling us what we are smaller than; and, contrariwise, because we also have a sense of being special, of being chosen, religion helps us by telling us what we have been chosen by, and what for. Secondly, we need answers to the unanswerable: how did we get here? How did "*here*" get here in the first place? Is this—this brief life—all there is? How can it be? What would be the point of that? And, thirdly, we need codes to live by, "rules for every damn thing." The idea of god is at once a repository for our awestruck wonderment at life and an answer to the great questions of existence, and a rulebook, too. The soul needs all these explanations—not simply rational explanations, but explanations of the heart.
>
> *It is also important to understand how often the language of secular, rationalist materialism has failed to answer these needs.*[1]

Pay close attention to Rushdie's three rough categories, which I'll label as "plot holes" in secular stories. First, a sense of awe and wonder is related to the human sense that we are significant, even though we often feel small in an overwhelmingly vast universe. Within this category, other related topics could be listed, such as love, purpose, and human dignity. Second, he relates the questions of origins, life after death, and human significance in light of death. Third, he lists issues of morality. This would include our sense of guilt, justice, good, and evil. Each of the three categories is related to the big questions of life that Rushdie admits secular accounts have often failed to answer—at least in a way he thinks most people find satisfying.

The assumed stories of secularity no longer take God for granted, yet even atheists such as Rushdie can't so easily shake the categories of personhood that have historically been inseparable from transcendence. Meaning, morality, beauty, hope, and love seem too etched into the core of who we are.

As we will see in more detail below, when God is removed from the warp and woof of everyday public life, many are left to grasp for a vague spirituality that seemingly allows them to design their own spiritual story. Others attempt to rigidly follow the story of scientific secularism, reducing the world to the sum of its material parts. Others tell a similar story of a world with no ultimate design and with us having a "this world only" existence but add in a narrative of human exceptionality and liberation. Yet no matter what story they tell, the script they actually live includes the key features of personhood.[2] We will love. We will live as moral agents. We will assign meaning. We will sense beauty. We will long to find hope. We will worship something.

John Polkinghorne, former University of Cambridge professor of mathematical physics turned priest, suggests a way to interact with these competing meta-stories:

> The theist and the atheist alike survey the same world of human experience but offer incompatible interpretations of it. My claim would be that theism has a more profound and comprehensive understanding to offer than that afforded by atheism. Atheists are not stupid, but they explain less . . . Although atheism might seem simpler conceptually, it treats beauty and morals and worship as some form of cultural or social brute facts, which accords ill with the seriousness with which these experiences touch us as persons.[3]

To get at what Polkinghorne is suggesting, we could speak in terms of comparing *worldviews*. Indeed, this is an apt description because each person you speak to will have a worldview—a perspective from which they view life. However, comparing *stories* will often provide a better bridge in conversation, because narrative "is the most characteristic expression of worldview, going deeper than the isolated observation or fragmented remark."[4]

A person's defining myth is not normally spelled out in a creedal-like formula, and it often even remains largely unarticulated, though inquiring about someone's most basic assumptions and most treasured values can help them begin to see the bigger narrative they, perhaps unwittingly, have been telling with their lives. From marketing to movies, we imbibe the narratives passed down and reinforced to us each day, so that our goals, our vision of the good, and our rationality begin to mirror the stories that surround our lives.

We are narrative creatures, which explains why approaching conversations in terms of offering a better story can be so powerful. Rather than relying on abstract logic or isolated facts, which can often appear fragmented and void of a larger context, a narrative approach frames logic and evidence in a larger vision of reality and invites the other person to imagine seeing the world through and living within a better story.

Story also strikes a more personal note and can be much less contentious. To put this practically, if you walk up to a new acquaintance and say, "What's your worldview?" you will probably get a confused expression or a defensive reaction. But if you ask them, "What's your story?" their eyes are more likely to light up and they engage in meaningful conversation. In a world of Facebook tirades and Twitter provocations, which have colored many of our conversational instincts, "What's your worldview?" can sound like you're looking for a fight, while "What's your story?" communicates you actually care and that you want to have a conversation. And if you listen closely as they tell their story, you'll likely hear how they make sense of themselves and the world around them.

TODAY'S POPULAR SECULARIZED STORIES

This section maps out three of the most popular of secular, grand story lines so that you can have a better sense of the narratives we must learn to interact with.

The pessimistic secular story. According to this story, the universe came into existence through a "big bang" billions of years ago with no divine cause or purpose for future inhabitants. Eventually, in one small corner of an immense universe, on the planet we call Earth, life began to emerge from chemicals. After a long unguided evolutionary history, billions of years in the making, which was characterized by natural selection and the "survival of the fittest," *homo sapiens* eventually emerged.

While in the past, humans embraced fanciful projections of deities, illusions of life after death, the rehearsal of sacred rituals, and a transcendent moral order, the use of reason and scientific discovery has awakened those who have the fortitude to face the harsh realities of a universe of natural causes and physical matter. Unfortunately, the human cowardice to face the fact that we are alone in the universe and to naively insist on maintaining values grounded in disproven myths continues to plague even apparently secular societies.

A truly unflinching commitment to follow this story to its end leads the pessimistic secular to conclude that human life has no *ultimate* significance. There is no cosmic order, no ethical order outside of our subjective preferences, no universal moral obligations, and even, many would maintain, no true free will—our actions are simply a product of our physical makeup and external stimuli. Reason leads to a grim reality: humanity will go extinct, and the solar system itself will as well. Everything eventually will run out of energy. No one will be alive to even remember human history; ultimately it will not matter that we ever existed. Our lives, if we are brave enough to face the truth, must be lived under the cloud of tragedy and absurdity.

The optimistic secular story. Much like the pessimistic secular account, this story begins with the beginning of the universe emerging out of natural causes. Eventually, against all odds, the physical conditions on a particular planet emerged as suitable for the beginning of life, and after a long unguided evolutionary process that favored the survival of the strong, the human species eventually emerged. For most of human history, our ancestors explained the world by appealing to a divine order, assuming an "enchanted" existence, and looking to an otherworldly existence after death. Like its secular counterpart, this more optimistic story finds its climatic turning point in Western Europe around the eighteenth century. Through reason and science, enlightened humans began to increasingly cast off the myths of deities and a divinely ordered cosmos. As indispensable or "reasonable" as such beliefs might have once seemed to be—perhaps even necessary as an evolutionary tool for survival—humans have progressed to the point of no longer needing such a theory.

Unlike its secular counterpart, which sees a godless world as a cold reality that the heroic grimly faces, this is an exhilarating story of liberation. Having escaped outdated, mythological conceptions of the world that were accompanied by stifling authoritarian dogma, we can now, individually and collectively, make our own meaning and set our own course. As rational beings set free from our cultural captivity to religion, we can now rise above the evolutionary forces of individual and tribal survival for the purpose of human flourishing—maximizing pleasure and minimizing pain, treating all people with dignity, creating systems for equal treatment for all, and taking personal responsibility to care for the earth and make it a better place. Yes, we will all one day die, but through no doing of our own and no plan of a divine being, we now find ourselves not only as actors in the story but as authors with the freedom to write the story for ourselves and to pursue meaning and happiness on our own terms.

The story of pluralistic and moral therapeutic spirituality. Though frequently under the guise of Christianity, this story is distinct from Christianity and the previous two secular stories. While not necessarily discounting the current secular models for the emergence of life, God—or at least some kind of divine force—is still seen as essential. God gives life meaning, morality, and significance. However, neither God, morality, nor our purpose is found by looking outside of ourselves to a divinely given order or traditional religious authority—such as written revelation or a religious institution. While ancient religions may provide some helpful wisdom for life today, the outdated portions of such teachings should be adapted for our modern world. Ultimately, we are to look inside of ourselves to listen to the unique human (or divine) spark within us and live authentic lives. God exists to help us find our true potential, feel better about ourselves, and guide us to treat others with dignity and respect. Diverse religious expressions, in their ideal forms, help us discover an inner peace and a love that makes the world a better place.

Three Micro-Stories

The three stories below aren't so much metanarratives that explain human origins or questions of the divine, but accounts that enter our lives and end up taking priority—they set the direction of life, even if most people aren't fully conscious of the script they are following.

The three examples are also only a quick sample of what could be a long list, but this is enough for you to get the idea.

The story of consumerism. Bombarded by ads, movies, and media, the default story sold to us from an early age is that the good life comes with a price tag. Built into the million-dollar ad campaigns that constantly flash across our eyes is the recognition that humans will pursue meaning—the golden ticket is to convince us that we can find it in what they are selling. As Naomi Klein has explained, humans need "community and narrative and transcendence," and the promise of the most successful companies is that you can find each of those things if you will just "go shopping again."[5]

The story of achievement. "You are what you accomplish." We are rarely explicitly told this; there's no need. The message is still loud and clear. The two-hundred-dollar study sessions for a leg up on standardized testing prep, the need to always be "winning," the celebrity culture painting the picture of what real success looks like—all of these are part of the collective story we hear and likely do our part in telling: "You can do it; you can be someone special—if you achieve, if you are noticed, if you become famous." This is an ancient story, but as James K. A. Smith has pointed out, it has metastasized within our Western meritocracy, where fame has become a sort of self-salvation: "We've traded the hope of immortality for a shot at going viral."[6]

The story of romance. Our loneliness, our insatiable desire to love and be loved, can be satisfied if we just find our "soul mate." Modern movies and songs, from *Beauty and the Beast* to Taylor Swift's "Lover," script for us the search for true love's kiss, with redemptive, yes even, salvific, hopes. If I can just find the "one," it will be heaven on earth—happily *ever after*.

It is important to be aware of different macro- and micro-stories. Yet given the piecemeal way many blend narratives together today and the unconscious nature by which our stories script our life, it would be a mistake to assume that people are always fully aware of the story lines they are enacting. Our life's scripts are more like the air we breathe than the items we select off a menu. As we will see, this means we have to find certain entry points that connect with their aspirations and longings to help people see their need for a better story.

HAVING A PLAN: TAKEN CAPTIVE BY THE RIGHT STORY

In various ways, the macro- and micro-stories haven taken us all captive. Contrasting the Christian story with these rival narratives sobers us to the way we are actually living despite what we confess. To counter these stories, we must embed our lives in the true story. Through the reading of the Scriptures, the fellowship of the saints, the partaking of the sacraments, daily prayers, and the preaching of the Word, God reorients the way we see the world. Constantly comparing the rival stories to God's story is essential to not being lulled to sleep in a secular age.

Thus, learning to view all of life through the lens of the gospel is essential for discipleship. Rather than seeing apologetics as tacked on to discipleship, apologetics becomes the natural outcome of discipleship. Basic Christian discipleship becomes the training ground for apologists. How do you become effective at talking about God in a skeptical age? Steep your life in the gospel story. Learn to see everything by way of *the* story. Study to see where the story of Christ challenges and overlaps with the dominant assumptions of culture around. By taking every thought captive to Christ and his story, you will grow closer to God, but you will also become the right type of person—a cruciform witness habituated in a pattern of thinking that serves as the foundation for our approach.

THE CHRISTIAN STORY

The Christian story is centered around a triune God. As an outpouring of his love, God created everything in the universe good. (There is disagreement among Christians on when and how God created, but that the universe was made inherently good is basic to the story.) As God's creatures, we have been created with inherit value, meaning, and purpose. As his image bearers, humans are made for a relationship with God, to love others, and to care for creation. And yet something has gone deeply wrong.

Endowed with the sense of moral obligation, the capacity for creative brilliance, and the desire for deep interpersonal relationships, humans were given the freedom to choose. Our problem is that we, quite absurdly, used our God given abilities to run from God. The result is a disordered world where we love things in the wrong order—we worship ourselves and the world around us rather than the Creator. We have become self-absorbed and fail to love others as ourselves. Having turned in on ourselves and away from God, we have become ill-equipped to live for what we were made. The result is the exclusion, enmity, and self-righteous superiority expressed in a myriad of seemingly ineluctable ways throughout history—testified to on a horrific scale by wars, genocides, and destruction of the earth and on the micro-level of our daily lives in our verbal spats, selfish tantrums, and desperate anxieties. The story of human failure fits with what we know all too well. While we have the potential for glorious achievements, we also have the tragic track record of misery and destruction. Facing this reality is essential for seeing the message of Christianity as good news.

The good news is not a series of abstract beliefs or an ideology or a list of rules to follow to be "good" people. While other religious "solutions" claim to offer salvation through obedience to a great prophet or a spiritual guru, the Christian story hinges on an *event*. The good news is a *person*. God himself entered our world as a man, offering forgiveness that transforms the broken and turns rebels into sons and daughters. To pay for sin and to mend the wounded, he bore on the cross the cost of rebellion. To defeat evil, he absorbed the worst of the malevolent powers of this world. While we ran away, Jesus came running to us with the Father's love. The good news is grace.

He came to save so that we might flourish as his image bearers. As the ideal human, Jesus charted the path of true human flourishing that combined authority with compassion, justice with mercy, and the freedom found in obedience. At the very heart of the Christian message is sacrifice and love for the stranger, for the marginalized, for enemies—a vision that has already transformed lives and the world in powerful ways, even as his followers continue to limp through a broken world. But one day, we will run and laugh and play in joy.

Broken and grief-stricken, Jesus willingly carried his cross to his own death. But then, surprising even his own fearful disciples, he rose from the grave in victory. Jesus' resurrection is the climactic event that proclaims to the world that God has conquered death. He is renewing the world. The disordered and broken world will ultimately be made right. Evil will be banished. The resurrection is the beginning of the great renewal. Christ's Spirit resides in those who turn from themselves and trust in him as Lord, liberating us to rest in God's eternal love in a new creation.

"INSIDE OUT" APOLOGETICS

To help us make this move from theoretical insights to everyday life, we now turn to "inside out" apologetics. "Inside out" begins by entering a person's social imagination and engaging their ideas from *within* it. This is critical. It's not enough to recognize that someone has different assumptions and "common sense" thinking that differs from us; we need to learn to step *into* their story before pointing them to the way *out*. Someone who has assumed the "givens" of late modernism brings deeply rooted assumptions, and they won't flippantly discard these assumptions in favor of the Bible or Christianity. We must then engage their story to tug at their assumptions and invite them to consider the Christian story. By beginning within their own story—listening for hints of the larger and smaller narratives that inform their life, paying attention to what they look to in order to fulfill the inescapable features of personhood—we are positioned to identify commonalities, listen so we can discuss points of disagreement, challenge their view on its own terms, and show how the prevailing cultural narratives fail to live up to their deepest aspirations.

Notice how in the familiar "building block" model (represented in the graphic on page 65), apologetics has a step-by-step feel. You start by establishing a basic and or an assumed universal logic and then proceed to argue for general theism, present historical evidence for the Bible's reliability, and finally share the message of the gospel. While it can seem like there's a lot of sense in these steps, the problem is that we can't expect unbelievers to build along with us as we leverage ideas grounded in a preconceived rational framework they don't necessarily share. Our unbelieving friends are often perplexed to understand why a Christian's "logical" steps should have any bearing on their lives. Another problem with the building block model is that it often doesn't lend itself to fostering conversations, which proceed with a healthy back-and-forth, often with a narrative feel. Stringing together premises and conclusions is not most people's idea of an engaging conversation.

In contrast to the way the building block model places the gospel at the end of interactions, "inside out" insists that the gospel be woven *into* the discourse, thus making it the thematic center of how we engage. By joining an unbeliever within their story and by keeping the gospel well integrated, we can more readily (and sincerely) identify points where Christianity overlaps with the other person's assumptions. While the gospel forms the lens through which we view all the world, this approach also emphasizes the importance of listening to understand the other person's view so we can see where their framework may have internal inconsistences and fail to make good sense of our human experience. In the graphic, the overlapping area represents common assumptions and connecting points that can be identified as things to affirm, while the area that does not overlap represents points at which the gospel can challenge the other person's views.

By interacting with alternative stories on their own terms before turning *out* to Christianity (what theologians refers to as "immanent critique"), we are not forced to play by the lowest common denominator and reason on the terms set by skeptics when discussing the Christian story. The goal is for both sides to be willing to "try on the other story" and see how it "fits" rationally, psychologically, and experientially. This will mean, instead of hiding our theological convictions, after inhabiting the other person's perspective we will ask the person to consider how Christianity's mega-story, along with all the Bible's little stories, better explains the world around us.

Accordingly, we don't have to wait until we've built a long and arduous apologetic chain of arguments to finally arrive (if we ever get there) at a closing gospel presentation. The gospel and its implications are present from the start and woven throughout, keeping the gospel central in our conversations. In this approach, recognizing the power of imagination and story does not exclude the importance of various types of evidence that both support and call into question other metanarratives. Yet the Christian narrative frames specific arguments and provides the needed context for people to make sense of and grasp the relevance of the evidence. "Inside out" incorporates arguments examining scientific and historical data, as well as utilizing inescapable aspects of personhood to compare views and ask, "What story about the world best fits?"

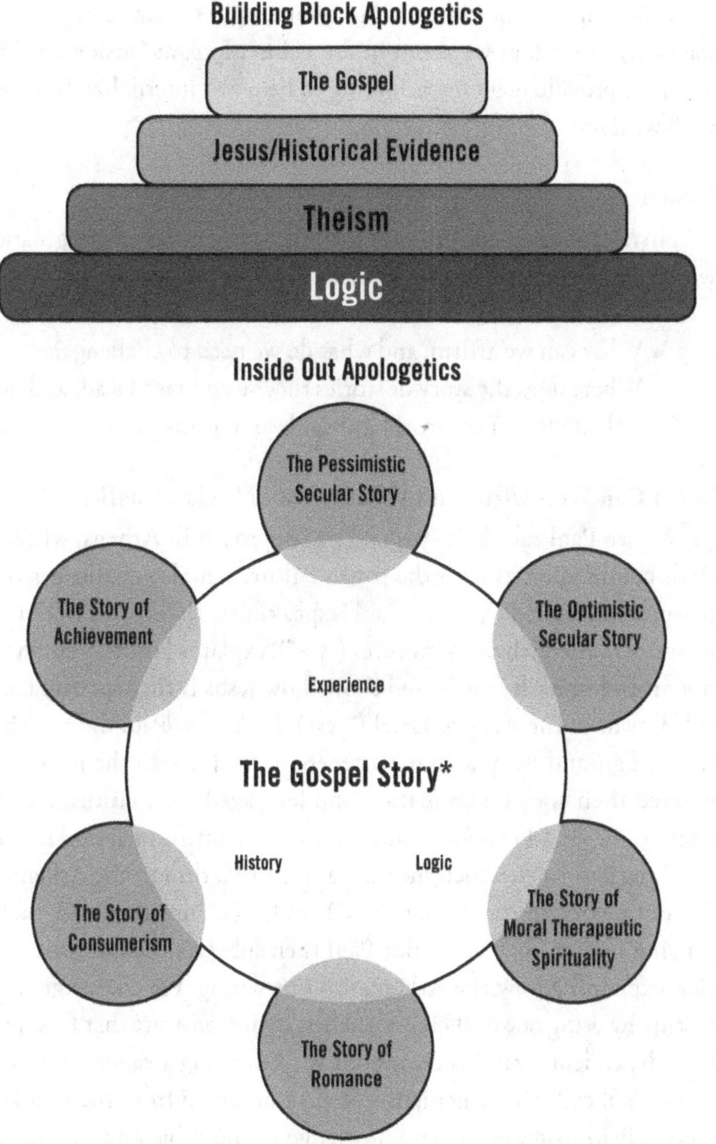

*The circle in the middle of the diagram represents Christianity with the gospel at the center as its core messsage. Of course, the Triune God—whose mission is expressed in the gospel—is at the center of all reality. However, we have placed the gospel at the center of this diagram because the Triune God reveals himself in the gospel, and it is in the gospel that we encounter him. For instance, the central proclamation in the New Testament, which Paul refers to as "of first importance" (1 Cor 15:3), is God's saving work in the life, death, and resurrection of Jesus Christ.

By placing the gospel at the center of apologetic conversations, the inside out approach understands logic, experience, and history in light of the gospel. Imagine these elements as not only floating around "the gospel" but also as entailments of Christianity that when viewed properly are part of the gospel's fabric and can extend out to bring someone to the core of the Christian message.

This chapter is not intended to offer a rigid system to be followed slavishly; instead, as we zoom in for a closer look at "inside out," the aim is to provide mental scaffolding to help you internalize and apply with wisdom.

Inside

First, starting on the *inside* of the other person's social imagination, we ask ourselves as we listen to others:

- What can we affirm, and what do we need to challenge?
- Where does the story or stories they've embraced lead, and how is their view of the world unlivable and inconsistent?

What Can We Affirm, and What Do We Need to Challenge?

We see Paul take this "yes and no" approach in Athens, where he finds commonalities with the pagan culture but also challenges their perspectives (Acts 17). When Paul is speaking with Jews (Acts 17:1–4), he starts in the Hebrew Scriptures ("yes"), explains how the Torah was not an end in itself ("no"), and shows how Jesus is the true and better fulfillment of the story of Israel ("yes"). In Athens Paul did not share the background story with his listeners, as he did with the Jews, so he entered their social imagination and leveraged their cultural stories (Acts 17:16–34). He quotes pagan sources and affirms where Athenian thinking is correct, which includes at least two things: the Athenians' desire to worship the divine ("yes"), and their intuition that they're missing something ("yes"). But Paul then subverts the dominant stories, explaining how the Athenians went wrong. He challenges their culture by using one of their own beliefs to demonstrate that God must be independent from his creation. Far from being a vague admonishment, Paul calls the Athenians to repent and turn from their idolatry ("no"). Paul displays a deep knowledge of the Bible and his context and skillfully maps the Christian story onto the prevailing cultural narratives of his particular audience.

As I'll discuss in later chapters, our secular culture possesses many things Christians can and should say yes to—the fight for human rights, the goodness of human diversity, the importance of serving society's oppressed and marginalized. As Jesus pointed out, even an evil person knows how to give good gifts to his children (Luke 11:11–13). By God's grace, there are often many points we can agree on with our unbelieving neighbors and friends.

We should follow Paul's example in studying the culture and being able to interact with and cite the authorities it respects. But as we do this, we also have to be prepared to do the hard work of wisely challenging these authorities and the underlying assumptions within their cultural stories. For example, in confronting Western culture, Christians would need to contrast (1) the culture's sense of moral autonomy ("How dare anyone, even God, tell me what to do!") with moral dependence on God; (2) the culture's denial of divine accountability ("A loving Creator wouldn't judge his creatures") with the reality of God's divine judgment; and (3) the culture's embrace of expressive individualism ("I look within myself to define myself") with finding identity in Christ and submitting to his lordship. In order to challenge these and other assumptions, we turn to the second question.

Where Do Their Stories Lead, and Are They Internally Consistent and Livable?

One way to help others see their blind spots is to trace where their assumptions and beliefs ultimately lead if applied consistently. Fallen cultures often contain assumptions that make Christianity seem implausible, yet those who hold these assumptions usually haven't worked them out in their head. Those assumptions are, after all, the very air they breathe. Because of this, by asking questions and discussing the implications of certain views, we can expose these views as overly simplistic and unlivable. This, of course, must be done with a sympathetic ear. We must listen well and admit when others make good points, but then push them to extend basic assumptions to their logical conclusions—help them see the problems and challenges within their own views. Sowing uncertainty in the other person toward their own views creates the space needed to discuss other options such as the gospel. The goal is to enter their story to challenge it on its own terms by helping them see where it's *inconsistent* and *unlivable* in order to lay the groundwork for them to take Christianity seriously.

Outside

Second, working *outside* their view to Christianity, we contrast the stories they've embraced with Christianity, asking where their stories borrow from the Christian story. The Christian story, while overlapping in certain ways, can weave in and out of the partial and fragmented narrative of the unbeliever. From this point we're inviting them to try on the biblical story to see how it fits with their experiences, observations, and history.

As is often the case when presenting models of various sorts, the distinction here between "inside" and "outside" may seem rigid and perfectly clear. It's not. Movement between the inside and outside of someone's view should be fluid, dictated by the unfolding conversation or by the opportunities found within a particular Sunday's Scripture text(s) but in neither case will it normally follow a textbook diagram. In fact, conversations will *hopefully* see you go back and forth as the discussion meanders along. I say "hopefully" because conversations are almost always unpredictable and rough around the edges. Moving back and forth from inside to outside, then, does not suggest a failure in applying "inside out," but rather that a real conversation marked by dialogue is taking place (and in conversation, we Christians need to be humble enough to admit when the other person has a point, as well as the real challenges for our own view). For our purposes, however, it will be most helpful to treat the inside and outside as two distinct sides of the same coin.

Where Do Competing Views Borrow from the Christian Story?

As we've seen, living as a Christian in post-Christendom has serious challenges. Rather than being a new and strange movement with a clean slate, as in the early church, Christians are now regularly viewed as an oppressive, antiquated holdover from the past. This default posture against Christianity poses a significant issue for Christian witness. Yet buried beneath the rubble of a fallen Christendom are the currents of the faith, carrying many of the secular world's most prized possessions. Secular author John Gray helps us here when he opens his book *Seven Types of Atheism* with refreshing frankness:

> Contemporary atheism is a flight from a godless world. Life without any power that can secure order or some kind of ultimate justice is a frightening and for many an intolerable prospect. In the absence of such a power, human events could be finally chaotic, and *no story could be told* that satisfied the need for meaning. Struggling to escape this vision, atheists have looked for surrogates of the God they have cast aside. But this faith in humanity makes sense only if it continues ways of thinking that have been inherited from monotheism [which do not find a register within their atheist account]. The idea that the human species realizes common goals throughout history is a secular avatar of a religious idea of redemption.[7]

Christianity has been transfused into the bloodstream of Western society. Though your secular friends may oppose Christianity, in many ways it is still pumping through their veins and directly linked to what they see as a healthy society. Your task is to help them see they are likely already personally borrowing from the Christian narrative and to wonder with them what might happen if Christianity—with its assumptions and ethics—were to be completely purged from our culture.[8] Many key features assumed in the Western moral, social, and judicial spheres originated in or have been profoundly impacted by Christianity. By learning to identify these features, you can explain how they seem to be smuggling resources from the Christian story in order to secure many of their most significant values and aspirations.[9]

In the following section, we'll address our current culture's moral aspirations with specificity, but for now the point is to show how this question promotes interaction. By working with an unbeliever and lovingly challenging them to see the ways they must borrow beliefs, norms, and practices from Christianity—ones that fit with some of their deepest desires but not their secular narrative—you have an opening to offer an invitation: *Why not try on this story and see how it fits in other ways as well?*

How Does the Christian Narrative Better Address Our Experiences, Observations, and History?

By working inside rival stories to show how their own narratives fail to adequately answer life's biggest questions we've created space for the other person to seriously consider how Christianity offers a more satisfying and rationally coherent story. By narrating how Christianity answers life's most fundamental questions and captures "the rich texture of this life and history," we open the door for them to come into the gospel story.[10] To paraphrase C. S. Lewis, we invite them to not only see Christianity, but to see a world illuminated by Christ. The ability to do this skillfully hangs on having a rich understanding of the gospel ourselves and learning to "take captive every thought to make it obedient to Christ" (2 Corinthians 10:5).[11] As we process our own life and the world around us through the spectacles of the gospel story, we will be equipped to explain how Christianity provides a robust vision of reality that illuminates everything else.

If you're thinking, *Okay, I think I see what you're saying, but what does this actually look like?* you are asking the right question. This chapter has provided the framework:[12]

Inside:

- Ask yourself:
  - What can I affirm, and what will I need to challenge?
  - Where does this story lead, and is it internally consistent and livable?

Outside:

- Ask yourself:
  - Where do competing views borrow from the Christian story?
  - How does the Christian narrative better address our experiences, observations, and history?

As we turn to part 2, you will see how this can work in practice.

NOTES

1. Salman Rushdie, *Is Nothing Sacred?* (New York: Granta, 1990), 8, emphasis original in the first paragraph; emphasis mine in the second.
2. N. T. Wright describes something similar and refers to them as "vocational signposts." He lists seven: "Justice, Beauty, Freedom, Truth, Power, Spirituality, and

Relationships" (*History and Eschatology: Jesus and the Promise of Natural Theology* [Waco, TX: Baylor University Press, 2019], 224). Later he writes that each of these "raises questions, questions which point beyond themselves and demand that some story be told which will provide the larger meaning for which they all long" (p. 233).

3. John Polkinghorne, *The Faith of a Physicist: Reflections of a Bottom-Up Thinker* (Minneapolis: Fortress, 1996), 70.
4. Wright, *The New Testament and the People of God*, 123. Michael Horton puts it simply: "All of our worldviews are stories" (*The Christian Faith: A Systematic Theology for Pilgrims on the Way* [Grand Rapids: Zondervan, 2011], 17).
5. "The Persuaders," directed by Barak Goodman and Rachel Dretzin, *Frontline*, aired November 9, 2004, www.pbs.org/wgbh/pages/frontline/shows/persuaders /etc/script.html.
6. James K. A. Smith, *On the Road with Saint Augustine: A Real-World Spirituality for Restless Hearts* (Grand Rapids: Brazos, 2019), 81.
7. John Gray, *Seven Types of Atheism* (New York: Farrar, Straus and Giroux, 2018), 1, emphasis in original. For another notable nonreligious scholar who recognizes how dominant secular narratives borrow from religious accounts and in particular the Christian story, see Jürgen Habermas, *Time of Transitions* (Cambridge: Polity, 2006), 150–51; Jürgen Habermas et al., *An Awareness of What Is Missing* (Cambridge: Polity, 2010), 18–21.
8. Gray adds that while secular humanists "imagine they stand outside the view of the world that monotheism expressed," they actually "have not shaken off a monotheistic way of thinking." He goes on: "The belief that humans are gradually improving is the central article of faith of modern humanism. When wrenched from monotheistic religion, however, it is not so much false as meaningless" (*Seven Types of Atheism*, 24). In this chapter ("Secular Humanism, a Sacred Relic," 24–51), he explains it wasn't until Christianity that people began to assume definite progress in history rather than a cyclical view that lacked definite progress within the course of history. While I don't agree with an absolute denial of any "thread of progress" and Gray's rather rosy picture of religious freedom, sexuality, and women in the pagan world prior to Christianity, his chapter correctly points out the serious moral failings that are often quickly glossed over in accounts of our current "civilized age." In contrast to Gray's overly sanguine remarks about the social life of the pagan world, the monumental impact Christianity had in the ancient world in shaping views on sex and the treatment of women as well as religious freedom, see, on the first topic, Kyle Harper's seminal book, *From Shame to Sin: The Christian Transformation of Sexual Morality in Late Antiquity* (Cambridge, MA: Harvard University Press, 2013), and on the second, Robert Louis Wilken, *Liberty in the Things of God: The Christian Origins of Religious Freedom* (New Haven, CT: Yale University Press, 2019), 7–23.
9. Christian Smith's *Atheist Overreach: What Atheism Can't Deliver* (Oxford: Oxford University Press, 2018) serves as an example of this approach. Smith offers a critique *inside* the skeptic's meta-story. He occasionally goes further, however,

and at important junctures shows how many atheists' most significant assumptions and deepest aspirations are borrowed from *outside* their framework, and particularly from devotees of the biblical story. His focus here lies primarily in the secular commitment to universal benevolence and human right. In order to maintain such high moral commitments and practices that require sacrifice, a society needs "at least implicit rationales in order for people to embrace and act on them over the long run" (p. 53). Smith models how to guide someone to see the possible long-term implications for themselves and society as a whole if they continue to embrace an overarching narrative absent of God. A society can't forever live off the fumes of a story no longer embraced. Without a coherent and rational framework that makes sense of high moral standards and motivates people to make personal sacrifices for the common good, the high ideals that most Westerners share hang by a tenuous thread.

10. Charles Taylor, *The Language Animal: The Full Shape of the Human Linguistic Capacity* (Cambridge, MA: Harvard University Press, 2016), 219. This section follows an approach similar to what Taylor refers to as "hermeneutical argument" (pp. 216–21).
11. It is important to keep in mind that the New Testament authors stress the importance of holding to the true gospel (e.g., Galatians 1:8–9; Jude 3) and give us formulas that summarize the content of the gospel (e.g., 1 Corinthians 15:1–4), and yet they do not offer a singular formulaic approach. Instead, the New Testament demonstrates a controlled flexibility, calling Christians both to faithfully communicate the message of the gospel and to tailor their presentation of that message to specific contexts. The gospel itself was originally articulated in certain languages and used imagery from specific cultures. Thus, to present the gospel faithfully means first to understand the Christian message within the context of the Bible and its native culture, and then to apply the message in a way that is understandable and relatable to those in your current context.
12. For a historical precedent for "Inside Out," see the structure of Augustine's *The City of God*, where the first ten chapters critique the pagan myths and Roman social order on their own terms before focusing on the biblical story in books 11–22.

PART

2

Offering a Better Story

The central aim of this book is not to help you tell stories in general but rather to help you be a better communicator of God's story in a world that no longer takes our plotline too seriously. The macro- and micro-stories described in the last chapter are like engines that power the way people think and live, even though most are not aware of what exactly is going on under the hood. Just because we drive a car doesn't mean we know how it works. For most of us, if a mechanic wants to convince us that we need costly work done on our car, his best bet is to explain why that sputtering sound will become a major problem if nothing is done. He will need to speak in ways we can understand, interpreting what that sound means and also explaining why it should actually matter to us.

Similar to a customer-oriented mechanic, we need to be aware of the points at which unbelievers sometimes sense something isn't quite right, while at the same time not assuming most people are fully aware of the story(s) that powers their lives. This section of the book models how the Christian story can be communicated to help people understand what is actually going on underneath the hood, as well as how the gospel can begin to repair what is broken.

Each chapter begins with a feature of the contemporary social imaginary—the way many today, due to the stories that fill our daily lives, tend to instinctively assume the world *is*. The chapters first describe a common assumption that makes everyday gospel communication challenging and then applies "inside out" to subversively challenge some of Western culture's most fundamental habits of thinking. A key distinction here is that the aim is to challenge, not to simply dismiss outright, as this allows for sincere engagement by which we can help others see how their deepest aspirations don't actually fit within secular narratives but find their home in the Christian story. The story of Christ is the true story of the God who is behind all that is true, good, and beautiful—"inside out" is about helping others see that what they have always been longing for can only be found in him.

Like my interaction with the student I shared in chapter 4, the goal in this section is not to give you a list of apologetic "moves," but instead to pass on a *way* to approach engaging others. These chapters offer key features of personhood and late modern culture's deepest aspirations (the very things that make up the stories we are most captivated by!), which opens up pathways to the gospel. Rather than strict step-by-step instructions, the goal is for you to come away with trajectories for talking about God in a post-Christian landscape. The secular terrain is just too varied to pass on a one-dimensional map with turn-by-turn directions. The rest of the book is more like riding around a region with a compass (the gospel) in hand, with the goal of gaining an intuitive sense, an "apologetic know-how" to navigate our cultural context.

chapter
6

Imagining a Better Meaning

Cultural Assumption #1:
"I don't need God or religion."

WHEN NOTHING SEEMS TO BE MISSING

The secular narratives that now loom large in our leading centers of culture no longer assume we live in a divinely ordered world filled with transcendent and eternal significance. As a result, instead of looking to God for significance or meaning in life, many "have constructed webs of meaning that provide almost all the significance they need."[1] For this reason, you will often meet people who seem far from being on any kind of search for religious meaning, neither looking for some missing bit of life-changing information about God nor waiting for someone—least of all a Christian—to answer all their spiritual questions. It is not "nagging questions about God or the afterlife" that drive many today, but rather, as philosopher James K. A. Smith explains, nonreligious longings, goals, and "quests for significance" that fill their lives to such an extent that they seem, for the most part, to be content if they merely have the right relationships and experiences—and they'll confidently tell you so.[2]

But despite such meanings that late moderns create for themselves, they still have their moments. Unable to shake the feeling that, as Luc Ferry puts it, they're not "on earth only to purchase automobiles or ever better stereo systems," they can experience a sense of loss despite having it all.[3] The longing for something beyond the payoffs of consumerism and self-actualizing relationships has long been expressed in the midst of this-worldly achievement and abundance. This restlessness is epitomized in the song "Something's Missing," as the popular artist John Mayer sings about the mysterious unease he feels despite his abundance of possessions, relationships, and comfort. After acknowledging he's obtained all the necessary elements that should seemingly furnish him with the American dream, the song admits life is lacking something, though he remains unsure of what it could be.

Yet when people living within this story begin to wonder if they are missing something and even come to realize there is in fact a "hole" in their lives, they often won't assume it's "God-shaped." Instead, given their framing narrative, they'll likely suspect, especially at first, that they must be missing something in this world, like wealth, achievement, sex, or friends. They assume they simply haven't reached *all* their goals yet, and so they put their heads down and recommit to frantically trying to achieve more.

Or in the cases where they've accomplished everything they thought would give their life meaning, only to admit to a growing sense that something is still missing, they will often assume they must have just adopted the wrong types of things in each category. They have, they tell themselves, pursued the wrong friendships, worked in the wrong jobs, purchased the wrong stuff, or married the wrong person. The remedy, they conclude, is to "trade up." And so the stereotypical midlife crisis—or as Mayer sings about in another song, a quarter-life crisis—ensues. The tendency among many late moderns, then, is to short-circuit deeper questions of life by assuming they can secure what's lacking through obtaining more or better things from this world while not taking seriously the possibility they might be missing something that can't be found in *this* world.

A LIVING APOLOGETIC

Encountering apathy toward questions of God can be disheartening, but there tends to be more going on beneath the surface than people admit. Even as late moderns enjoy abundance and comfort, the sense that "somewhere there is a fullness or richness which transcends the ordinary" still haunts many.[4] The secret is discovering what spooks them.

First and foremost, our lives are to be a kind of friendly, otherworldly "haunting," as our priorities are set by a King who is not of this world. Cultivate friendships with your neighbors and coworkers, identify as a Christian, live out your faith, invite them to your home to spend time with you and your friends, live sacrificially, and be ready to speak into their lives.

Life has a way of tearing through complacency and naive senses of control and immortality. People's apathy can be quickly shaken when the realization hits them that their "webs of meanings" are much more fragile than they had imagined.[5] The question is, *Who will they turn to in those times of fear and angst?* If you have been a friend and have consistently modeled hope in the midst of sorrow and bold humility during difficult times, doors are more likely to open for you to give "the reason for the hope that you have" (1 Peter 3:15).

We also should become adept at interacting within the secular webs of meaning they've constructed for themselves, pressing through to the vulnerability and anxiety they sense from being cut off from transcendence.[6] The rest of this chapter focuses on how the most significant and universal experiences of life—the sense of purpose, the experience of beauty, the need for something more, and the reality of death—call for a better story and point to a better meaning.

Purpose

"Inside" their story. In the simple, everyday experiences of life, most take purpose and meaning for granted. As atheist philosopher John Gray has written, "Other animals are born, seek mates, forage for food and die. That is all. But we humans—we think—are different."[7] Or perhaps more accurately, as humans, we sense that we *are* different. We don't simply wish our lives had purpose and meaning; we instinctually live with purpose and meaning. Yet within the purely secular story lines, there is no ultimate, transcendent meaning to life. Thus we must either go against our instincts and own up to a meaningless existence (the pessimistic story) or create meaning for ourselves (the optimistic story). Neither option is free from problems.

The optimistic story not only lacks logical consistency, but it also fails to bear out experientially—the webs of meaning we construct for ourselves are at best temporary and frail. In his book *Straw Dogs*, Gray argues that in a godless world, human life is only composed of physical matter, and as such, we are left without choice, selfhood, and free will.[8] But if this is the case, how can we be free to create our own meaning? Furthermore, if all that exists is matter, then even if you manage to construct meaning and do something that the human race recognizes as monumental, ultimately what difference will it make in the grand scheme of things?

Even if you forge ahead with the greatest of philanthropic deeds, to be remembered for generations to come, it doesn't change the fact that the solar system will still implode and all humankind's achievements, big and small, will disappear into utter insignificance. This is a harsh reality for those who accept the story that says this world is all we have. In the end, as the secular philosopher Thomas Nagel says, "It wouldn't matter if you had never existed."[9] This bitter pill lines up with the pessimistic story, but the problem is that when someone claims they have completely swallowed it, normally they've actually had a kind of visceral reaction that doesn't allow them to fully absorb it. Does anyone really have the stomach for it? It seems for those who feel most acutely the implications of this story and come the closest to actually absorbing the pill, they end up gutted. Life becomes empty of *life*.

The character Ivan from Fyodor Dostoyevsky's novel *The Brothers Karamazov* serves as a powerful example of this problem. Ivan is known for his denunciation of God, and yet throughout the novel, he finds that he cannot help but be deeply moved by "irrational" things, such as an intense desire to live:

> Do you know I've been sitting here thinking to myself: that if I didn't believe in life, if I lost faith in the woman I love, lost faith in the order of things, were convinced in fact that everything is a disorderly, damnable, and perhaps devil-ridden chaos, if I were struck by every horror of man's disillusionment—still I

> should want to live . . . I have a longing for life, and I go on living in spite of logic. Though I may not believe in the order of the universe, yet I love the sticky little leaves as they open in spring. I love the blue sky. I love some people, whom one loves you know sometimes without knowing why. I love some great deeds done by men, though I've long ceased perhaps to have faith in them . . . It's not a matter of intellect or logic, it's loving with one's inside, with one's stomach.[10]

The question is what story best explains this sense that comes from within "one's stomach," which seems so difficult to shake—that there is purpose in life, and that even life's most mundane stuff is meaningful, and that the people of our daily encounters are worthy of being loved?

"Out" to a better story. Christianity says that humans find a nihilistic life difficult, if not impossible, because we have been hardwired by God to live with purpose and meaning. It is for this reason that even if people deny God and can't find a rational reason to live with purpose and meaning, they still work, marry, raise children, think, build, plan, and play as if there is a point to it all. Even if our lives are aimed at the wrong goal, we still aim it at something—something we believe is valuable. But where does value come from?

The Christian story makes sense of these experiences and explains why humans, even those who deny God and have no explanation, live as if they have purpose. The reason we intuitively aim our lives at certain ends and find meaning in our tasks is that we are made in the image of God. The problem is that because of sin, our inherent longing for purpose is thwarted, so no matter what we do, we know we will die and our accomplishments will turn to dust. When people slow down to actually consider such futility, it is difficult to not be shaken by feelings of despair. Yet at the heart of the Christian story is the claim that through the death and resurrection of Jesus Christ, God has rescued us from sin and futility, giving our work eternal significance and fulfilling our longing for purpose. Moreover, in the person of Jesus, God has given us a model of how we are to live with purpose and aim at the true and eternal goal.

Beauty

"Inside" their story. The sense of awe we feel when we hear and see beauty has a way of challenging spiritual lethargy. We all know what it feels like to be deeply moved by a summer sunset, a masterful painting, a song that leaves us speechless, the sight of our children curled up in bed, or the smile of our spouse. Beauty moves us in profound ways, often to tears and with long-term effects. We are amazed by it. We seek it out. But we rarely wonder where it comes from. What is its source?

What if this joy we find in beauty is "merely the accidental by-product of our evolutionary history, a vestigial memory of hunting prospects or mating opportunities?" As N. T. Wright asks, "Would we still find it beautiful if we knew that to be true?"[11]

If the earth and mankind are simply accidents of nature, a chance collection of atoms, then what is beauty? Can we speak of the glorious sunset as beautiful without impoverishment? A lover as beautiful? One of Mozart's compositions as beautiful? The sight of a boy compassionately helping his widowed neighbor cross the street as beautiful? And if we persist in naming such things as beautiful, what do we really *mean* by this?

If you tell your fiancée you find her beautiful, do you mean to say you prefer her random conglomeration of atoms over others, while admitting your preference is itself a product of neurons firing in your body over which you have little to no control? Embracing this perspective would seem ridiculous to most people. When we look at a gorgeous sunset or at our child, we intuitively assume significance and beauty much deeper and fuller than what a purely secular framework can provide.

Experiencing beauty evokes a sense of longing for something more than this life can offer. In their song "Somewhere Only We Know," the English rock band Keane expresses the bittersweet longing that beauty often evokes in people, no matter how religiously lethargic they may be. It's interesting how people, in an effort to recapture the sublime feeling they've experienced in their past, will sometimes return to the places where they encountered beauty, hoping to find it again. But they are almost always disappointed when they realize the places from their past aren't what they once were. Keane's song speaks to people's desperate longings to reexperience these feelings because they sense something meaningful and perhaps even transcendent that is calling them to something higher—something that cuts to their very purpose in life.

"Out" to a better story. Christians believe that true beauty exists because God exists; all that is good, true, and beautiful is from God himself. God created the world for people to enjoy and delight in, and though the beauty in this world exists in a fallen state, marred by the effects of sin, it witnesses to himself, pointing us to his lovingkindness. Moreover, the fallen beauty we see in this world is but a shadow of what is to come; the beauty we see here, though it brings us joy, also makes us long for the coming day when beauty will be fully renewed to a perfect state. One of C. S. Lewis's central characters in his novel *Till We Have Faces* expresses this yearning that is felt in the midst of beauty: "It was when I was the happiest that I longed most . . . And because it was so beautiful, it set me longing, always longing. Somewhere else there must be more of it."[12]

In *The Weight of Glory*, Lewis argues that the reason for beauty's longing—how it promises much and yet remains fleeting, how it fills us with joy while breaking our hearts—is that it points to a reality beyond itself:

> [Those things] in which we thought the beauty was located will betray us if we trust to them; it was not *in* them, it only came *through* them, and what came through them was longing . . . They are not the thing itself; they are only the scent of a flower we have not found, the echo of a tune we have not heard, news from a country we have never yet visited . . . We cannot mingle with the splendours we see. But all the leaves of the New Testament are rustling with the rumour that it will not always be so. Some day, God willing, we shall get *in*.[13]

The Christian explanation of beauty also provides a reason for Christians to create and admire beautiful things, such as music, plays, paintings, sculptures, novels, and movies.[14] Because beauty, creativity, and design point beyond the creation to the ultimate Creator, our impulse to invest in and enjoy the beautiful is infused with a higher meaning. Creating and admiring beautiful things are tangible ways for Christians to worship the Creator. While committed materialists may experience the same impulse to create as Christians do, they cannot provide such a powerful justification and meaning for their work.

Something More

"Inside" their story. Even when someone sets out to construct their own web of meaning apart from God, they do so in hopes of finding fulfillment and happiness—of finding the good life. Despite the incredible diversity of cultures and different types of people in the world, doesn't everyone ultimately want the same basic things? Everyone wants purpose. Everyone wants to be a part of something bigger than themselves. Everyone wants to find true joy. These desires cut to the heart of humanity. We are always searching for it, and when we find something that does seem to satisfy, it's never enough. We always set out looking for more. Yet when we pursue happiness, we do so only to find it's remarkably fleeting. Even if we manage to grab hold of happiness for a while, experience tells us it will one day slip through our fingers, disrupted by life's trials and disappointments.

"Out" to a better story. C. S. Lewis argued that every natural desire has an object within this world toward which it is aimed. We get hungry and thirsty, and we live in a world where there is food and water. We have sexual desires, and sex exists. Thus, when humans have a desire that "no natural happiness will satisfy,"[15] it should give us serious pause about the possibility of the existence of something beyond this world that is made to fulfill that desire. As Lewis put it, "If I find in myself a desire which no experience in this world can satisfy, the most probable explanation is that I was made for another world."[16]

People, if honest with themselves, will admit to wanting at certain times in their lives something or someone that feels just outside their reach. Channeling Lewis, we should point to the Christian story, affirming an unbeliever's longings, and encourage them to see how their longings suggest they were not made for only this world and its ways, but rather something—someone—much greater. They were made for God, and in the words of Augustine, their heart will be restless until it rests in him.[17]

Again, we should not underestimate the powerful witness of living our lives grounded in the Christian story's conception of beauty and longing. Even in this life, the Christian will experience foretastes of the good life, yet their hope rests in something beyond just this life, where their desires will one day be fully satisfied. Fellowship with Christ in the present, then, offers a fuller experience of life, including hope amid loss, joy amid suffering, and the promise of a future, deeper satisfaction found in God's eternal love.

Death

"Inside" their story. A fear of death seems to haunt us all—so much so, according to cultural anthropologist Ernest Becker, that we try our best to ignore the reality of our own mortality.[18] Despite our efforts, death remains, underlying everything. It is a reality, and it does no good to deny this fact. A popular secular sentiment is to dismiss death by saying that in death we merely cease to exist. In death there is no meaning, no life, and no hope, so the best thing we can do, they say, is to embrace life. While easy to say, it is difficult, if not impossible, to live consistently.

Some say scarcity creates value, so the fact that our lives are so short is what gives them meaning. But does it really? If everyone fades to nothing, then nothing about them finally matters.

The secular philosopher Luc Ferry asserts that the question of death, and in particular our awareness of it, far from being a matter we can easily ignore or dismiss, is at the heart of our distinctiveness as humans: "As distinct from animals . . . a human being is the only creature who is aware of his limits. He knows that he will die, and that his near ones, those he loves, will also die. Consequently, he cannot prevent himself from thinking about this state of affairs, which is disturbing and absurd, almost unimaginable."[19] When people honestly consider what it means to die, they cannot help but feel disturbed.

Ferry recounts Edgar Allan Poe's "The Raven," in which the titular bird hauntingly utters "nevermore"—a powerful illustration of the existential terror that death brings. "Poe is suggesting that death means *everything that is unrepeatable*. Death is, *in the midst of life*, that which will not return; that which belongs irreversibly to time past, which we have no hope of ever recovering."[20] Death casts a shadow over all of life. Death is seen in every idyllic experience of our childhood that we can never get back and in every one of our irreversible mistakes. Death is every friend, child, or loved one we have buried. Death is the future, our inevitable fate. Silent darkness. Cut off from all we love. All we hold dear. The finality of love and relationships makes death intolerable. By empathetically helping someone consider what will happen to them after they die, we place a sobering existential weight on an unbeliever's shoulders that is difficult to simply shrug off.

"Out" to a better story. In an age in which people assume they can create their own webs of meanings and significance in life, death serves as "God's dismantling tool."[21] If late moderns are forced to face the thought of death, it will sober, humble, and even confuse them. As Old Testament wisdom reminds us:

> It is better to go to a house of mourning
> than to go to a house of feasting,
> for death is the destiny of everyone;
> the living should take this to heart.
>
> ECCLESIASTES 7:2

Yet while death alerts us to important realities, for Christians the story doesn't end there. If Jesus rose from the dead, then we too, though we die, will be made alive in him (John 11:25–26; 1 Corinthians 15:12–28). Death has lost its sting, and life has new meaning. As Ferry explains, our greatest desire as human beings is "to be understood, to be loved, not to be alone, not to be separated from our loved ones—in short, not to die and not to have them die on us."[22] Christianity's response to this universal human desire *not* to die is that, in Christ, death fails to spell the end of life, love, community, and meaning. Christ has opened the door for us to experience all these things in our fullest capacity. For this reason, Christianity is something the unbeliever should at the very least want to be true. The beauty and hopefulness of the Christian story certainly do not prove it is true, but the horror of death and the implications of Christ's resurrection can awaken the spiritually lethargic and point them toward a future that infuses our lives with eternal meaning and significance.

NOTES

1. James K. A. Smith, *How (Not) to Be Secular: Reading Charles Taylor* (Grand Rapids: Eerdmans, 2014), vii.
2. Smith, *How (Not) to Be Secular*, vii.
3. Luc Ferry, *Man Made God: The Meaning of Life* (Chicago: University of Chicago Press, 2002), 8.
4. Charles Taylor, *A Secular Age* (Cambridge, MA: Harvard University Press, 2007), 677.
5. Smith, *How (Not) to Be Secular*, vii.
6. See Taylor, *A Secular Age*, 594–617.
7. John Gray, *Straw Dogs: Thoughts on Humans and Other Animals* (New York: Farrar, Straus and Giroux, 2002), 38.
8. Gray, *Straw Dogs*, 38.
9. Thomas Nagel, *What Does It All Mean? A Very Short Introduction to Philosophy* (New York: Oxford University Press, 1987), 96.
10. Fyodor Dostoyevsky, *The Brothers Karamazov*, trans. Constance Garnett (New York: Macmillan, 1922), 241–42.
11. N. T. Wright, *History and Eschatology: Jesus and the Promise of Natural Theology* (Waco, TX: Baylor University Press, 2019), 227.
12. C. S. Lewis, *Till We Have Faces: A Myth Retold* (New York: Harcourt, Brace and World, 1980), 74.
13. C. S. Lewis, *The Weight of Glory* (1949; repr., San Francisco: HarperSanFrancisco, 2001), 30–31, 43, emphasis in original.
14. See Andy Crouch, *Culture Making: Recovering Our Creative Calling* (Downers Grove, IL: InterVarsity, 2008).
15. Lewis, *Weight of Glory*, 32.
16. C. S. Lewis, *Mere Christianity* (1943; repr., New York: Macmillan, 1960), 120.
17. Augustine of Hippo, *Confessions*, trans. Henry Chadwick (Oxford: Oxford University Press, 1991), 3.
18. See Ernest Becker, *The Denial of Death* (1973; repr., New York: Free Press, 1997).
19. Luc Ferry, *A Brief History of Thought: A Philosophical Guide to Living* (New York: HarperCollins, 2011), 2–3.
20. Ferry, *Brief History of Thought*, 5, emphasis in original.
21. David Gibson uses this terminology in reference to death in his contribution to Kevin J. Vanhoozer and Owen Strachan, *The Pastor as Public Theologian: Reclaiming a Lost Vision* (Grand Rapids: Baker Academic, 2015), 131.
22. Ferry, *Brief History of Thought*, 4.

chapter

7

Imagining a Better True Self

Cultural Assumption #2:

"You have to be true to yourself."

In *Habits of the Heart*, the sociologist Robert Bellah tells of how he and his team of researchers interviewed a woman whose faith became paradigmatic of a growing brand of American spirituality:

> Sheila Larson is a young nurse who has received a good deal of therapy and describes her faith as "Sheilaism." "I believe in God," Sheila says. "I am not a religious fanatic. I can't remember the last time I went to church. My faith has carried me a long way. It's Sheilaism. Just my own little voice." Sheila's faith has some tenets beyond belief in God, though not many. In defining what she calls "my own Sheilaism," she said: "It's just try to love yourself and be gentle with yourself. You know, I guess, take care of each other. I think [God] would want us to take care of each other."[1]

Sheilaism is clearly distinct from Christianity and the story of scientific secularism. When a transcendent reality is not woven into the social imaginary of a culture, no longer directing people to look outside of themselves to the divinely given fabric of the universe, people will still look for something to guide them. For many, rather than looking outside themselves for a divinely given story that summons them to submit, they choose to look inside themselves, eventually considering this to be the only true way to live freely. This story doesn't always include an appeal to the divine, yet sometimes, as with Sheila, "God" is still a viable option—though in this telling, a God who does not comply with my feelings remains largely irrelevant, if not implausible.

The result is what Robert Bellah labels "expressive individualism"—the belief "that each person has a unique core of feeling and intuition that should unfold or be expressed if individuality is to be realized."[2] And this individuality is to be lived out by refusing to "[surrender] to conformity with a model imposed . . . from outside."[3] Each person is to throw off the shackles of expectations imposed by anything on the outside and look within to be true to themselves.

Self-authorizing morality, which holds personal choice as the highest good, is a natural extension of this self-oriented outlook on life. Personal freedom is seen as an end in itself. And once a culture makes individual choice and independence from external norms the ultimate good, a deity of some kind might still be affirmed, but traditional religion—with its overt call to submit to something beyond ourselves—is seen not only as boring and antiquated, but also as dangerous and oppressive.

An example of our culture's shift from looking outward to looking to ourselves is found in a recent Jeep Renegade commercial. The advertisement focuses on a group of young female music stars posed by the titular car, firing off the short axioms they live by: "I have chosen to be . . . unapologetically me." "A renegade is someone who doesn't seek the approval of other people." "A renegade sets their own standard." Meanwhile, a line of text appears at the bottom of the screen, reading, "Be unique. Be authentic."[4]

Upon the slightest reflection, one should wonder how purchasing a mass-marketed Jeep (and being persuaded by a commercial to do so) could ever constitute as being unique or "unapologetically me." In this way, in one beautifully produced and self-contradicting minute, the commercial presents the defining moral ethos of our time. But we miss an opportunity if we simply mock such expressions as juvenile self-centeredness. Most people reading this will have had the freedom to make decisions in the important areas of their lives, such as whom to marry or what occupation to pursue. We know this hasn't always been the case, and in some ways, expressive individualism is a correction gone too far.

In the past, societies possessed a hierarchical structure that generally made social advancement a hopeless endeavor for the poor and was an oppressive environment for those lacking social status. Too often this led to the denigration of the individual. This contemporary "me"-centered script, which denies a *givenness* to the universe, is the result of a long-developing reaction against an oppressive "we," who maintained the hierarchical structures that kept the marginalized in their place. The promise of returning to an alleged golden age with such structures is naive nostalgia. We should explain to our secular friends that we're not suggesting we go back.

SUBVERSIVE FULFILLMENT

Yet we also need to explain how today's secular narratives fail to deliver on their promises. For one, basing our identity solely on our internal feelings and desires is unstable, since feelings and desires often change—from day to day and year to year. The fluctuation leads to a persistent identity crisis, with its accompanying anxieties.

Second, it's also not actually possible to look inside ourselves and find our identity, since culture is always cultivating our desires and telling us how we should feel about and respond to our impulses. We cannot help but act according to the expectations and opinions of those around us. As Charles Taylor puts it, "No one acquires the languages needed for self-definition on their own."[5] We are always defining our personal identity and ethic in relationship with a community.

Third, beyond its instability and impracticality, the pursuit of unfettered freedom in the name of being "true to yourself" also undermines some of our culture's deepest aspirations and humanity's most basic existential needs. In this chapter, we will explore four of these: a stable identity that can't be lost, a real morality, a rationale for pursuing justice, and a love that truly sets us free. We will see that expressive individualism actually hollows out these ideals. Since discovering our true self is about knowing where we stand,[6] we need a story that gives us a bedrock outside of ourselves to stand on. Christianity not only offers a footing to support these four ideals, it also offers the path to fulfill our deepest longings—a path that leads to the only person in whom we can discover our true self.

IDENTITY

"Inside" their story. Nearly all people at some point in their lives find themselves searching for self-worth, and if we're honest, we never simply look inside and find the answers. We can't help but look to the outside, to the culture and those around us, for affirmation that we are valuable and worthy. It is for this reason that the "hero" stories our culture tells us—whether in Disney movies, Fourth of July parades, or Nike commercials—resonate so deeply, for they provide deeply embedded, living pictures that we strive to emulate. We see an ideal and subconsciously think, *If I could be like that, then I'd be significant, and others would hold me in high esteem.*

Everyone looks to other people and embodied ideals to discover what is important and what they should find their identity, worth, and happiness in. We all have someone (or a group of people) we consider the "ultimate authority" in a practical sense, and so we place great amounts of trust and concern in his or her opinions, decisions, standards, or requirements. Everyone pays homage to something in hopes that it will validate us in the eyes of others. In a quest for cosmic validation, then, we all eventually "sell out."

But as the novelist David Foster Wallace famously said, whatever you sell out to in this world "will eat you alive."[7] If you sell out to success, you will always fear failure. If you sell out to receive the love of others, you will live a fragile existence, constantly striving to secure affection. If you sell out to your career, you will end up bitter and lonely. We all source our identity in someone or something, and we would be foolish to underestimate how doing so shapes our identity and, just as important, shapes how we interpret our identity.[8]

Yet in life, the people or things in which we source our identity are constantly threatened or taken from us. And whenever that happens—whenever the thing, person, or symbol we deify is taken away—we feel as if we have been robbed of our true self. We are left without an identity; we feel faceless, nameless, and insignificant. Wallace, who was not known for his religious piety, explains this existential reality for all humans: "In the day-to-day trenches of adult life, there is actually no such thing as atheism."[9] You don't have to be religious to feel the effects of worshiping something that leaves you empty, something you were not made to worship. That's why we don't need to use overly religious terminology when having this discussion, at least initially. We can leverage terms and ideas that all people, regardless of belief, can relate to (*identity*, *selling out*, *validation*, etc.), and we can build common ground with an unbeliever through our shared desire to soundly secure our identity and worth.

"Out" to a better story. After first focusing on their story, encourage others to imagine how the Christian story could map onto their life. In the same way that pain warns us to pull our hand off a hot stove, the empty feeling we get when our "gods" fail us is God's way of saying, "Something is desperately wrong—*change course*." What if there is a source for identity that provides an emotional strength capable of weathering even the most tumultuous seasons of life? The claim of the Christian story is that there is.

The good news of Christianity is that we can know and live in a right relationship with the One who will always prove stable and, rather than destroying us, will sustain, love, and care for us. When we are restored to God, we are freed to live in a right relationship with the rest of the world. Jesus entered the world to save us from the slavery of idolatry in order that we might know the One we were designed to love, the One who *is* the source of our value and significance. When we find our identity in Christ, our lives are at last oriented correctly, allowing us to treat people and things, not as false sources of worth, but as good gifts from the Lord and extensions of his love.

God affirms the goodness of creation throughout the entire story, from the opening chapters of Genesis where creation is described as "good" to when God becomes flesh and lives the human life to the vision of a restored creation in the closing chapter of Revelation. Things like work, relationships, play, and even our physical bodies themselves are good and will one day be fully redeemed. Yet Scripture shows these good gifts become life-destroying when we make them ultimate, when we hold on to them with clenched, white-knuckled fists. It's no surprise, then, that when these idols are wrested from our grasp, we feel deep insecurity, angst, and anger. Our unstable responses only confirm how these false gods never deliver; they merely enslave and control. Even when we possess them, we feel dissatisfied and want more. When they are taken from us, we will wade through endless burdens to get them back, or we will sink into despair because our idol has become unattainable and all is lost.

Idolizing anyone or anything apart from God will destroy us. Yet the answer is not to shun others and give up the things of the world altogether—after all, God commanded that we love others and accept all good gifts with thanksgiving as coming from him. The answer, then, is that we accept the Christian story's teaching that we are to find joy, value, and significance in Christ, the One who is eternally secure and who enables us to enjoy the good gifts of his provision while protecting us from the burden of being defined by them.

Morality

"Inside" their story. Expressive individualism, with its drive to free people from external norms and expectations and help them arrive at their true self, produces an ethics based on personal preferences. This morality, constructed around "*nothing but* expressions of preference, expressions of attitude or feeling," has famously been labeled *emotivism*.[10]

Even if one refuses to accept that morality exists independently of our perception or feelings, people still find universal and objective moral judgments to be irresistible in practice. Though someone might affirm expressive individualism in theory and a laissez-faire, "you be you" ethic, their everyday reactions point in the other direction—such as when they see the brutal oppression of the poor, the hypocrisy of powerful politicians, or another report of the selfish negligence of a drunk driver who destroyed the lives of an innocent family.

Even materialists, as secular philosopher Luc Ferry points out, "have never been able to refrain from passing continuous moral judgement on all and sundry, which their whole philosophy might be expected to discourage them from doing."[11] People committed to a purely materialist story still make moral judgments and live as if humans have the ability to make choices and be held accountable by a standard beyond themselves.

Ferry, recognizing this reality in himself, admits that he "cannot invent . . . the imperatives of the moral life" and that truth, beauty, justice, and love seem to "impose themselves on [him] as if they [came] from elsewhere."[12] Since moral imperatives seem to impose themselves on us, the questions become: *Where do they come from? How might we ground this morality "from elsewhere"?*

Grounding morality in culture? Some have argued that morality is completely dependent on cultural attitudes and assumptions. In other words, we judge something as "good" or "bad" because of our social location. According to this view, culture is what imposes morality on us from the outside. What is viewed as "good" in one culture may be viewed as "bad" in another. While dialoguing, you can agree with this last statement—cultures certainly view things differently. But the question is not whether cultures differ, but rather, "Is it possible to judge a cultural view or individual behavior as 'right' or 'superior,' and the opposite as 'wrong' or 'inferior?'" If someone answers affirmatively, then they've admitted there is something that transcends culture and determines morality. If we say, for instance, that it is better for cultures to allow women to have the same rights as men, then we are admitting there is something that stands above culture and provides a moral standard.

If they answer negatively and claim there is nothing that stands above culture, then additional questions are necessary. As C. S. Lewis pointed out, what, then, can we conclude about Nazi Germany?[13] Is our condemnation of the Holocaust or our advocacy of human rights just a reflection of cultural bias? This is too bitter of a pill for most to swallow. But if someone tries to do so, and insists that we have no right to say a cultural practice is evil—even the Holocaust—then we could ask on what authority they say this. Telling others they cannot call a cultural practice evil is itself a moral judgment that transcends any particular culture.

Grounding morality in science? Attempts have been made to claim that science and naturalistic evolutionary theories can explain morality. For instance, some may suggest to you that morality is merely an evolutionary development, with the most beneficial adaptations for survival being passed on. How might we respond?

Science is helpful in *describing* aspects of morality in a physical sense, and it can certainly assist us in exploring certain questions of morality. Its usefulness, however, is largely dependent on what is meant by *morality*, for this term is used to mean at least three different things in these discussions.

First, morality can be used to mean the realm of right and wrong. In this sense, it prescribes something; there is an obligation. If I say, "Murdering innocent people is wrong," or "We are responsible to care for the most vulnerable in our society," I mean we have an obligation to live (or not live) in a certain way. Most of us will find it unacceptable to say such morals are just a matter of personal taste. For me to say something along the lines of, "You value caring for the poor and keeping people alive, while I value the rich and am not concerned about those who are a drain on our society—to each his own"—would be deeply disturbing to most of us because we assume that humans have a responsibility to live in certain ways. This is sometimes called "real" or "authoritative" morality.

Second, morality is sometimes used to mean the social rules and practices of a given society at a purely descriptive level. In this sense, the morality of a culture or the stages of moral development are described but are not evaluated on any basis of what is *really* right or wrong.

Third, morality is used to mean something that is more practical. In this sense, something is being prescribed. Someone says, "Do this; don't do this," but it is not a moral obligation, as with the first definition. It is more instrumental in nature, like someone saying, "If you want to score a goal, you should shoot." Or, "If you want to be happy, you should do this." The "should" is directed at achieving a purpose, but it does not say whether the purpose is good or bad.[14] One is not obligated to pursue a certain goal.

Distinguishing among these definitions is crucial if we are to avoid talking past each other. Empirically based scientific studies can address the second and third types of morality but are unable to adequately address the first—which we might call "real morality." It is important to note that, as we engage others, it may not be enough to identify the category of morality being discussed just once. As James Davison Hunter and Paul Nedelisky point out, conversations involving morality often look like a shell game. A claim is made early in the conversation that "real" morality is being addressed, but before long—"through a sleight of hand"—one of the other categories is used in a way that conflates the definitions.[15]

This "sleight of hand" suggests secularists face serious challenges fitting "real morality" into their story. Secular sciences can describe a goal within a society or even how best to achieve a certain goal, but they cannot provide what goal one *ought* to pursue. Atheist philosopher Thomas Nagel admits as much, saying that "from a Darwinian perspective our impressions of value, if constructed realistically, are completely groundless." And if true for basic values, Nagel adds that "it is also true for the entire elaborate structure of value and morality that is built up from them by practical reflection and cultural development."[16]

At times people will suggest that according to science our goal is survival, but this misses the point. Science only observes that animals adapt and strive to survive; yet this alone does not oblige us morally to live certain ways. It is one thing to *describe* why we behave a certain way, but no purely scientific theory can provide a moral obligation that says if we *should* or we *shouldn't* conform to what we observe in nature.

However, since nature (as well as survival) is, after all, a brutal and bloody affair, most agree that the violence we observe within nature is not a model for how humans should live. We don't judge an animal to be *wicked* for killing their rivals. Yet we do judge humans for such a thing, which suggests many today recognize that we should rise above the violence of the natural world. Most see our own human history of aggression done for the advancement of our own tribe as something we need to overcome. And yet despite science's inability to adequately explain morality in its fullest sense and justify our obligation to rise above our base instincts, Nagel admits (along with many others) that he can't shake his belief that "good" and "bad" are more than an individual's personal preferences.[17]

We sense an obligation to live moral lives. To whom do we sense this obligation? I ask "to *whom*" because obligation exists in relationship.

We sense we owe our friends our care and concern, but we don't feel an obligation to an inanimate object. "Aha," some will reply at this point, "we don't need God for moral obligation; we simply owe each other moral lives." But that isn't enough. For one, this doesn't settle the questions of *what* is "moral" and *why* we owe humanity this. Plus, when we speak in terms of "obligation," we normally assume that whoever we owe can free us from our responsibility. While a friend could release us from an obligation to a debt we owed her, we can't free ourselves or each other from the obligation to live a moral life in general. So if someone isn't willing to cast off moral obligation as an illusion, the question remains: To whom are we ultimately responsible?[18]

"Out" to a better story. In searching for answers to our deepest questions, like those concerning moral obligation, it becomes necessary to move beyond science and culture to the questions of purpose. For example, what do we mean when we consider a watch to be "good"?[19] A positive evaluation relies on an understanding of the watch's purpose. Someone made it for a certain end. If we think a watch is designed to serve as a weapon, we will evaluate the watch differently than if we understand the watch to be made for telling time. Understanding an object's purpose is essential for knowing whether it is "good" or "bad." The same is true with morality. If humans were made with no purpose in mind, then there is no real morality. If we are left to make up our own morality as a society, then who is to say that one culture's values are better than another's?

Understanding the purpose for our existing, then, is essential for distinguishing "real" morality.[20] For this, we need to know the purpose for which we were made. Looking to a transcendent, personal, and good agent as the one who designed the world and gives direction to our lives is the simplest and most coherent grounds for moral truth in all its categories. For Christians, the clear source and basis for morality is the triune God. We are obligated morally to the God who made us for himself. As his image bearers, we are moral agents made to reflect his glory and enact a morality that comes from him. The Christian story, thus, provides a framework to support the human need for value, moral obligation, and purpose in life—the very points we all intuitively sense but secular stories fail to adequately explain.

Justice

"Inside" their story. Despite accusations of simple moral relativism often leveled against late moderns, many balk at this suggestion. Most nonbelievers I talk to have a strong reaction against injustices in the world, coupled with a sincere impulse to do something about it. Social action and human rights are in vogue, and rather than misrepresent unbelievers, which is a sure conversation-stopper, these impulses should be affirmed. Countless organizations have been formed to help serve the poor, end sex trafficking, provide disaster relief, curtail racism, and cure diseases. These causes are grounded in two foundational assumptions of our modern morality: basic human dignity and universal benevolence. The interesting question is why so many people believe in human dignity and universal benevolence. Below we will see that while Christians have compelling reasons to affirm them, secular narratives lack the resources to offer sufficient (1) grounding, (2) motivation, or (3) hope for these modern ethical intuitions.

According to your story, what grounds universal human dignity and our obligation to care for others? Basic human dignity and universal benevolence have not been universally held.[21] The standard assumption in ancient cultures was that different people groups were unequal. This is why, for example, practices such as slavery, infanticide, the mistreatment of women, and even, in some cases, human sacrifice and widow burning were accepted. Only later, after the biblical story infiltrated the Western world, did the idea of basic human dignity begin to change moral conceptions. In some instances, changes came fairly quickly; in other cases, the fruit was slow to arrive. Yet when changes did occur in favor of a morality based in the ideal of love for all people and human rights, it is difficult to escape the fact that the history of these developments can be traced back to the biblical story. For centuries, this story served as the backbone of the Western tradition and has remained a central feature in modern morality. Beginning with the Enlightenment in the 1700s, late modernism has attempted to formally sever the connection that runs from Christianity through dignity and benevolence, while still living off of its heritage.[22]

The question, then, is, "If you deny the Christian assumptions that were essential for the formation, what reasons do you have for believing in universal human dignity and rights?" Nature doesn't provide a basis for human dignity any more than it gives us a comprehensive moral instruction manual. What we observe in nature, as we've already noted, is that the strong eat the weak, "red in tooth and claw."[23] Insiders within a group might help each other, such as when animals hunt for their prey in packs, but this is ultimately for their own tribe's advancement and often at the expense of other groups. Observations from nature alone can't lead us to modern conceptions of justice. Again, this is not to say that many unbelievers don't live lives of high moral integrity, respecting the dignity of all humans and seeking to care for others. This question is whether their story grounds such a high level of morality and if secular narratives themselves can sustain these moral aspirations for society in the future.

Some unbelievers propose that the grounding for these high-level values is found in their ability to promote peace and order. In other words, people should strive toward these moral ideals and encourage others to do the same so they themselves can live in a society that will bring them the most happiness. Christian Smith, however, points out that while this argument has some practical merit in promoting some "ethical" behavior rooted in a morality of self-interest, it fails to provide a convincing rationale for "obligations to promote the good of all other human beings."[24] This reasoning can *only* warrant concern for a limited number of people with whom they have a vested self-interest. Why should someone work (often with much personal sacrifice) for the welfare, prosperity, and happiness of other people, say on the other side of the globe, when they are utterly extraneous to one's personal well-being? "If morality only exists to benefit us, then I will be moral with people I wish to benefit and who might benefit me."[25]

And when local cultural conditions become highly polarized and the well-being of certain other groups has a perceived negative impact on oneself, the logic grounding "good" behavior will no longer stand. If people do not have a vested self-interest within a secular story line to maintain, justice, compassion, and equality for all, *rationally* it seems they have two choices: they can jettison these values and simply do what seems best for themselves, even if that comes at the expense of others, or they can look to a different metanarrative that can support these ideals.

According to your story what motivates people to act justly and with high moral standards? For secularists concerned with the world's injustices, their inability to understand and articulate the basis for this moral conviction is not their only problem. Though many strongly and sincerely believe they should do something about injustice, their feelings and behavior often stop there. It is one thing to have a general desire for justice; it's a very different thing to labor self-sacrificially against injustice and steadfastly pursue just circumstances for others. Quite simply, most people are committed first and foremost to their personal welfare, not to the welfare of others.

And why shouldn't they be? Expressive individualism provides shallow motivations to give selflessly of one's money, time, health, social standing, and even one's life for the good of others. After all, if we are to be "true to ourselves," why should I give of myself for others' sakes? To take naturalism at its word, we are all heading toward an inglorious final act—decomposition in the ground, no memory, no lasting meaning. Why, then, should we care so profoundly for others? Why suffer for people we don't know? Why not seek pleasure for ourselves while we can?

We can also raise the problem of what Christian Smith calls the "shrewd opportunist," which asks, If there is no God, why should rational persons "uphold a culture's moral norms *all* of the time?" While agreeing that it is *personally* beneficial to keep up appearances and support standards that will lead to general orderliness in society, the shrewd opportunist asks, "Why not be good when it serves one's enlightened self-interest but strategically choose to *break* a moral norm at opportune moments, when violation has a nice payoff and there is little chance of being caught?"[26] Smith shows that even the brightest secular ethicists have yet to provide a satisfactory answer to this question. If we're going to motivate people to commit to high moral obligations, we'll need to borrow resources from another story.

According to your story, is there any ultimate hope? Even as we challenge the ability of late modern frameworks to adequately ground quests for justice and provide reasons to act on them, we should still affirm people's intuitive desires to right wrongs, as well as their efforts to do so. Yet conversations can make one take interesting turns here, as people may express their own desperation. For instance, one thing most people will concede is that satisfying their deepest desires for justice often seems to be a hopeless endeavor. Fighting injustice can feel like trying to plug holes in a dam that's on the brink of failure. The problem is that once you cover one hole, three more sprout open and the water pours through. The fight quickly becomes overwhelming. And it only gets worse if we look beyond the present moment. We know our efforts are futile, because most certainly the dam will collapse. In the end, the world will cease to exist, and justice—ultimate justice—will be left unserved. Our cosmic insignificance casts a very dark shadow over our best intentions and most selfless acts. What will our efforts come to in the end? Is the answer really, *Nothing*?

"Out" to a better story. Our culture's aspirations for justice and human rights include the obligation to respect all people—even those you find personally appalling—and as Smith puts it, to "identify and empathize with the needs and sufferings of every person, even those on the other side of the earth whose cultures are alien to ours." He goes further, "And we are to devote to them not merely passing sympathetic feelings, but understanding, material aid, and resources."[27]

These humanistic ideals require that we make sacrifices to our welfare for the sake of others—and "others" includes those we don't know, those who don't impact our lives, those who are very different from us, and even those who are antagonistic toward us and our values. This is a high bar, and for the unbeliever, it can become uncomfortably apparent that secular narratives provide neither the grounding, motivation, nor hope to maintain such idealistic moral aspirations.

A better grounding. According to Christianity, we have a sense of right and wrong because there is a God whose moral law stands above that of individual people or cultures. The pursuit of justice resonates with us because God created us in his image and desires that we seek his righteousness as a way of representing his very nature to the world. When God entered the world as a human in the person of Jesus Christ, the universal ethic he taught—which commands that we love all people, even our enemies—was shocking in the ancient world. This, as we will see in the final section of this chapter, makes sense in the Christian framework in which self-giving love is the very center of eternal reality.

A better motivation. It was not, however, simply Jesus' teaching that was revolutionary. Jesus' followers also stood out because Jesus provided them with compelling motivation to serve others selflessly. God's very being not only provides an unchanging standard of justice, but also because of his love for his creation, God made it possible for all people to be forgiven and to be set free from their own acts of injustice. God himself entered the world as a man, a completely innocent victim, to endure our suffering so that he could declare us innocent. He did this while knowing it would lead him to absorb the violence of this world and take on himself the judgment we deserve. What moves Christians to give themselves for others is the reality that Christ has given himself for us. In his mercy, he has freed us from our own self-absorption so we may reach out to love the world and sacrifice ourselves for justice. He taught us that sacrificing our self-centeredness to serve others is actually the way to be most fully human, to become the "true you."

A better hope. Jesus' resurrection and ascension point us to his return, when he will usher in a new world and right all wrongs. In the end, justice will be fully and perfectly satisfied. Yet through his death and resurrection, he offers now to all who would humbly turn to him the opportunity to be on the right side of justice. Only by his sacrifice do our sacrifices have meaning—and through Christ *they do have meaning.* Our strivings for peace and our efforts to restore dignity and worth to our sisters and brothers will have tangible, eternal significance. Even in the darkest of times, then, when the dam collapses and the flood overwhelms, the Christian story provides an enduring vision of hope that truly upholds a long-suffering pursuit of justice.

To Love and Be Loved by Others

"Inside" their story. We long to know and to be known, to love and to be loved. We desire to belong to something bigger than ourselves, whether it's family or some other group devoted to a common, greater cause. This is the human condition.

Our culture's pervasive emphasis on authenticity can make it seem like our desire for community and relationships is subsiding, but in reality, the decision to "find oneself" is just one's search for a new community to find love in. Notice how when someone "expresses their individuality" with a certain style of music, a car, or a set of beliefs, there are an awful lot of people expressing their "individuality" in the same way. We've already pointed out the problem of thinking that someone is expressing inner "authenticity" when buying a mass-produced Jeep.[28] In fact, most Jeep owners take pride in *joining* the Jeep community or in giving the "Jeep wave" when passing other Jeep owners on the road. No matter what we tell ourselves, the way people actually live is proof enough that a longing for community and life-giving relationships is very much alive today.

In fact, many people will agree with you that the most important part of our existence as humans is finding true love—with a romantic partner, friends, and family. So you might ask them, "What do you mean when you talk of love?" According to a scientific secular account, if there is no God and we are simply the result of natural processes, then love is nothing more than a physical reaction in the brain—a mere chemical condition or a drive passed down from our ancestors as a cold instrument of survival.

You might also ask, "Does the story you have assumed actually commodify love? And if so, can love truly flourish?" Expressive individualism corrodes the deep bonds we desire by causing us to view neighbors, friends, and marriages as instruments for our own self-actualization. And the culture narrative of achievement teaches us that we have to do things to merit love. But when we feel like we are "paying in" more than we are receiving, we either abandon these relationships or struggle with bitterness. If the ultimate purpose in life is self-fulfillment and the means is achievement, it will be difficult to treat others as anything more than commodities that help us get more of what we want.[29]

Yet even apart from expressive individualism, in our current human condition we normally expect more than we give in our relationships, and expressive individualism only exacerbates this tendency. One of the vices of a fallen human nature—pride—makes it very difficult not to resent the success or happiness of others. "Pride is *essentially* competitive—is competitive by its very nature—while the other vices are competitive only, so to speak, by accident. Pride gets no pleasure out of having something, only out of having more of it than the next man."[30]

Have you ever had this experience? A friend has done something wonderful and is being recognized for her accomplishment. You want to be happy for her. Instead, though, you hate her for it, or, at the very least, resent her in secret. All you can think is, *If I had just had a little more time,* I *could have done a better job, and it would have been* me *who is being recognized. If only they could have seen what* I've *done—what* I'm *capable of doing.* We already have a difficult time celebrating others, but when a relationship with someone is built on a foundation of self-interest, truly loving others becomes an even deeper problem.

In summary, the modern quest for self-fulfillment actually undercuts our ability to truly know others and to be fully known. (1) Deep relationships are undermined because there are only shallow motivations to keep a sacred vow to one another and hang through tough times and stay committed to one another. In the modern search to find our "true self," (2) we also lose the ability to truly receive and rest in the love of another as a gift, for we always feel we have to earn love, to achieve something worthy of the transaction. And finally, (3) we lose the ability to truly love others because love is given based on self-interest; that is, it is based on whether the other person aids in my personal actualization.

"Out" to a better story. At some point, however, an unbeliever might reply, "I don't live like that. I understand the pull of expressive individualism, but I do have relationships that are altruistic." This is significant. Many who have generally assumed expressive individualism do strive to live sacrificially in some of their most intimate relationships.

When people refuse to abandon important relationships in the name of personal freedom and instead value others more than their own self-actualization and autonomy, they seem to be admitting something parallel to the Bible's teaching, namely, that saying no to some desires is an important part of genuine flourishing. They are admitting that personal sacrifice is essential for deep, life-giving relationships. This concession opens the door for Jesus' teachings to be seen in a new light. When Jesus tells us we must die to live and gives us rules to live by, he is inviting us to a deeper, truer kind of flourishing.

Christianity teaches that we are to weep with those who weep and rejoice with those who rejoice (Romans 12:15). Everyone longs for genuine community, where people truly love and care for one another; the problem is, of course, that this sort of flourishing community isn't possible if everyone is utterly self-interested.

The foundation of the Christian life is finding your true self in Christ. By trusting in Christ, your primary identity changes and you are now a child of God, fully *known* and fully *loved*. In discussing the ingredients for a healthy marriage, Tim Keller offers a picture that is supremely true of God's love for his children:

> When over the years someone has seen you at your worst, and knows you with all your strengths and flaws, yet commits him- or herself to you wholly, it is a consummate experience. To be loved but not known is comforting but superficial. To be known and not loved is our greatest fear. But to be fully known and truly loved is, well, a lot like being loved by God. It is what we need more than anything. It liberates us from pretense, humbles us out of our self-righteousness, and fortifies us for any difficulty life can throw at us.[31]

Beyond any human love, this divine love will change a person—giving them the ability to truly receive and give love. The love of God turns the believer away from the need to secure love through performance or by one-upping others—a radical posture in an era of competition and individualism—and frees one to pursue the good of others and the good of the world. In this way, Christianity offers not only a vision for life and true friendship; it has the resources to cultivate thriving relationships and flourishing communities.

This profound human yearning for relationships also points to a mysterious and distinctly Christian view within the gospel story: God himself has always existed as a relational being; he exists in three persons—Father, Son, and Holy Spirit. God has never been lacking in relationship, even before he created angels or human beings. Relationality has always been fundamental to reality. God is eternally personal.[32]

This notion of eternal, personal love as essential to God's being differentiates the Christian conception of him from all other world-explaining stories. For instance, Muslim theology emphasizes the absolute oneness of Allah. In eternity past, before Allah created anything, he was entirely alone. Because love requires an object, and a relationship between at least two persons, Allah could not have been a loving, relational being before he created the universe, for he had no one with whom to relate. In order to be a loving being, Allah needed his creation. In contrast, the Christian God, because he has always existed in community, has always been a loving, relational being. His love is not contingent on creation; he is an eternal communion of self-giving love.

The Christian story offers a richer basis for love than any other meta-story: Love is an ultimate reality found in God himself. And because we are made in the image of a self-giving God who has always existed in love, we are designed to lovingly give ourselves to others. When we are self-centered instead of selfless, we act against our very nature. In our fallen, broken state, we find it difficult, if not impossible, to truly love others as we are designed to. Yet Christ has made it possible for humankind to enter once again into the eternal reality of God's love. In extending God's love to us, he enables us to truly love others. In a world created by a personal God, love is at the very center of reality—and resting in this love is the only way to discover our "true self."

NOTES

1. Robert N. Bellah et al., *Habits of the Heart: Individualism and Commitment in American Life*, rev. ed. (Berkeley: University of California Press, 2008), 221.
2. Bellah, *Habits of the Heart*, 334.
3. Charles Taylor, *A Secular Age* (Cambridge, MA: Harvard University Press, 2007), 475.
4. "Release Your Renegade," Jeep Renegade TV Commercial (2017), www.ispot.tv/ad/wC8G/jeep-renegade-release-your-renegade-feat-halsey-chloe-nixon.
5. Charles Taylor, *The Ethics of Authenticity* (Cambridge, MA: Harvard University Press, 1991), 33.
6. See Charles Taylor, *Sources of the Self: The Making of the Modern Identity* (Cambridge, MA: Harvard University Press, 1992), 27.
7. David Foster Wallace, "Transcription of the 2005 Kenyon Commencement Address—May 21, 2005," http://web.ics.purdue.edu/~drkelly/DFWKenyonAddress2005.pdf.
8. Here I am summarizing Wallace's much longer quote.
9. Wallace, "Transcription of the 2005 Kenyon Commencement Address."
10. Alasdair MacIntyre, *After Virtue: A Study in Moral Theory*, 3rd ed. (Notre Dame, IN: University of Notre Dame Press, 2007), 11–12, emphasis in original.

11. Luc Ferry, *Learning to Live: A User's Manual* (London: Canongate, 2010), 229.
12. Ferry, *Learning to Live*, 236–37.
13. See C. S. Lewis, *Mere Christianity* (1943; repr., New York: Macmillan, 1960), 25.
14. See James Davison Hunter and Paul Nedelisky, "Where the New Science of Morality Goes Wrong," *Hedgehog Review* 18, no. 3 (Fall 2016): 48–62, www.iasc-culture.org/THR/THR_article_2016_Fall_HunterNedelisky.php. Also see their book, *Science and the Good: The Tragic Quest for the Foundations of Morality* (New Haven, CT: Yale University Press, 2018). In response to the claim that happiness and well-being provide such a moral ideal, they conclude, "We have observed already just how historically and culturally tendentious the concept of happiness is in the new moral science, and how poorly it is operationalized for scientific studies. The prima facie case against happiness as a scientifically useful concept is very strong: people find subjective well-being in as many different sources as one can imagine . . . On the face of it, there is no way to compare one person's happiness to another's, or even to compare a single person's experience of happiness at one moment to anything she experienced in the past. There are not units by which comparison can be made" (p. 210). They go on to observe that there have been times when large numbers of people have found subjective happiness within regimes, such as the Hitler Youth, that most would be uncomfortable describing with positive moral terms.
15. Hunter and Nedelisky, "Where the New Science of Morality Goes Wrong," 56.
16. Thomas Nagel, *Mind and Cosmos: Why the Materialist Neo-Darwinian Conception of Nature Is Almost Certainly False* (New York: Oxford University Press, 2012), 109.
17. Nagel, *Mind and Cosmos*, 110.
18. For more on this, see C. Stephen Evans, *God and Moral Obligation* (Oxford: Oxford University Press, 2013).
19. See MacIntyre, *After Virtue*, 57–59.
20. MacIntyre uses an analogy of a hypothetical culture that loses a coherent framework for science while still retaining scientific terminology, which serves to illustrate the current cultural situation in which moral language has been retained without a larger teleological framework. In the absence of such a framework, the moral language ceases to be coherent (see *After Virtue*, 1–5).
21. See Christian Smith, "Does Naturalism Warrant a Moral Belief in Universal Benevolence and Human Rights?" in *The Believing Primate: Scientific, Philosophical, and Theological Reflections on the Origin of Religion*, ed. Jeffrey Schloss and Michael Murray (Oxford: Oxford University Press, 2011), 295–98.
22. See Nicholas Wolterstorff, *Justice: Rights and Wrongs* (Princeton, NJ: Princeton University Press, 2008); Taylor, *Sources of the Self*.
23. Alfred Lord Tennyson, *In Memoriam A. H. H.* (London: Bankside, 1900), canto 56, p. 60.
24. Christian Smith, *Atheist Overreach* (Oxford: Oxford University Press, 2018), 18.
25. Smith, *Atheist Overreach*, 22.
26. Smith, *Atheist Overreach*, 25, emphasis in original.

27. Smith, *Atheist Overreach*, 24.
28. Ironically, the capitalistic forces within a consumeristic society are happy to capitalize on the quest for true freedom, in essence selling the idea, "You can be like the other truly authentic ones . . . if you buy our product!"
29. In *Tribe: On Homecoming and Belonging* (New York: Hachette, 2016), Sebastian Junger offers a revealing historical case that illustrates how serious losses often accompany "progress" when rooted in individualism and consumerism. Junger recounts how years before the Revolutionary War, Benjamin Franklin observed that English settlers were often giving up their more civilized life in settlements to join Indian tribes, and Indians, even when given the opportunity, rarely chose to transition into the more "advanced" settlements. The reason for this surprising one-way migration: the desperate human need for resources that support committed long-term relationships that advanced individualistic societies, despite significant gains in certain areas, have tended to undervalue, to their own detriment. Recent writers such as Andrew Delbanco (*The Real American Dream*) and Yuval Levin (*The Fractured Republic*), both drawing on Alexis de Tocqueville's *Democracy in America*, have made the point that the individualism the culture has embraced fails to provide a unifying vision for a cohesive society or a productive political system.
30. C. S. Lewis, *Mere Christianity* (1943; repr., New York: Macmillan, 1960), 109, emphasis in original.
31. Timothy Keller, *The Meaning of Marriage: Facing the Complexities of Commitment with the Wisdom of God* (New York: Dutton, 2011), 95.
32. For a practical introduction to the doctrine of the Trinity, see Michael Reeves, *Delighting in the Trinity: An Introduction to the Christian Faith* (Downers Grove, IL: IVP Academic, 2012).

chapter
8

Imagining a Better Happiness

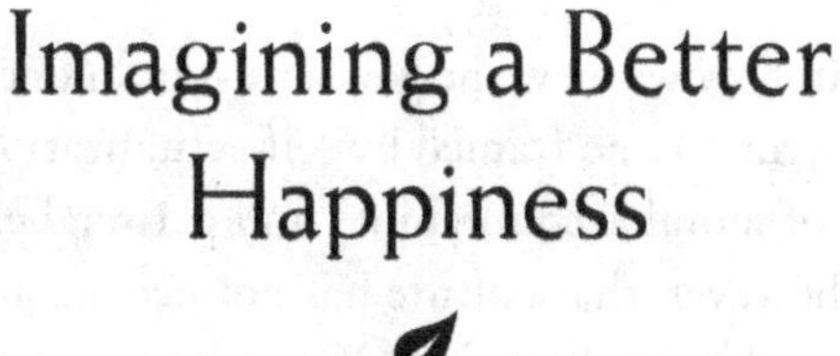

Cultural Assumption #3:
"The ultimate goal in life is to be happy."

Should happiness be the ultimate goal in life? In posing the question, it is immediately important to point out the difference between happiness as a momentary feeling that is dependent on circumstances and a deep happiness that remains amid life's trying circumstances. On the one hand, given that suffering, loss, and death are universally inescapable human experiences, a life built on a happiness rooted in fleeting circumstances will eventually be undermined. Merely considering our inevitable demise and the eventual loss of everything we hold dear can undercut the happiness we seek in the present. On the other hand, a deeper type of happiness is rooted in something beyond the contingencies of life. The challenge is to help people realize the futility of our contemporary secular scripts of the good life and begin to imagine a way to face life's changing circumstances with joy and hope.

THE GOOD LIFE?

Rather than the good life being defined in predominately moral terms (i.e., seeking virtue, shunning vice, and conforming to a divinely given "way"), now the good life is often defined by a pursuit of a feeling, which is won by the accumulation of all the things you would find if one were to weld together ideal versions of a job résumé, dating profile, and Christmas list. By achieving success, wealth, power, and the right body type, we've allowed a modern combination of meritocracy and consumerism to cast an imaginative and alluring vision of "happily ever after."

This shift in how we view the good life—from one that is framed by a code of virtue to one framed by self-actualization, has resulted in a lost sense of moral accountability and personal guilt *before God* (we shall see, however, that culture has not necessarily lost personal accountability and guilt altogether). When looking at society around him, C. S. Lewis lamented in the middle of the twentieth century that "a sense of sin is almost totally lacking," and that a moral register had been traded for a therapeutic rationalism.[1] So we see it today too. People once assumed that humankind's main problem was that we had turned against the universe's moral fabric and our Creator. Today, physical and psychological disorders are the root problem. "Sickness" has become the dominant description for our modern malaise.[2]

In 1966, sociologist Philip Rieff composed a seminal work, *The Triumph of the Therapeutic*, in which he foresaw an age when the pursuit of "feeling better" will overshadow the quest for justice, forgiveness, or redemption. In this new cultural context, he asserts, the main core value of society will be happiness, and thus the religious person, who was "born to be saved," will be overshadowed by the psychological person, who is "born to be pleased."[3]

Rieff's main contentions have proven true. To most late moderns, the goal of life is to make oneself happy on one's own terms.[4] And this belief has had a direct impact on our culture's assumptions concerning what is wrong with the world, that is, the "sickness" we face. If someone feels overwhelming guilt or sadness, they don't suspect they need to make any fundamental change in their beliefs, and they certainly don't think they need to "repent" of anything to God.

We no longer see the problem as being sourced in our sinfulness, selfishness, or disobedience, but only that our mind-set is skewed, perhaps a bit off. Our problems, we tell ourselves and each other, are primarily psychological, and with the right amount of time and resources, we can work them out. We may require therapeutic fine-tuning now and then or, in more serious situations, perhaps even serious professional help. But traditional religion, far from being a viable solution, is now seen as being part of the problem. Its external moral constraints rub against our individualism and make us feel guilty, suggesting it's not okay to be true to oneself.

THREE POINTS OF CONTRAST

First, in contrast to the story of therapeutic rationalism, a central idea in the Christian story has always been that because of sin and the fall, which have marred both human nature and the natural world, humans will never be perfectly happy in this life.[5] In this life, pain and suffering can't be completely escaped. Our most prized achievements will be undermined. We will fail in our most worthy endeavors. We will watch loved ones die. We will, inevitably, lose our own health. Then one day we will die.

If our joy is contingent on circumstances, we will be fragile, anxious, or on the brink of despair because we know we can't actually escape pain and loss. In response to these experiences, some have suggested seeking to avoid the pain of inevitable loss by never fully giving ourselves to anything. While perhaps safeguarding (at least in part) against the sorrow of loss, the result is a numbing of the very affections that make us human—and the more powerful the anesthesia, the more we lose the capacity for the joy we were made for.

In contrast to the secular therapeutic approach to life that seeks to escape such pain as the foundation for the good life, the Christian approach is more realistic about the inevitable circumstances of this life. Suffering is an inescapable part of our present human existence, and only by learning from our pain can we become fully human—and truly flourish. Experiencing great sorrow is not the antithesis to the good life but can instead be a result of knowing true joy. For to truly love also means to feel the pain of loss. To delight in the light within the world means you will lament the darkness. Knowing the true story, sensing the echoes of Eden and the inbreaking of God's future reign, makes us feel the pain and sorrows of our present evil world all the more acutely. As Jesus taught, "Blessed [flourishing] are those who mourn" (Matthew 5:4).[6] This is not a mourning that is absent of joy. Happiness in hope buoys the soul, for a better day *is* coming.

Second, the Christian story sees physical pain and emotional distress as a sign that beneath the surface of suffering, *deeper* problems exist. But it is not just Christianity that takes this opposing view, as David Foster Wallace points out. This contrast exists between our late modern therapeutic age and almost every culture in human history:

> In most other cultures, if you hurt, if you have a symptom that's causing you to suffer, they view this as . . . a sign that your nervous system knows something's wrong. For these cultures, getting rid of the pain without addressing the deeper cause would be like shutting off a fire alarm while the fire's still going. But if you just look at the number of ways that we try like hell to alleviate mere symptoms . . . you can see an almost compulsive tendency to regard pain itself as the problem.[7]

Wallace observes that the utilitarian approach, which views the maximization of pleasure and minimization of pain as the meaning to life, actually undermines true joy as it ignores what humans have basically always assumed: we are supposed to learn from pain. Pain, rather than being the root problem itself, is a symptom that something more foundational has gone wrong.

Third, Jesus taught that the only way to find true joy is to deny yourself. We were made to love God and to love others. Our design is patterned after the tripersonal self-giving nature of God himself. God is perfectly joyful because he lives to give of himself. The way to find ultimate joy, according to the Christian story, is to decenter ourselves and to step into relationship with this loving, personal God.

This is the "paradox of joy." If you pursue happiness as an end in itself, you will spend your life trying to minimize self-sacrifice and pain by getting everything and everyone to rotate around you. Yet a self-centered life pushes against the very fabric of the universe. The more we demand to be in the center, the more we feel like we are losing control when things don't respond to our wishes, which leads to frustration, anger, and a debilitating egotism. Self-absorption dehumanizes us, eventually leaving us bitter and alone, because we were made to turn outwardly rather than inwardly on ourselves. Hence Jesus' command to pick up our cross and follow him is indeed a call to die, but it is also a call to live with the grain of the universe and discover true joy.

In summary, as we engage others, it's important to understand that many now view the "good life" largely in terms of personally "feeling good" rather than "feeling bad," and then assume that with the right psychological balancing and therapeutic practices, they can be happy. By comparing the modern story about happiness with the Christian story, we can invite others to consider which narrative actually *fits*.

FEATURES OF HUMAN EXPERIENCE

One way to begin such an interaction with someone who has assumed a therapeutic rationalism is to discuss specific features of human experience that don't seem to fit in their story. Our first topics below—evil, as well as dignity and death—are features of life that seem inescapable, but like puzzle pieces put in the wrong box, they don't neatly interlock with the secular therapeutic picture of reality. And while the "therapeutic turn" holds out the hope of an abiding happiness, the second set of three topics will discuss the ongoing disappointment and despair in the midst of prosperity, the continual struggle with guilt, and the crisis of a divided society. All of these are reasons for you to ask others to imagine a better way to put the pieces together—one that can lead to an undergirding contentment and peace, no matter the circumstances.

Evil

"Inside" their story. In his book *Unapologetic*, Francis Spufford reflects on the then recent atheist bus campaign in London, which triumphantly declared, "There's probably no God. Now stop worrying and enjoy your life." He takes particular issue with the implication that since there is no God, people can be carefree, not worry about judgment, and simply enjoy life. After describing three people who are themselves facing horrific circumstances, Spufford asks what this bus message would mean for them:

> So when the atheist bus comes by, and tells you that there's probably no God so you should stop worrying and enjoy your life, the slogan is not just bitterly inappropriate in mood. What it means, if it's true, is that anyone who isn't enjoying themselves is entirely on their own. The three of you are, for instance; you're all three locked in your unshareable situations, banged up for good in cells no other human being can enter. What the atheist bus says is: there's no help coming . . . But let's be clear about the emotional logic of the bus's message. It amounts to a denial of hope or consolation, on any but the most chirpy, squeaky, bubble-gummy reading of the human situation. St. Augustine called this kind of thing "cruel optimism" fifteen hundred years ago, and it's still cruel.[8]

How does one live a good life amid the brutal realities of our modern age? For most, personal experience is enough to attest to the cruelty of this world, but if we ever find ourselves in need of reminding, the twenty-four-hour international news cycle offers a window into the apparent "evils" of society. The strength of our responses and ability to cope with the atrocities of our world, as well as our capacity to not be overcome by the anguish of suffering under cruel injustices, is contingent on the story we embrace.

The end of the nineteenth century was accompanied by a growing sense of optimism among many prominent Western intellectuals. Technological progress, advances in knowledge, and the hope of freedom from perceived antiquated religious myths were all interpreted to be a sign of blossoming moral sophistication that would produce the most peaceful stage in human existence. But then came the twentieth century—the bloodiest in all of human history.

The same technological advancement that led to many remarkable achievements and engendered boundless optimism was also leveraged by Western nations to unleash the first "modern war." Among World War I's defining legacies is the way in which men mechanized brutality, as seen in the use of chemicals and artillery to kill from the trenches and in numbers that were, at the time, beyond imagination. Twenty years of further technological advancement culminated in World War II, and tens of millions more slaughtered. Wrapped up in the Second World War was, of course, the Holocaust, whereby one of civilization's most cultured and educated societies mechanized murder in an utterly systematic way, enabling the killing of more than ten million Jews and other "undesirables." Vacuum salesmen, teachers, milkmen, and average college students went from tackling the mundane issues of everyday life to following orders to murder civilians, women, children, and entire families—thousands each day. Mass violence has persisted since the World Wars, as leaders and nation-states conduct state-sponsored famine, genocide, and civil war. Even times of peace, such as the Cold War period, were marked by fear of nuclear proliferation and the potential destruction of entire societies.

And in the twenty-first century, despite our incredibly high moral aspirations and strides in some areas, it often feels like we take one step forward and two steps back. The reality is that things aren't getting better in any simple or linear way. Terry Eagleton, a leading British intellectual, has rightly criticized leading atheists who have suggested otherwise:

> The true anti-realists are those like the scientist Richard Dawkins, with his staggeringly complacent belief that we are becoming kinder and more civilised . . . It is true that some things get better in some respects . . . But some things also get worse . . . Nobody would gather from his smug account of the evolving wisdom of humanity that we are also faced with planetary devastation, the threat of nuclear conflict, the spreading catastrophe of AIDS and other deadly viruses, neoimperial zealotry, mass migrations of the dispossessed, political fanaticism, a reversion to Victorian-type economic inequalities, and a number of other potential catastrophes.[9]

As pessimistic as Eagleton may seem, don't miss that even he admits that *some* things are getting better. His emphatic gesticulating serves the purpose of getting his enlightened Western readers to look up and avoid tunnel vision. Your view about whether things are getting better or worse depends on your vantage point and whether you are willing to see other pieces of the landscape. If we take the wide-angle view, "progress" on some fronts seems clear enough, but, nonetheless, the carnage and barbarisms of the twentieth and twenty-first centuries can make even the most steely-eyed champion of "modern progress" dumbstruck. What is the correct word for such horrifying realities? The Christian story calls them *evil*—rebellion against God and the order of his good creation. But does the language of *evil* make sense within secular stories?[10]

The first line of University of Columbia professor Andrew Delbanco's book *The Death of Satan* reads, "A gulf has opened up in our culture between the visibility of evil and the intellectual resources available for coping with it."[11] He goes on to say:

> The repertoire of evil has never been richer. Yet never have our responses been so weak. We have no language for connecting our inner lives with the horrors that pass before our eyes in the outer world. Philanthropy and protest seem empty gestures, arbitrary in their choice of beneficiary or occasion. It is now commonly remarked . . . that technology has carried us to the point where death by fire is indistinguishable from the puffs and crackle of a video game; and when some shocking cruelty does seize our attention, it is likely to be met with consternation or annoyance. We shudder or wince; then we switch the channel.[12]

Even when we keep the channel on long enough to be moved beyond a wince, when we can't so easily turn ourselves off to the cruelties that confront us, our therapeutic age lacks a sufficient moral vocabulary to understand or to cope well. The story of good and evil that echoes in the human heart is now buried beneath language of disorders, antisocial behavior, and cultural conditioning.

And with "evil" and "sin" cast aside, what then? We must still face the reality of monstrous deeds—rape, mass shootings, torture, acts of terrorism; what is left to be said to the victims and the bereaved? "Your child was killed by someone who acted on the prescriptions of his social environment and genetic arrangement." This is a frustratingly vacuous account that leaves most people not only unsatisfied but also deeply disturbed.

Delbanco illustrates this problem with a scene from the book turned movie *The Silence of the Lambs*. Dr. Hannibal Lecter is an imprisoned serial killer who cannibalizes his victims. In one scene, he sits straitjacketed in a Plexiglas cell and addresses the young FBI agent, Clarice Starling, sitting on the other side:

> "Nothing happened to me, Officer Starling. *I* happened. You can't reduce me to a set of influences. You've given up good and evil for behaviorism, Officer Starling. You've got everybody in moral dignity pants—nothing is ever anybody's fault. Look at me, Officer Starling. Can you stand to say I'm evil?"[13]

The irony is that while Hannibal is the one locked up, it's Clarice who finds herself trapped. We all find ourselves trapped when evil isn't allowed to be called by its true name.

"Out" to a better story. The biblical story names evil. Anything that slanders God and harms the creation he loves is evil. According to the Christian story, the knowledge of evil's reality resides deep within the human heart (Genesis 6:5; Jeremiah 17:9). Each person knows it, not simply because they see it in the world, but because they feel it in their own hearts. If one is attentive, they sense their own dark side—their capacity for selfishness, their disregard for the needs of others, and their prideful scorn for people who are different. We admire the ideals of love and peace, but when we search ourselves, we find that the ancient account told in Genesis 3 also rings true with what lurks beneath the surface of our souls: we each want to write our own story with ourselves as the ruler, not step into the story as a humble servant, and we possess a frightening capacity to think and do evil things in order to get what we want. And when wholesale massacres of millions occur or seemingly "normal" people show up at peaceful gatherings to murder strangers, even the most secular person can be tempted to believe that forces well beyond human comprehension are at work, akin to what the New Testament refers to as "the powers of this dark world and . . . the spiritual forces of evil" (Ephesians 6:12).

The gospel, however, does not imply the abandonment of belief in social and psychological disorders. Sickness is a reality, just not the *whole* of reality. The Christian story incorporates the therapeutic story into its narrative, resulting in a more compelling account of humanity. Humans are multidimensional—God created humans as embodied and social beings. When humans rebelled against God, the world became disordered—spiritually, physically, and relationally. But while affirming sickness, the biblical story refuses to *reduce* people to a conglomeration of atoms that simply becomes sick. We are spiritual beings living in a spiritually charged world, one that's not simply "sick" but ensnared in a moral and spiritual rebellion.

Once evil is named, there is hope. And courage is often not far behind. The answer to evil in the Christian story is found on the cross, where Jesus absorbed evil and suffered with us and for us. The cross is a just and loving God's way to pay for our evil without us paying for it ourselves. In the death of the only pure and innocent One, evil was sentenced. A sure victory over the cosmic evil forces was declared, with the resurrection as a climactic inbreaking of a renewed reality, the beginning of a restoration project that will lead to eternal joy.

But at least for now, we must live with evil. The gospel story, however, refuses to let it have the final word. And that is reason enough for joy. Better days are coming.

Dignity and Death

"Inside" their story. As we've already seen, late modernism places a premium on human dignity. At first glance, trading sin for sickness may seem to heighten human dignity because it removes the embarrassment and shame of knowing we have violated our Creator's laws and that our nature is marred and broken. In reality, however, redefining our primary problem as sickness instead of sin degrades human dignity because, as Charles Taylor describes, we are now to view ourselves as simply "incapacitated"—helpless victims who need to be "manipulated into health."[14] We are simply the sum of our physical parts—machines needing reprogramming to operate better, to keep us going until our batteries run out or a virus corrupts our code.

And, of course, our batteries will run out and the virus will come.

The dignity of life and the problem of death, then, are crucial ideas to explore with those who have embraced the therapeutic turn. As Luc Ferry has written:

> Psychology, it is a well-known fact, has dethroned theology. Yet on the day of burial, at the foot of the grave and the coffin, a certain discomfort takes hold of us. What are we to say to the mother who has lost her daughter, to the grief-stricken father? We are dramatically confronted with the question of meaning or, rather, with its eclipse in a secularized world . . . Whatever comfort a few compassionate gestures may bring, however precious this is, it does not measure up to the question posed by an absence that we know well has become, in a strict sense of the word, meaningless. Whence the banalities one always hears. They do not, however, conceal that the king is naked . . . Without being completely useless, the crutches offered by psychoanalysis are only that: clever prostheses.[15]

At times even leading advocates of "self-help" wonder, given the secular story line, why more people aren't depressed. Reflecting on "why has evolution allowed depression and pessimism to exist at all?" Martin Seligman writes, "Many people believe there is no God, that the only purposes in life are those people manage to create for themselves, and that when they die, they rot. If this is so, why are so many of these same people cheerful?" Seligman puts his finger on a problem that can't be fully resolved through techniques: "As a therapist I was trained to believe that it was my job to help depressed patients both to feel happier and to see the world more clearly. I was supposed to be the agent of happiness and of truth. But maybe truth and happiness antagonize each other. Perhaps what we have considered good therapy for a depressed patient merely nurtures benign illusions."[16] Accordingly, honesty *or* happiness become options we must choose from—unless there is a better way.

"Out" to a better story. The Christian story recognizes the multiple dimensions of our problem, and this includes the reality of illness and the good and important progress of modern medicine. In fact, the Christian should see this progress as part of God's providential care for this world. Sickness itself is a result of sin entering the world, and part of the human vocation is to bring holistic healing to the world, which includes alleviating suffering and caring for those who are physically, emotionally, or psychologically sick. This kind of care will often take the form of sacrifice on the part of the caregiver. Christianity provides a thick motivation, and even a moral obligation, to make scientific discoveries and to care for the world, especially for those who cannot care for themselves.

Instead of reducing humans to biological machines or determined products of culture that can be reprogrammed, Christianity emphasizes that all of us—the least to the greatest—have inviolable dignity as God's image bearers. God deems us worthy to be redeemed for a meaningful life and allows us to make significant choices in that life. At our most fundamental level, we are not physical parts that will be discarded but multidimensional beings with a soul and an eternity to be saved for. Death, then, is not the final word.

Jesus' resurrection was a universal declaration that what every human heart already yearns for is possible: to love and be loved, fully restored (body and soul), forever. Because the mind often has to catch up to the heart, wishing this was true might be the first step in discovering it is true. But as we will see in chapter 10, there are good reasons for the mind to catch up and trust that Jesus' resurrection is true, not mere wish fulfillment. For among other historical reasons we will see later, the resurrection came as a surprise even for his disciples. No one seemed to be "wishing" for a resurrected Messiah in the first century.

Disappointment and Despair

"Inside" their story. Late moderns often see their personal "sin," a violation of a divinely given command, as something to giggle about—an outdated notion that the grown-up modern mind need not be afraid of. Even those willing to consider a belief in God tend to dismiss their own transgressions as small missteps, because, after all, who doesn't make mistakes? If there is a God, isn't it his job to forgive? In a therapeutic culture that doesn't take sin too seriously, how should Christians approach conversations about it?

One familiar way to explain sin is by using the Old Testament law to demonstrate one's need for forgiveness and reconciliation. The law was given, not only to live by, but also as a mirror so that people can see how far short they fall of God's standard. This use of the law to reveal sin is biblical, and in some more traditional contexts, it still can prove quite effective in conversation. However, for many today it will not register if you first present the concept of sin by discussing a divinely instituted law that "they must be accountable to, or else . . ."

While breaking a divine law is something that late moderns might shrug off, what they cannot so easily dismiss is the existential weight they feel in the face of the pressures of limitless choice and possibility—the pressure of being successful, having the latest things, finding fulfilling relationships, discovering themselves, and curating their image. Beyond feeling the constant pressure to perform, late moderns must endure the disappointment and despair that come from failing to measure up. And as Charles Taylor notes, even when they do measure up, they are left feeling discontented: "Even people who are very successful in the range of normal human flourishing (perhaps especially such people) can feel unease, perhaps remorse, some sense that their achievements are hollow."[17]

When visiting America in the nineteenth century, Frenchman Alexis de Tocqueville observed that despite America's prosperity, there was a "strange melancholy which oftentimes . . . haunt[ed] [its] inhabitants . . . in the midst of their abundance."[18] If only he could see us now. For those who have embraced the therapeutic turn, the melancholy, unrest, and sense of being haunted that de Tocqueville observed seems now even more ubiquitous.

Tyler Durden, the main character in the movie *Fight Club*, captures this discontentment poignantly: "We have no Great War. No Great Depression. Our Great War is a spiritual war. Our Great Depression is our lives. We've all been raised on television to believe that one day we'd all be millionaires and movie gods and rock stars, but we won't. And we're slowly learning that fact. And we're very, very pissed off."[19]

Novelist Matias Dalsgaard describes how even when someone does achieve worldly success, they are plagued by an abiding insecurity, "Such a person must have no stable or solid foundation to build upon, and yet nonetheless tries to build his way out of his problem. It's an impossible situation. You can't compensate for having a foundation made of quicksand by building a new story on top. But this person takes no notice and hopes that the problem down in the foundation won't be found out if only the construction work on the top keeps going."[20] When one builds without paying attention to the foundation, as Dalsgaard describes, the result is inevitably disappointment and despair.

These diverse voices, speaking from different professional perspectives and worldviews, are pointing to the alarming inability of the modern person to cope with life. Increasingly it is becoming apparent that we are now facing "the loneliness crisis," which is evident by the alarming increases in reports of chronic loneliness, single-person households, mental illness, depression, and suicide.[21]

"Out" to a better story. Despite the enormous prosperity of the West and the vast resources poured into the medical industry to help us "feel better," restlessness and anxiety continue to characterize the modern world.[22] There's solace in the fact, though, that once again the issues that plague our time can set the table for a sincere conversation about the human diagnosis and possible remedies. It is often when someone is struggling with the weight of discontentment and sadness that we find an opening to introduce the concept of idolatry—one of Scripture's primary ways of describing sin.

As we've already seen in our discussion of identity, the human heart is shaped and guided by whatever it is that one worships and desires above all else—whether it's money, sex, power, fame, success, or something else. This is a fool's errand, however, for by making these temporal things ultimate, one opens themselves up to disappointment and despair. The late modern person knows what it's like to feel devastated at the loss of something they had placed all their hope in or, worse, the hollow, lonely feeling of acquiring that which was supposed to satisfy, only to find it exacerbating an already miserable state of mind. This disappointment suggests that something is not right. We should lean into this existential angst as a way into the topic of sin and our deepest problem—namely, idolatry.

We find a helpful illustration of this point in a short novel titled *The Pearl*. The story describes *a* poor diver named Kino, who one day discovered a pearl of immeasurable value. Gradually, Kino became obsessed with the pearl, and it ruined his life. He was nearly killed; his hut was burned down; and worst of all, he hurt his wife for trying to destroy the pearl. While Kino initially saw the pearl as a blessing he could sell to save his son's life, it became a corrupting curse that led to his son's death. Kino's greed and love of the pearl blinded him to what really mattered in life. As his wife declared early in the book, "This pearl is like a sin! It will destroy us."[23]

The pearl, of course, was not actually evil and was not what destroyed. Kino's ultimate devotion to the pearl is what brought ruin. The story is powerful in that it illustrates how people are inclined to take that which is good and make it an *ultimate* good, thereby allowing it to enslave and enable evil. The Christian story speaks into the despair that results from the disordering of our loves, offering hope in leading others to their ultimate good—God himself—through whom all other things can be enjoyed as good gifts pointing back to their source.

Guilt

"Inside" their story. Even within a secular culture that has largely dismissed sin, there remains a "strange persistence of guilt."[24] Wilfred McClay, a historian at the University of Oklahoma, has observed that guilt has not just remained: "It has grown, even metastasized, into an ever more powerful and pervasive element in the life of the contemporary West," and yet both the categories to make sense of this experience and the means to escape guilt have been lost.[25] So, while the person you're talking to may claim they don't believe in "sin" or even that neither they nor their closest friends feel pangs of guilt or shame, you have reason to be skeptical. Guilt lies beneath the surface, mysteriously haunting even those who claim to have cast off the weighty requirements of a divine Lawgiver.

In some ways, this person's thinking is in line with the logic of Friedrich Nietzsche, who when he proclaimed the "death of God" more than one hundred years ago, also believed that the moral framework and the guilt it produced would soon die as well.[26] Nietzsche was only partly right. Western culture has largely lost a coherent and transcendent moral framework grounded in the givenness of creation. But he was also partly wrong: we haven't escaped the experience of guilt.

McClay points to Sigmund Freud's influence in recognizing the modern abiding sense of guilt and the therapeutic methods we've turned to in order to save ourselves: "Freud declared the tenacious sense of guilt to be 'the most important problem in the development of civilization.' Indeed, he observed, 'the price we pay for our advance in civilization is *a loss of happiness* through the heightening of the sense of guilt.'"[27]

Freud's claim is compelling when we consider our present age's continuous efforts to appease conscience by separating the psychological feeling of guilt from the moral reality of guilt. Our culture has often attempted to "'demoralize' guilt by treating it as a strictly subjective and emotional matter."[28] You might "feel" guilty, but you're told not to worry; you aren't really. Some have attempted to discredit the feeling of guilt as simply a repressive emotion that is best to be downplayed or ignored. But this hasn't worked. We still feel guilty, even if we don't know why or to whom we feel accountable.

First, our attempt to explain guilt away has not worked because to do so involves prying moral dimensions from our understanding of guilt, and this has proven to be as difficult as ceasing to be moral beings altogether. One can, for example, deny that one should feel guilty for putting their own self-actualization before their children's needs, as, for instance, Teal Swan, one of the leaders of the "authenticity" movement, says should be done: "I can't [prioritize my son over my other interests]. I can't do that and be authentic."[29] Yet Swan, rather than avoiding a universal morality, is actually seeking to replace a traditional moral code with a new code grounded in self-actualization. *Everyone* is responsible to be "authentic to themselves." Yet even if one can fully make this switch, which is highly doubtful, wouldn't one then begin to feel guilty for living something less than an "authentic life"?

In listening to Swan, one can sense that behind her bold assurances that she is freeing herself from repressive cultural expectations and that there's nothing to feel bad about, yet she still does. Seeping through her protests seems to be a measure of suppressed but very real guilt over her pursuit of authenticity.

Though it is an extreme example, Swan is paradigmatic for our age. Our ongoing fight against our own shame is a sign that guilt, despite our best efforts, is powerful and is not going away. In fact, the rise of virtue signaling and social media shaming, both of which rely heavily on appeasing personal guilt and pressuring others by making them feel guilty, suggests its existential and practical impact. Though the objective category of moral guilt is regularly disregarded, the psychological power of guilt is ubiquitous, which is why virtue signaling and shaming feel so good and, in one sense, seem to "work."

Second, through technological advancement we have gained a sense of power, agency, and interconnectedness that has only added new dimensions to our sense of guilt. As Wilfred McClay observes, what I do or don't do with my recyclables and what kind of transportation I use impact the environment and therefore impact everyone. I have the power to feed starving people and house the homeless. Most people who are reading this will have the resources to adopt kids from orphanages in starving and dangerous regions of the world, raising them in safe, loving homes. But even if we do a great deal of such noble work, we must admit that it will never be enough: "Whatever donation I make to a charitable organization, it can never be as much as I could have given. I can never diminish my carbon footprint enough, or give to the poor enough, or support medical research enough, or otherwise do the things that would render me morally blameless."[30]

This is a painful conclusion to reach, and one that leads to the root problem: we live in a world that carries around an enormous and growing burden of guilt and yearns—sometimes even demands—to be free of it. Finding ways to press into this emotional reality can wedge open the cracks within secular narratives. People, as it turns out, still long—even if it is subconsciously—for a release from the gnawing feeling of guilt that casts a shadow over even their most "successful" pursuits of pleasure and well-meaning philanthropic efforts.

"Out" to a better story. Rather than freeing us from guilt, the secular therapeutic story has left us to drown in it and has tossed us a life preserver with gaping holes—it may float for a minute, but the air escapes fast. As we've seen, simply denying the reality of the objective moral dimension in our experience of guilt doesn't save us from its emotional currents. It only leaves us with the feeling of treading water, with no shoreline in sight.

The Christian story says that feelings of guilt cannot be wished away, because they're given to us by God as existential warning signs. Like a lifeguard's flag, our sense of guilt is God signaling to us, "Danger!" Thus, rather than trying to sever feelings of guilt from moral reality, Christianity says we must pay attention to both. God made us with consciences that, though imperfectly, still work. If we listen closely, we will hear them pointing to a moral universe and a Creator, to whom we sense an obligation. This may seem or feel repressive, like a lifeguard telling you not to swim, yet accepting this reality is the only way to experience true flourishing, because it leads to God's redemptive plan for freeing people from their guilt—both the objective legal reality and the emotional by-product.

God sent his Son, who came to take our guilt—in its totality—on himself, that we might be forgiven and healed. And hundreds of years before Jesus entered the world, God proclaimed how this would come to be through the words of a Hebrew prophet:

> But he was pierced for our transgressions,
> he was crushed for our iniquities;
> the punishment that brought us peace was on him,
> and by his wounds we are healed.
> We all, like sheep, have gone astray,
> each of us has turned to our own way;
> and the LORD has laid on him
> the iniquity of us all.
>
> ISAIAH 53:5–6

MORAL OUTRAGE

"Inside" their story. If questions of guilt fail to resonate in conversation, the current state of public discourse is another doorway for engagement. Do you find that our society is plagued by a bitterness toward "the other"? Why does everyone seem so angry at each other? What do you think is the cause of the deep divisions and animosity we are experiencing, and what can be done about it? Though these may seem like strange ways to embark on a conversation about faith, in our therapeutic age these questions can actually serve as a backdoor entrance into a discussion of sin and guilt.

Wilfred McClay goes on in the above-mentioned article to argue we all feel a need to escape the indictment of our conscience and achieve release from the emotional weight of our guilt. Traditionally, the same God who sets the moral standards and pronounces final judgment is also the means by which holistic forgiveness is offered and accepted. Yet out of a desire to eliminate what is viewed as oppressive doctrine, therapeutic rationalism has cut us off from the traditional remedy. The assurance to those who avail themselves of God's grace is that the verdict against the sinner has been paid and the impurity removed. The result is a freed person who is able to enjoy true psychological relief from guilt.

But with no God and no substitutionary death on the cross, our culture has turned to its own type of "scapegoat" to remove the guilt. Our culture looks for someone to blame for our problem. We seek someone or some group to bear all of our collective guilt so we can feel relatively free and innocent. Though, as McClay observes, "almost none of [this] has occurred consciously," the approach ironically ends up borrowing, albeit with disastrous results, from a religious paradigm: "it is a story of people working out their salvation in fear and trembling."[31] McClay elaborates:

> With moral responsibility comes inevitable moral guilt . . . So if one wishes to be accounted innocent, one must find a way to make the claim that one cannot be held morally responsible. This is precisely what the status of victimhood accomplishes. When one is a certifiable victim, one is released from moral responsibility, since a victim is someone who is, by definition, not responsible for his condition, but can point to another who is responsible.

This is not to deny that there is a real moral struggle between victims and oppressors. McClay does not—and nor should any Christian—suggest otherwise. Rather, his point is that *all* sides are now rushing to identify as the victim—claiming the status for themselves. And when this happens, it undermines the hope for true reconciliation and the embrace of "the other" because it justifies animus and malice:

> But victimhood at its most potent promises not only release from responsibility, but an ability to displace that responsibility

onto others. As a victim, one can project onto another person, the victimizer or oppressor, any feelings of guilt he might harbor, and in projecting that guilt lift it from his own shoulders. The result is an astonishing reversal, in which the designated victimizer plays the role of the scapegoat, upon whose head the sin comes to rest, and who pays the price for it. By contrast, in appropriating the status of victim, or identifying oneself with victims, the victimized can experience a profound sense of moral release, of recovered innocence. It is no wonder that this has become so common a gambit in our time, so effectively does it deal with the problem of guilt—at least individually, and in the short run, though at the price of social pathologies in the larger society that will likely prove unsustainable.[32]

Welcome to our world of microaggressions, fanatical student protests, and Twitter wars. The ability to seek the common good through compromise is a mere pipe dream because the other side is determined not merely to be wrong. Those on the other side are deemed morally reprehensible so that I and my group can be completely innocent. All guilt falls on "the other," and the only proper response is to silence the guilty. The result of this new response to personal guilt and shame is that "all moral striving" is politicized, and "instead of seeing moral struggle as something between you and God (the religious version) or as something that happens between the good and evil within yourself (the classical version), moral struggle now happens primarily between groups."[33]

Hence, it is common for all sides to have what Alan Jacobs calls the "problem of the repugnant cultural other" or, as he shortens it, the RCO.[34] "If I'm consumed by this belief that that person over there is both Other and Repugnant," then there is no reason to interact with them as a neighbor or to consider their perspective. As Jacobs explains, "The cold divisive logic of the RCO impoverishes us, all of us, and brings us closer to the primitive state that the political philosopher Thomas Hobbes called 'the war of every man against every man.'"[35]

"Out" to a better story. Christianity tells a different story about our guilt, social interactions, and hope for how humans might live together with both diversity and unity. First, the Bible tells a story that indeed says we are each guilty, objectively before God—no matter how much we might try to suppress the subjective feelings of guilt. Since the blood of Christ is on our hands, we can't simply blame others to relieve our guilt. We've all turned away and sought to hide from God, sometimes in direct, conscious rebellion and sometimes in shame. None of us can claim superiority, because salvation doesn't come from our own righteousness but from the righteousness of God himself. When someone truly believes this, the temptation for public shaming or to flaunt their own moral superiority is undermined. Belief in the Christian story also undercuts the assumption that we are always "right." Coming to grips with God's mercy despite our rebellion melts away prideful scorn and produces genuine humility that admits personal failures and a willingness to forgive those who have wronged us.

Second, at the heart of the gospel is a crucified King who forgave his murderers while he hung on the cross. Jesus' most famous sermon taught his followers to be meek, merciful, and committed to peacemaking. Jesus commanded them to love their enemies and pray for those who mistreated them, and he modeled this message throughout his entire life. In contrast with ancient norms, Jesus universalized benevolence. The parable of the good Samaritan taught that seeking the common good of others was not to be limited to one's political or social tribe; everyone becomes a neighbor whom you must love as yourself.

Third, the Christian story is antithetical to coercion. While this story presses up against modern sensibilities by including a God who will one day deliver final judgment, this should *free* individuals to *not* seek vindictive retribution and a will to power. While Christians are to pursue justice and have an objective standard by which justice can be measured, the confidence that God will one day bring a final judgment frees one from the all-consuming lust to "get even" (see Romans 12:19). The biblical story also assumes human agency; each of us will be held accountable for our choices. Coercive or manipulative behavior that sows public discord and distrust is never the way of the kingdom. As New Testament scholar Richard Bauckham has stressed, "Coercion contradicts the nature of truth . . . It is in the very nature of Christian truth that it cannot be enforced. Coerce belief and you destroy belief and turn the truth believed into a lie."[36]

The fact that Christians have not always embraced their own stories' resources to find freedom from personal guilt and to motivate them to care for "the other" is not evidence that these resources do not exist. As we will examine more closely in chapter 11, these resources have provided the very means to offer a prophetic course correction, not only to society in general, but also for Christians themselves who have failed to live according to the narrative they confess to believe.

Since we can't live in isolation from the community and social structures we find ourselves in, this final section has touched on the collective aspect of what we've called the quest for the good life. But this can also raise a problem that contemporary people have with religion. Many assume that the exclusive claims of religion, and Christianity in particular, are a major part of our current social problem. We turn to that issue next.

NOTES

1. C. S. Lewis, *God in the Dock: Essays on Theology and Ethics* (Grand Rapids: Eerdmans, 1970), 95.
2. See Charles Taylor, *A Secular Age* (Cambridge, MA: Harvard University Press, 2007), 618–23.
3. Philip Rieff, *The Triumph of the Therapeutic: Uses of Faith after Freud* (1966; repr., Chicago: University of Chicago Press, 1987), 25.
4. Gabe Lyons and David Kinnaman cite a survey that supports this claim, with 84 percent of Americans believing that "enjoying yourself is the highest goal of life," 86 percent indicating that to enjoy yourself you must "pursue the things you desire most," and 91 percent agreeing that "to find yourself, look within yourself" (*Good Faith: Being a Christian When Society Thinks You're Irrelevant and Extreme* [Grand Rapids: Baker, 2016], 57–58).
5. See Taylor, *A Secular Age*, 635–36.
6. For more on "flourishing" as a translation of Matthew 5:4, as well as in the rest of the Beatitudes, see Jonathan T. Pennington, *The Sermon on the Mount and Human Flourishing: A Theological Commentary* (Grand Rapids: Baker, 2017).
7. Larry McCaffery, "A Conversation with David Foster Wallace," *Review of Contemporary Fiction* 13, no. 2 (Summer 1993), www.dalkeyarchive.com/a-conversation-with-david-foster-wallace-by-larry-mccaffery.
8. Francis Spufford, *Unapologetic: Why, Despite Everything, Christianity Can Still Make Surprising Emotional Sense* (San Francisco: HarperOne, 2013), 11.
9. Terry Eagleton, *On Evil* (New Haven, CT: Yale University Press, 2010), 155–56. The world can simultaneously be getting better and worse. After all, the "world"

covers many different locations and aspects of life. For instance, medicine and comforts can increase, while the quality of our emotional and relational lives is suffering.

10. I am in debt to the stimulating thirty-six-part lectures by Charles Mathewes that led to this section ("Why Evil Exists," *The Great Courses*, www.thegreatcourses.com/courses/why-evil-exists.html).
11. Andrew Delbanco, *The Death of Satan: How Americans Have Lost the Sense of Evil* (New York: Farrar, Straus and Giroux, 1995), 3.
12. Delbanco, *Death of Satan*, 3.
13. Thomas Harris, *The Silence of the Lambs* (New York: St. Martins, 1988), 21; quoted in Delbanco, *Death of Satan*, 19.
14. Taylor, *A Secular Age*, 620.
15. Luc Ferry, *Man Made God: The Meaning of Life* (Chicago: University of Chicago Press, 2002), 3.
16. Martin Seligman, *Learned Optimism: How to Change Your Mind and Your Life* (New York: Vintage, 2006), 108.
17. Taylor, *A Secular Age*, 621.
18. Alexis de Tocqueville, *Democracy in America*, trans. George Lawrence (New York: Harper, 1988), 296.
19. *Fight Club*, directed by David Fincher, screenplay by Jim Uhls, based on the novel by Chuck Palahniuk, distributed by 20th Century Fox, September 10, 1999.
20. Matias Dalsgaard, *Don't Despair: Letters to a Modern Man* (London: Pine Tribe, 2014); quoted in David Brooks, *The Second Mountain: The Quest for a Moral Life* (New York: Random House, 2019), 24.
21. See Brooks, *Second Mountain*, 32–33; also see the studies cited in Arthur C. Brooks, "How Loneliness Is Tearing America Apart" *New York Times*, November 23, 2018, www.nytimes.com/2018/11/23/opinion/loneliness-political-polarization.html.
22. This trend is particularly alarming in America; see, for instance, Joel Achenbach, "'There's Something Terribly Wrong': Americans Are Dying Young at Alarming Rates," *Washington Post*, November 26, 2019, www.washingtonpost.com/health/theres-something-terribly-wrong-americans-are-dying-young-at-alarming-rates/2019/11/25/d88b28ec-0d6a-11ea-8397-a955cd542d00_story.html.
23. John Steinbeck, *The Pearl* (1945; repr., New York: Penguin, 1992), 38.
24. Wilfred M. McClay, "The Strange Persistence of Guilt," *Hedgehog Review* 19, no. 1 (Spring 2017): 40–54, https://hedgehogreview.com/issues/the-post-modern-self/articles/the-strange-persistence-of-guilt.
25. McClay, "Strange Persistence of Guilt."
26. See McClay, "Strange Persistence of Guilt."
27. McClay, "Strange Persistence of Guilt," emphasis mine.
28. McClay, "Strange Persistence of Guilt."
29. Teal Swan and Ralph Smart, "How to Be Authentic," YouTube, June 24, 2015, 11:10–20:10, www.youtube.com/watch?v=irxqCDeQulk. Thanks to my former student Daphne Edmonston for pointing me to this video.

30. McClay, "Strange Persistence of Guilt."
31. McClay, "Strange Persistence of Guilt."
32. McClay, "Strange Persistence of Guilt."
33. David Brooks, "Guilt, Victimhood and Moral Indignation," *Seattle Times*, March 31, 2017, www.seattletimes.com/opinion/guilt-victimhood-and-moral-indignation.
34. Alan Jacobs, *How to Think: A Survival Guide for a World at Odds* (New York: Currency, 2017), 26. Jacobs is borrowing this term from Susan Friend Harding, "Representing Fundamentalism: The Problem of the Repugnant Cultural Other," *Social Research* 58, no. 2 (Summer 1991): 373–93.
35. Jacobs, *How to Think*, 27.
36. Richard Bauckham, *The Bible and Mission: Christian Witness in a Postmodern World* (Grand Rapids: Baker, 2003), 99.

chapter
9

Imagining a Better Inclusiveness

Cultural Assumption #4:
"It's okay to be spiritual, but not to say that your religion is the only way, or attempt to bring it into the public square."

COEXIST?

Our acquaintances, friends, coworkers, and neighbors have diverse views on religion and life. This itself is not completely new. In *The City of God*, for instance, Augustine cites the pagan philosopher Varro, who was writing hundreds of years before him, as calculating 288 variations of answers to the question, What is the good life?[1] While you might not typically view ancient societies as beacons of diversity, in Varro's time, and later in Augustine's, the educated elite had the opportunity to read and discuss a wide variety of ideas. And even for the common person, diversity was at times apparent, particularly visible, for instance, at major trade routes where even the average person could rub shoulders with a diverse population. So, then, what is so different about our experience today?

Throughout most of human history, even when diversity was present, there tended to be one dominant religious view among the general population, and minority communities learned to operate as tight-knit, family-like groups. Given these conditions, the insular quality of social life meant that most people did not have to deal seriously with the religious claims of other communities. Now we face a situation where there is no longer one dominant and overarching *explicitly religious* culture that is given "overwhelming credibility" or is seen as being "beyond challenge."[2] And the more people within a culture who can imagine other belief systems as possible options, the more religious commitment becomes psychologically fragile.

Consider how this vulnerability can play out for Christian teens enrolling at major universities. Stories of students leaving Christian homes only to find their faith shaken by the diversity they encounter on campus are told so often they can't help but feel cliché. Johnny, who was a leader in his youth group and from a Christian family, unexpectedly experiences a gnawing angst during his first semester. His angst morphs into a crisis of faith as he befriends atheists and takes classes with secular professors, who, to Johnny's surprise, don't all drip with elitist arrogance and bark patronizing insults as portrayed in popular Christian movies. In fact, many are friendly, smart, and really quite normal.

Meanwhile, there's Sally. She had a dramatic conversion experience in high school, leading to a newfound seriousness about her faith. After leaving home and settling into her dorm, she builds relationships with several students from other faiths. To her surprise, they equally testify to their own spiritual and conversion experiences. To her greater surprise, she finds that their testimonies seem sincere and even compelling.

For Christian students, many of whom are facing modern pluralism in a personal way for the first time, the diversity of the university setting can be a confusing experience. Initially, they may wonder why other students don't see how "obvious" the truth is and can be tempted to think, rather triumphantly, that their own acceptance of Christianity proves their superior intellect. However, if they don't simply hide away in the safe confines of Christian enclaves, they soon discover, if they're honest with themselves, that many of their peers view the world differently, not because they are unintelligent—quite the contrary—but because they are interpreting the same world through a different story.

This is a disorienting experience for a Christian student because she must now reckon with the fact that the beliefs of her secular friends cannot always be so quickly dismissed as the result of ignorance or the inability to think critically. Reality, it turns out, is more complicated, and she eventually must recognize that it is not simply a lack of logic that is the problem. Her unbelieving friends harbor interpretive lenses for viewing the world that are fundamentally different and lead to starkly different conclusions.

Within this new landscape, any ground of certainty is shaken, loosened, and primed for either a brittle skepticism toward all religions or a privatizing and relativizing of faith. Regarding the former, the newfound religious skeptic will feel compelled to reject all faiths as merely culturally conditioned human expressions, thereby denying the truthfulness of any religion. There are no ultimate religious truths, only regional opinions produced by culture. Regarding the latter, the new optimistic pluralist will go the other direction: "Perhaps everyone can be right. Perhaps we are in fact all talking about the same things, each on a journey leading to the same place."

A modern parable of this second outlook, the optimistic relativist, is found in the acclaimed television series of the mid-2000s, *Lost.* The co-producer Carlton Cuse explains that the six-year television phenomenon was about much more than a group of people trapped on an island:

> Very early on we had decided that even though *Lost* is a show about people on the island, really, metaphorically, it was about people who were lost and searching for meaning and purpose in their lives. And because of that, we felt the ending really had to be spiritual, and one that talks about destiny. We would have long discourses about the nature of the show, for many years, and we decided it needed to mean something to us and our belief system and the characters and how all of us are here to lift each other up in our lives.[3]

In the finale, after all leading characters have died and have entered a church, representing a "purgatory-of-sorts" vision of the afterlife, the camera pans to an array of symbols representing different religions.[4] This sentiment that all major religions lead to a common destiny is widely appealing. Drive into any U.S. city and you'll probably spot a handful of "coexist" bumper stickers. While Christians are called to love their neighbors, to "coexist" with people of other beliefs, the collection of symbols on these stickers and in shows like *Lost* is not simply signaling peaceful interaction, but rather the sentiment that while it's okay, even good, to be on a spiritual quest, it's dangerous and intolerant to suggest that one religion is the only path.

RESPOND, DON'T REACT

For most Christians, bridging the gap between culture's pervasive "coexist" mentality and Jesus' words in John 14:6—that he is the *only* way to the Father—is daunting, if not outright frightening. The temptation for many of us is to simply remain silent. Others can fall into the trap of reacting with frustration, demonizing both the skeptical and optimistic pluralist. But it is important we learn to avoid reacting out of fear or frustration.

The late sociologist Peter Berger saw that modern pluralism, despite its challenges, had a tangible upside for the Christian, because "it is better for social conditions to encourage us to decide upon faith than for us to live amid circumstances that 'give' us faith, making our religious identity akin to our hair color or our particular allergies rather than a personal quality that arises from our free assent."[5]

Furthermore, because modern pluralism has weakened the conditions that support belief in Christianity, it has made it necessary for Christians to be more intentional with their faith than they were in past times when Christianity was taken for granted. To Berger's point, these instances often produced a weak, insincere "cultural Christianity" that people treated as little more than something they were born into, like their hair color. Modern pluralism, then, presents an opportunity to strengthen the church by intentionally focusing on her internal culture. The internal culture of the church, which comprises, for example, the way Christians conduct worship, maintain relationships with each other, choose leadership, determine the content of preaching, order their calendar, teach their children, produces its own framework for living and thinking. Christian communities seeking to thoughtfully engage the diversity of the modern world should intentionally build their own Christian social imaginations.

Globalization, too, should give Christians genuine reason to find hope amid the challenges of pluralism, for through it, the world has come to the West. Globalization has its own challenges, of course, but Western Christians should see how it provides opportunities to take the gospel to the world by simply crossing the street. The Western church should also find great encouragement in the newfound access and communication we can have with Christians from other nations who are already bearing—and will likely increasingly bear—the responsibility of being the center of the global church.[6]

And yet we shouldn't be overly sanguine. Problematic assumptions that have accompanied the rise of modern pluralism are now seen as "common sense" to many people. As discussed, it is common today for Westerners to insist that all religious traditions—or at least all major religious traditions—describe the same reality and lead their adherents to the same ultimate destination. Religions, then, are simply different paths up a single mountain, each path being unique but trustworthy in its directions. Or in more popular discourse: "Of course there can't be just one way to God." What is important according to this view, then, is not religious doctrine but recognizing that we are all on different routes to the same place, and therefore no one should be excluded.

This new kind of "tolerance" places an overwhelming pressure on others to relativize and privatize their religious commitment. Of course, because this perspective will seem obvious to the person you are talking to in a given conversation, they likely won't see that they themselves are forcing an exclusive, ideological framework on others. In order to make headway, you will need to step inside their story, show its inadequacies, and narrate a better way to live for the common good in a pluralistic world.

Cultural Expressions Can't All Be Wrong

"Inside" their story. You can partially agree with the critic who claims religions are cultural expressions. We are historically conditioned, insofar as we are strongly influenced by our cultural contexts. But once the religious skeptic tries to assert that cultural context is the sole determining factor for what people believe, religious skepticism becomes self-defeating. From this perspective, religious skepticism itself must be deemed as nothing but a conditioned response to culture, and therefore as untrue. Atheists, after all, are hard to find in traditional cultures. Does this mean all atheists are simply a product of their culture? Of course not. While our cultural context conditions us in many ways, it is not singularly decisive in what we believe as individuals. If that were the case, how would one explain a pluralistic culture where people who grew up in Christian families share deconversion stories and atheists share conversion stories?

A Different Kind of Intolerance

"Inside" their story. With respect to the optimistic relativist, who takes the "all religions are basically the same" approach, at first glance this person's view can sound humble and tolerant, but ask them to consider their approach more closely. If someone says they are against any one path to salvation, they themselves are articulating a doctrine of salvation. Further, by claiming there are many paths to salvation, they automatically contradict how most religious adherents—irrespective of which religion—understand their faith. This means, by this person's own standards, that while seeking a flawed form of pluralism, they are in some sense being intolerant of the world's sincerest religious believers.

Some optimistic relativists will describe a transcendent reality or god residing at "the top of the mountain"—a mountain on which all humanity is traveling up. This spiritual being at the peak is sometimes described as an all-loving divine spirit that is beyond our grasp. Those who go so far as to suggest this idea will also find themselves offending people of countless religions for how it completely glosses over the genuine distinctives of others' faiths.

On the whole, religious adherents find it offensive when others grossly misinterpret or ignore the actual tenants of their religious doctrine. Buddhists, for instance, would disagree that their religion could be described as a "way to God," because belief in a personal God isn't a feature of their belief system. As for Christians, while we would agree that God is love, we would also assert that what we mean by "love" is distinct and that God has many other essential attributes that this "mountain peak" fails to include.

To the optimistic relativist, an important question is, "What do you mean by salvation?" Religions describe what the final stage of existence will be in conflicting terms—from affirming an immaterial, impersonal eternal existence, to the Christian view of an embodied person, resurrected to live in a new creation, to views suggesting no afterlife existence at all.[7] If all these paths lead to the same salvation, what are we saved *to* and what are we saved *from*? The world's religions are far from an agreement on how these questions are answered.

Somewhat ironically, people who hold to the "all religions are basically the same" perspective under a mantle of inclusivity and tolerance actually engage in a form of progressive colonialism that runs over views they don't find palatable. It's as if they've placed themselves on top of the mountain, with truth in hand, looking down on myopic religious adherents scrambling up their intolerant "one way." The problem isn't that they think others are wrong and they are right. We all do that. The problem is that this view is often held because it is thought to be more tolerant than those views that make exclusive claims, all the while making its own exclusive claim.

Our Lives Together

"Inside" their story. This perspective is not limited to matters of ultimate salvation. *New York Times* columnist Nicholas Kristof, a secular man himself, sees this sharp intolerance masked by language of "tolerance" to be a problem: "Too often, we liberals embrace people who don't look like us, but only if they think like us."[8] However an online commenter disagreed, protesting against Kristof's call for a robust and inclusive conversation: "Why should we debate the merits of something dehumanizing and harmful, in so doing legitimizing it as a valid option?" The problem is that the commenter assumes that what is "harmful" is also "common sense," when in actuality the questions of "harm" and "flourishing" are the very issues up for debate.

The respondent to Kristof goes on to say, "You may disagree, but calling for us to debate and elevate these opinions is going to fall on deaf ears for most people our age. We don't care about civility." In other words, he is uninterested in dialogue because he sees his own group's vision of human flourishing as above dissent and disconnected from the way they treat others who don't share the same assumptions. Yet what prevents brutal coercion from being justified by such reasoning?

Kristof's critique makes clear that not every secular person shares the commenter's desire to ignore others. Still, this intolerant exclusivism is representative of Harvard Law School professor Adrian Vermeule's concern with our culture's dominant qualities: "Liberal society celebrates toleration, diversity, and free inquiry, but in practice it features a spreading social, cultural, and ideological conformism."[9]

On the topic of "ideological conformism," it can be incisive to pose certain questions: What resources are available in the secular story to undermine the human proclivity for self-righteousness and coercive intimidation toward those who don't share your values? Or, to put it bluntly, why not be insulting and even abusive to other groups if that is deemed the best tactic to gain your group's concept of "justice"?

Some might answer, "Because wouldn't you want to live in a world where people are considerate and kind to one another?" But what about those who don't value civility and inclusion of different ideas. Such people, like the commenter to Kristof's article, would likely conclude that pursuing their own (superior conceptions of) justice outweighs the trivialities of civility and "playing nice." What within the secular story provides the thick motivation needed to resist the impulse to be coercive and even vicious toward people who aren't like you, if one's actions are justified by being done in the name of some higher goal (especially if one can get away with it)? And who gets to determine what higher goal is worth such exclusion and coercive treatment?

This is not to suggest that Christians have always lived up to the ideals of toleration, diversity, and free inquiry. Far from it. Christians, as we will discuss in chapter 11, have too often failed to live out the resources available within our story. The goal here, however, is to get to a point in the conversation where you and your secular friend can agree on factors that make living peaceably in a pluralistic society difficult.

It should be no surprise that both secular and religious people can be narrowly and harshly judgmental. As the work of the NYU professor Jonathan Haidt has shown, self-righteousness is deeply embedded in human nature. Christians don't need empirical studies to tell us humans are self-centered; the Bible has long told us this story. Yet when cultural authorities such as Haidt point this out and the daily media barrage reflects widespread tribalism, identity politics, and denunciations of entire swaths of people who vote or worship differently, we are left with what could be a common concern that sparks a deeper apologetic conversation.[10] Given our ingrained impulse to view ourselves and our groups as morally superior, as well as the fierce animosity bubbling over in our public interactions, what hope do we have for moving toward a more peaceable and inclusive society?

Since all sides can be guilty of not living up to the high aspirations of diversity and free inquiry, the key question becomes: What story about the world has the resources to (1) undermine coercive pressure against those who don't share the same story, (2) encourage adherents to embrace people who are ethnically and culturally different, (3) respect others by not acting like major differences don't exist, and (4) motivate people to live peacefully with those who do not think like them?

The Dignity of All

"Out" to a better story. The Christian story, while recognizing that cultural and social contexts affect beliefs, upholds the dignity of each person by refusing to reduce them to a mere product of cultural conditioning. Moreover, Christianity acknowledges that different religions have beliefs that overlap, without ignoring the major differences between them or flattening them to the lowest common denominator.

Just like any group that gathers around a common interest or belief, Christianity is exclusive—as we have seen, even groups that gather around a belief in tolerance embrace a form of exclusivism as they define their own exclusive brand of tolerance. The question, then, is which meta-story has the resources to enable people to treat others, especially those who don't agree with them, with respect, dignity, and love? And what narrative can attract people from different times, places, races, and socioeconomic standings to unite around such goals?

Religious Freedom

"Out" to a better story. The first Christians uniquely appealed to an unprecedented diverse demographic and were the first in the ancient world to introduce the idea of religious liberty. Some early Christian leaders argued that people should have the right to their own beliefs, free from the coercion of the state. The first person we have on record to claim liberty of religious faith is Tertullian, the third-century Christian, who argued that "religious faith is an inward disposition of the mind and heart and for that reason cannot be coerced by external force."[11] Tertullian went on to say, "It is only just and a privilege inherent in human nature that every person should be able to worship according to his own conviction . . . It is not part of religion to coerce religious practice."[12]

Though Tertullian's point may seem obvious or standard for us today, it was a novel idea in the ancient world. As Larry Hurtado, a historian who specialized in the study of Christian origins, pointed out, in antiquity (and for many parts of the world today) "conformity in religion was required as an expression of solidarity with your family, your people, and your ruler. So any serious religious diversity or dissent raised questions about your loyalty to these groups."[13]

Robert Wilken—who championed the aforementioned research on Tertullian and the later development of what we now know as religious freedom—concludes this same study by summarizing the historical basis for this modern ideal that began with this small group of third-century dissenters:

> It was early Christian teachers who first set forth ideas of the freedom of the human person in matters of religion; it was Christian thinkers who contended that conscience must be obedient only to God; and it was the dualism of political and spiritual authority in Christian history that led to the idea that civil government and religious belief must be kept separate. The process by which the meditations of the past become the certainties of the present is long and circuitous. But by the eighteenth century ideas on religious liberty advanced by earlier thinkers had become the property of all.[14]

It was the Christian story that planted and nurtured the seeds from which religious freedom blossomed. And without a coherent framework—which includes such convictions as belief in "one transcendent God who welcomes all peoples," an absolute moral standard beyond a particular society, religion as more than outward rituals, and humans as moral agents[15]—the future prospect of religious freedom is unknown. Many find it doubtful that a purely secularized story has either the resources to produce or maintain such ideals over the long term. For example, Jürgen Habermas, a leading philosopher who once insisted on an exclusively secular framework for public life, changed his posture toward religion because he saw "there is no alternative to" the heritage of the "Judaic ethic of justice and the Christian ethic of love" for the ideals of "freedom and a collective life in solidarity, the autonomous conduct of life and emancipation, the individual morality of conscience, human rights and democracy."[16]

Diversity

"Out" to a better story. From the outset, the gospel was proclaimed as both an exclusive and all-inclusive message in that while Jesus is the only way to salvation, the salvation made possible through Jesus is extended *to all people*—not just to the elite or to people from a certain culture. One of the features that set apart Christianity from other religions in the ancient world was its "transethnic and translocal" quality, "addressing males and females of all social levels."[17] In other words, one of Christianity's unique features in its original ancient context was that while it denied that its God could be worshiped along with other gods, it attracted people from all sorts of regions, ethnicities, and races.

Today Christianity itself is still proving to be remarkably inclusive and is the most geographically diverse belief system in the world. Its growth in the non-Western world is incredible: More Christians attend church in China than in all of Europe. East Asia is projected to have 171.1 million Christians by 2020, which will be 10.5 percent of its population. Africa will have 630 million Christians by 2020—that will be 49.3 percent of its population.[18] Furthermore, while the hubs of other major religions remain in the same places in which those religions were founded, Christianity's geographical center has quite remarkably migrated throughout its history.[19] This migration further testifies to Christianity's unique transcultural message. For these reasons, it isn't hyperbole to describe Christianity as the most culturally, racially, ethnically, and socioeconomically diverse worldview in history.

The Narrow Path to Peace

"Out" to a better story. The final chapters of the biblical story present a picture that helps explain Christianity's ability to appeal transculturally and to bind people together for the common good. The vision prizes cultural diversity, with people from every nation, tribe, people, and language retaining their cultural distinctives, while uniting as they live together in harmony (Revelation 7:9). In line with this closing biblical vision, New Testament scholar Richard Bauckham has stressed how the biblical story gives the Christian resources to encourage diversity and unity:

> The biblical story is not only critical of other stories but also hospitable to other stories. On its way to the kingdom of God it does not abolish all other stories, but brings them all into relationship to itself and its way to the kingdom. It becomes the story of all stories, taking with it into the kingdom all that can be positively related to the God of Israel and Jesus. The presence of so many little stories within the biblical metanarrative, so many fragments and glimpses of other stories, within Scripture itself, is surely a sign and an earnest of that. The universal that is the kingdom of God is no dreary uniformity or oppressive denial of difference, but the milieu in which every particular reaches its true destiny in relation to the God who is the God of all because he is the God of Jesus.[20]

When one embraces the Christian story, she can appreciate cultures while addressing and saying no to its blind spots. Bauckham puts it well, "When Paul states that in Christ there is no longer Jew, Greek, barbarian, or Scythian (Colossians 3:11), what he denies is cultural privilege, not cultural diversity."[21] The gospel frees the Christian to be open to what other cultures offer for the common good and frees them to challenge the sins of particular cultures, starting with our own.

This has the power to keep one from being swept away by the blind spots found in even the most sophisticated cultures (consider, for instance, the powerful and dominant nationalist story line within Germany during the 1930s), while simultaneously keeping one from demonizing everything in a culture that is not their own.

At the core of Christianity is a person who was not a political figure asserting coercive authority, or an elite philosopher looking down on the unenlightened, or a spiritual guru affirming others in their misguided quests. Instead, the heart of the story is a person whose love drove him to teach that there are paths, that if chosen, will ruin you. In his love, he warned against the brutality of false gods and false stories and offered himself as the true God and the true way. And his way didn't lead to shedding any blood—except for his own.

At the heart of this story, we find a humble and courageous Savior forgiving his enemies and teaching his disciples to do the same. Even those who were by natural temperament "fighters," literally ready to wield their swords against Jesus' enemies, were radically changed by their leader's nonviolent and nonretaliatory approach: "When they hurled their insults at him, he did not retaliate; when he suffered, he made no threats" (1 Peter 2:23). Looking back to his Lord's costly sacrifice, Peter instructs the church, who at the time was being persecuted unfairly, to respect everyone and care for the very people who were mistreating them. How could they do this?

The true believer sees that while he once stood as an enemy, a rebel against God and his image bearers, yet Jesus died to absorb the judgment he deserves. When someone experiences this kind of unmerited mercy, grace becomes the theme of her life. When one accepts the reality of God's grace, how could she not also, as Jesus commanded the crowds after they heard him tell the story of the good Samaritan, "go and do likewise" (Luke 10:37)?

Christians, for now, only get a glimpse at the incredible cost Jesus paid for securing this forgiveness, but this "good news" provides unrivaled resources to generate forgiveness and compassion toward all people. Compared to the late modern story that attempts to ground neighborliness in personal self-interest, if you *try* this story on, you will be motivated to accept the price of loving all people, even if the cost seems to far outweigh your personal benefit. Our best hope for a better "inclusiveness" is paradoxically found on the narrow path that leads to the cross.

NOTES

1. See Augustine, *The City of God against the Pagans* (Cambridge: Cambridge University Press, 1998), book XIX, chapters 1–2, pp. 909–16.
2. See James Davison Hunter, *To Change the World: The Irony, Tragedy, and Possibility of Christianity in the Late Modern World* (New York: Oxford University Press, 2010), 201. Granted, much of the West today is said to be ruled by the "iron cage" of achievement, consumerism, and individualism, which leads to certain moral norms and conceptions of the good life. Attached to these key features of modern society are practices and "idols" that are *implicitly* religious. However, explicit belief in some kind of actual divine being is still often affirmed alongside these features—so the "cage" does not imprison most to the same explicitly religious confessions of faith.
3. Kristin dos Santos, "*Lost* Bosses Finally Answer: Was Everyone Really Dead the Whole Time? What Was the Show About? Find Out!" *ENews*, March 16, 2014, www.eonline.com/uk/news/521692/lost-bosses-finally-answer-were-they-really-dead-the-whole-time-what-was-the-whole-show-about.
4. Jacob Stolworthy, "*Lost* Ending Explained: What Actually Happened in the Most Misunderstood Finale of All Time," *The Independent*, February 12, 2019, www.independent.co.uk/arts-entertainment/tv/news/lost-ending-explained-finale-jj-abrams-damon-lindelof-anniversary-8-years-what-happened-a8365081.html.
5. Peter L. Berger, "The Good of Religious Pluralism," *First Things* (April 2016), www.firstthings.com/article/2016/04/the-good-of-religious-pluralism.
6. See Philip Jenkins, *The Next Christendom: The Coming of Global Christianity*, 3rd ed. (Oxford: Oxford University Press, 2011), which argues that the center of Christianity has already moved to Africa, Asia, and Latin America and will continue to do so.
7. See, for instance, different religious stances on the afterlife in John Gray, *Seven Types of Atheism* (New York: Farrar, Straus and Giroux, 2018), 4.
8. Nicholas Kristof, "Stop the Knee-Jerk Liberalism that Hurts Its Own Cause," *New York Times*, June 29, 2019, www.nytimes.com/2019/06/29/opinion/sunday/liberalism-united-states.html.
9. Adrian Vermeule, "Liturgy of Liberalism," *First Things* (January 2017), www.firstthings.com/article/2017/01/liturgy-of-liberalism.
10. See Jonathan Haidt, *The Righteous Mind: Why Good People Are Divided by Politics and Religion* (New York: Vintage, 2012).
11. Cited in Robert Louis Wilken, *Liberty in the Things of God: The Christian Origins of Religious Freedom* (New Haven, CT: Yale University Press, 2019), 1.

12. Cited in Wilken, *Liberty in the Things of God*, 1; Wilken notes (p. 11) that Tertullian is the first in the history of the West to use the phrase "freedom of religion" (*libertas religionas*).
13. Larry Hurtado, "Religion and National Loyalty," *Marginalia: Los Angeles Review of Books*, April 12, 2019, https://marginalia.lareviewofbooks.org/religion-and-national-loyalty/.
14. Wilken, *Liberty in the Things of God*, 187.
15. Wilken, *Liberty in the Things of God*, 9, 11.
16. Jürgen Habermas, *Religion and Rationality: Essays on Reason, God, and Modernity* (Cambridge: Polity, 2002), 149.
17. Larry W. Hurtado, *Destroyer of the Gods: Early Christian Distinctiveness in the Roman World* (Waco, TX: Baylor University Press, 2016), 186.
18. See Timothy Keller, *Making Sense of God: An Invitation to the Skeptical* (New York: Viking, 2016), 26.
19. See Andrew F. Walls, *The Missionary Movement in Christian History: Studies in the Transmission of Faith* (Maryknoll, NY: Orbis, 1996), 16–25.
20. Richard Bauckham, *The Bible and Mission: Christian Witness in a Postmodern World* (Grand Rapids: Baker, 2003), 110.
21. Bauckham, *The Bible and Mission*, 110.

chapter

10

Imagining Better Reason(s)

Cultural Assumption #5:

"We've progressed beyond faith and myths to reason and science."

Paul Kalanithi grew up in a devout Christian home. His passions and giftedness eventually led him to earn degrees at the University of Cambridge and Yale School of Medicine before becoming a renowned neurosurgeon. Along his academic journey, he moved away from his religious upbringing and adopted what he called an "ironclad atheism." He concluded that "enlightened reason offered a more coherent cosmos" than Christianity, and "it is unreasonable to *believe* in God."[1]

Kalanithi embraced a narrative that many people you encounter might share. The narrative says something like this: We should have the courage to embrace the cold, hard facts that science presents to humankind. We bravely have chosen to let go of comforting, childish religious beliefs and have grown up, taking an adult stance on reality.[2] Life's most important questions, according to this story, are no longer to be solved by "faith," for we—the enlightened members of society—have come of age. Given what we know, we can reason from the ground up, one logical truth at a time, and build a robust fortress of truth. Religious faith is wishful thinking for the weak. Reason and evidence, in contrast to faith, are the characteristics of maturity and serve as the neutral arbitrators for deciphering reality. Like all coming-of-age stories, this can be an enticing narrative to accept as it gives the illusion of strength and control.

Eventually, however, before Kalanithi's untimely death in his late thirties, he saw major problems with the narrative he had so quickly accepted and long considered concrete but which in fact turned out to be, among other things, utterly thin. In his *New York Times* #1 best-seller, he explains:

> The problem, however, eventually became evident: to make science the arbiter of metaphysics is to banish not only God from the world but also love, hate, meaning—to consider a world that is self-evidently *not* the world we live in. That's not to say that if you believe in meaning, you must also believe in God. It is to say, though, that if you believe that science provides no basis for God, then you are almost obligated to conclude that science provides no basis for meaning and, therefore, life itself doesn't have any.[3]

He goes on to explain that while science rooted in "manufactured objectivity" makes it "the most useful way to organize empirical, reproducible data," at the same time "its power to do so is predicated on its *inability* to grasp the most central aspects of human life: hope, fear, love, hate, beauty, envy, honor, weakness, striving, suffering, virtue."[4]

One cannot begin to capture the multiple dimensions of these ideals or answer the important questions associated with them through science alone, which means a person is either left with a superficial picture of human life or must look elsewhere for answers to humanity's biggest questions. This realization eventually led Kalanithi to leave behind what he came to see as a reductionistic view of the world while being drawn back to the church by what he calls "the central values of Christianity—sacrifice, redemption, forgiveness."[5]

If we respond to this scientific coming-of-age narrative by assuming we can simply reason from the ground up with our secular friends and lead them to Christianity, our conversations will likely take a different and wholly unproductive course. Reasoning from the ground up is not what pulled Paul Kalanithi out of his atheism, but rather Christianity's ability to illuminate the most important parts of life. Recall Charles

Taylor's explanation of the "immanent frame" discussed in chapter 3 (p. 35), in which people are no longer inclined to see nature as pointing to divine realities. Since the plausibility of arguments for Christianity "is shaped by cultural pressures and imaginative constructions which ultimately transcend the rational arguments which underlie it,"[6] how do we have a constructive conversation with those whose "reason" has been shaped by this imaginative coming-of-age story that pits adult atheistic reasoning against childish faith?

In his book *Re-Imagining Nature*, Alister McGrath offers an illuminating answer that both serves our question here and casts a helpful vision for the "inside out" approach altogether. He writes, "The best way of engaging a closed reading of the 'immanent frame' would thus seem to be to provide an imaginatively compelling alternative, which is seen to have rational plausibility." A more promising approach, then, is to "open up alternative readings of our world" by "capturing the cultural imagination with a richer and deeper vision of reality." This will not come "from the cold certainties of closed logical argument, but from the open imaginative embrace of a luminous and compelling vision of truth, beauty, and goodness which stands at the heart of the Christian faith."[7]

This means helping others reimagine the world by casting a more compelling vision for human reason, which is how this chapter begins (part 1). Rather than reason or science alone, we need a reimagined rationality that doesn't achieve a "manufactured objectivity" at the cost of "the most central aspects of human life."[8] Within this renewed framework for reason, this chapter turns to offer reasons for believing (part 2). Rather than isolated logical "proofs," these lines of evidence become most persuasive when they are seen as signposts that fit within the larger context of the Christian story.

PART 1: REIMAGINING REASON: REASON ALONE?

Though many people you talk to will still hold the cultural assumption that appears at the beginning of this chapter—"We've progressed beyond faith and myths to reason and science"—and you will hear this story told in various ways, many have pointed out its serious philosophical and historical problems. For starters, it is widely recognized by scholars that what is judged to be rational is dependent on at least three factors: (1) basic logic, (2) prevailing cultural metanarratives, and (3) the evidence available.[9] When answering the big questions of life, such as questions of meaning, purpose, morality, and God, there is no single agreed-on way to approach them, certainly not one that makes use of basic logic and evidence alone. The overarching frameworks used to reach conclusions on life's most significant questions are themselves contested. This is why philosopher Alasdair MacIntyre has stressed that the important question one must ask when speaking about larger worldview questions is which rationality we are talking about.[10] Even if the person you are talking to is not aware of it, they, like everyone else, make their "rational" judgments based on a metanarrative in which they've placed their confidence and trust, given a combination of logical, cultural, emotional, and existential reasons.

For example, if someone claims that science is the only way to determine truth, consider asking, "How can science prove that science is the only source of truth?" This claim cannot be supported by evidence or reason alone. It takes a leap of faith to believe it.

While no metanarrative can be proven by reason alone, this doesn't mean we cannot or should not compare views sincerely. Like the questions we've addressed in previous chapters, we must learn to meet people inside their story, while at times challenging the very foundational assumptions by which their story hangs together. To effectively do this, we can begin by asking questions, such as: Which metanarrative best accounts for human experience and scientific findings? Which story is the most consistent with itself? Which story is best able to incorporate the insights of rival stories? Can the story be lived out consistently? As we've already seen and will continue to see in this chapter, these questions can serve as a springboard to turn *outside* their own narratives and to Christianity.

Scientism

"Inside" their story. Modern science is an unquestionably critical enterprise in grasping truth, so we should be quick and sincere in affirming our thankfulness for it. What we must take issue with, however, is the claim that science is the *only* means by which one can obtain truth. When you encounter a person who makes this claim, try to help them better understand your position by prompting them to reflect more deeply on the assumptions on which modern science necessarily predicates itself.

The problem with the scientism narrative is that it has its own set of beliefs and values that cannot be proven and therefore require a type of faith.[11] For example, two of the assumptions essential to modern science—the rationality of the universe and the reliability of basic cognitive faculties—cannot be proven by science. Scientists cannot explain why or how these are true; they simply believe that they are.

Even the less weighty, more manageable types of questions that science seeks to answer require more than bare logic and empirical facts. Despite how it may seem, scientists cannot *simply* observe significant facts and then form a hypothesis. After all, what makes a fact *significant*? How does one determine whether the problem is *worth investigating*? There is no scientific way to determine beforehand what problems are *worth* solving or which facts are *significant*. Scientists must trust their intuition, personal experience, or some other source beyond science.[12] Moreover, once the data has been examined, what are the rules for forming a hypothesis? The history of science teaches that accepted theories are not simply the straightforward results of accumulating the "right" facts.[13] Imagination, intuition, and historical contingencies all play significant roles in successful hypothesizing.

And what about the meta-questions of life? While modern science has given us access to important knowledge about the world, the scientific method cannot prove or even explain much of the knowledge and experience that nearly everyone agrees to be true. Science alone, for instance, cannot account for logical and mathematical truths; it simply assumes them. It cannot prove many beliefs that everyone takes for granted. For instance, how would someone prove scientifically that other people don't only have brains but also have minds? How would someone prove that our memory beliefs (i.e., what we remember) actually happened?

Beauty is also outside its purview—how would the scientific method account for aesthetic truths without undermining the sublime, which it is seeking to account for? Neither can science sufficiently ground ethical statements. One cannot, through scientific methods, determine if certain actions are morally wrong. Consequently, science cannot account for justice, human rights, or good and evil. The list goes on, and it demands we be honest with ourselves: if we seek to apply an absolutist view of science consistently across our lives, we would be left without many of the most important truths on which we base our existence.

Moreover, if science proceeds by assuming only "natural" causes (sometimes referred to as methodological naturalism), then it eliminates itself from even presuming to speak on the question of God. If someone pursues science based solely on this approach, then their experiments are limited to answering questions about and considering factors within this world alone. In adopting this approach, they are not warranted in answering questions about things beyond the material world, because the method screens out such a world from the beginning. There is nothing necessarily faulty with this approach or its results, if one is searching to discover a cure for a disease or test the results of a physics experiment. However, if one is asking the deepest questions of life or wondering if miracles are possible, screening out the possibility of anything behind the material world unnecessarily and without warrant limits the answers.[14]

"Out" to a better story. We've seen some of the internal shortcomings and inconsistencies of using science to make belief in God obsolete. In actuality, skeptics are like everyone else. They believe what they do about the world for a variety of reasons, many of which are not "provable" by any type of scientific method. Scientific study and discovery raise important questions that people must answer with a story that cannot be narrated solely by the results of empirical tests. As two Oxford scientists and a Princeton philosopher have asked each other when discussing the emergence of earthly life:

> But what is the story of this story? What kind of a narrative do we have here? Is it tragedy? Or a comedy of errors? Or a heroic epic? Or farce? Or is it a tale of boundless exploration? Or a triumph of the aggressive? Or a triumph of the adaptable? Is it the story

of brute force? Or is it the story of courage in spite of brute force? A story of increasing depth of experience? Is it a good story? Is it a story of good? Is it good?[15]

Questions of personhood—such as meaning, morality, significance, beauty, and love—are precisely the questions that scientism fails to answer. They also are the questions we can't help but ask. As Briggs, Halvorson, and Steane—the aforementioned Oxford and Princeton scholars—explain, "We detect what we think matters in the world around us, and we contribute to that. This is what each of us does . . . We talk of things going *wrong* when someone suffers some affliction, a cancer or a famine or an enslavement. We say we are trying to make things *right* or *better* when we study medicine or develop agriculture or liberate slaves. These are all judgements about value and significance."[16] Those who try to live by a story of scientism must answer life's most important questions by borrowing from another story. Instead of science alone, they draw on science *plus* something else, a bigger story that encompasses both the emergence of science and the universal features of personhood.

The Christian story was a crucial factor in providing the setting and resources for modern science to develop and flourish. When in conversation with an unbeliever about this, you might ask them, "What assumptions are necessary for modern science to flourish?"

Historian Rodney Stark has shown there are religious reasons why modern science emerged in Christian Europe and not in the sophisticated societies of China, ancient Greece, and the Islamic world.[17] The Christian story about the world provided assumptions that were vital to the rise of modern science. It was the Christian belief that the universe is contingent—formed by a personal and sovereign Creator who ordered the universe—that enabled science to mature. The doctrine of creation implied regularity and orderliness to the universe, giving early scientists confidence that nature could be studied and understood. A world that was not structured and stable would be impossible to study. Even the doctrine of original sin played an important role, leading to a suspicion of contemplative reason alone and to the view that experimentation was necessary to gain knowledge about nature.[18]

Thus, far from there being a deep conflict between science and faith, modern science is a "legacy of Christianity."[19]

Trusting in Our Cognitive Faculties

"Inside" their story. The world is something that we can understand. All human reasoning and scientific disciplines depend on this. We can't fully know everything we'd like to know, but we *can* understand it in part. We are so accustomed to being able to comprehend aspects of the world around us that fundamental questions are quickly passed over: What makes science and understanding in general possible? Why is it that the structures of the universe can be charted mathematically?

Theoretical physicist John Polkinghorne explains: "The universe might have been a disorderly chaos rather than an orderly cosmos. Or it might have had a rationality which was inaccessible to us."[20] But this isn't the case. Our minds fit the world around us, as is evident by how what begins as theorical mathematics turns out to fit with the external world. The Oxford mathematician John Lennox explains: "It is very striking that the most abstract mathematical concepts that seem to be pure inventions of the human mind can turn out to be of vital importance for branches of science, with a vast range of practical applications."[21] What best explains the ways our minds "fit" with the universe?

Some argue that the human mind is simply imposing its structure on the world. The world only seems to be structured because that is how we are looking at it—it's actually an illusion. Yet this fails to account for the precise agreement between many scientific theories, observations, and correct predictions about the physical world. Can an illusion be right so many times?[22]

Others explain this fit as simply a cosmic coincidence. The correspondence between mathematics, the universe, and the comprehensibility of natural laws has happened by chance. This "explanation" is woefully unsatisfying, for what does it actually explain? Still others say our cognitive ability to make sense of the world can be explained by our evolutionary drive to survive. But assuming that our cognitive faculties are simply materials produced by natural forces, how does this give us any reason to trust such faculties?

Philosophers of different stripes have argued that if naturalism and evolution are both true, "our cognitive faculties would very likely not be reliable."[23] Many prominent nonbelievers—such as Friedrich Nietzsche, Thomas Nagel, and John Gray—agree with theists on this point.[24] They take naturalistic evolution to its logical end and conclude that it is concerned with the way we behave (i.e., survival and reproduction) rather than the truthfulness of our beliefs. John Gray, for example, contrasts the secular scientific story—in which the human mind "is programmed for survival, not for truth"—with the Christian view, which claims "the human mind mirrors a rational cosmos."[25] From a naturalistic perspective, there is no reason to suppose content generated by neurological structures is true—which, of course, would then undercut one's own claim to possess knowledge of *any* kind.

"Out" to a better story. The assumed relationship between our minds and the world does not prove Christianity. However, belief in God, who created us, makes better sense of this phenomenon than secular frameworks do. Since God has created both our minds and the universe, the Christian story gives good reason to trust our cognitive faculties to connect up to the world around us, a belief that science has taken for granted. This belief led Christianity to be ahead of its time in providing a framework for explaining the intelligibility of the universe. McGrath writes:

> God created the world with an ordered structure, which human beings are able to uncover by virtue of bearing the "image of God." That has been a settled conviction of the Christian faith since its earliest days, a thousand years before anyone started to do science seriously and systematically. Yet this intellectual framework fits what we now know—and *did not* know until the 1700s.[26]

The Christian framework, thus, gives us reason to expect that our cognitive faculties will match up with the world around us; naturalism has no reason to expect such. This is one of the reasons why many philosophers see a "deep concord between science and theistic belief."[27]

PART 2: REASONS TO BELIEVE[28]

Apparent Design for Life

"Inside" their story. There is a growing awareness that a great deal had to go right for life on earth to occur. By analogy, imagine that our universe was regulated by a complex system of dials, with each having to be at a surgically precise position for life to exist. These include the cosmological constant, the strong and electromagnetic forces, carbon production in stars, the proton/neutron difference, the weak force, and gravity. From these "dials," the fine-tuning needed for life-giving conditions range from 1 part in 10 to 1 part in 10^{53}.[29] If one dial was off, even in the slightest, human existence would not be possible. Alvin Plantinga concludes that "on balance, the sensible conclusion seems to be that there is indeed an enormous amount of fine-tuning, although the precise amount isn't known."[30]

A popular explanation of our universe's fine-tuning is that it may be one of zillions, and the odds are that one of a gazillion universes is finely tuned for life. Though this theory of countless universes is only conjecture (believing it takes a leap of faith), let's for the sake of argument assume there are in fact zillions of universes and that the "cosmic dials" happened to land in the right place in ours. Like the lottery, where the odds for an individual who buys a ticket to win are not good, yet someone *does* in fact win, such could be the case for our universe. Indeed, if one accepts by blind faith that zillions of universes exist, then perhaps our universe is the result of fine-tuning by blind irrational force. We are the luckiest people living on the luckiest planet in the luckiest universe, and if we weren't, we wouldn't be here to speculate about it.

Yet many don't find it quite so easy to shake off the universe's fine-tuning by dismissing it as coincidence. Alvin Plantinga's analogy of an *apparent* cheater in the Wild West illustrates why such multi-universe theories shouldn't placate this intuition of design.

> I'm playing poker, and every time I deal, I get four aces and a wild card. The third time this happens, Tex jumps up, knocks over the table, draws his sixgun, and accuses me of cheating. My reply:

> "... have you considered the following? Possibly there is an infinite succession of universes, so that for any possible distribution of possible poker hands, there is a universe in which the possibility is realized; we just happen to find ourselves in one where someone like me always deals himself only aces and wild cards without ever cheating" ... Tex probably won't be satisfied; this multi-game hypothesis, even if true, is irrelevant.[31]

Why would the multi-game hypothesis be irrelevant? Plantinga continues: "No doubt *someone* in one of those enormously many poker games deals himself all the aces and a wild card without cheating; but the probability that *I* (as opposed to someone or other) am honestly dealing in that magnificently self-serving way is very low ... It is vastly more likely that I am cheating; how can we blame Tex for opening fire?" It is analogous for those arguing in this way against the fine-tuning argument: "The fact, if it is a fact, that there are enormously many universes has no bearing on the probability (on atheism) that *this* universe is fine-tuned for life; that remains very low."[32]

"Out" to a better story. The question is not, "What can we *prove*?" but "What is the best explanation for the apparent fine-tuning of the universe for life?" For many scientists, like Francis Collins, one of the world's leading geneticists and director of the National Institutes of Health, the best explanation is the existence of a fine-tuner: "To get our universe, with all of its potential for complexities or any kind of potential for any kind of life-form, everything has to be precisely defined on this knife edge of improbability." Thus, he concludes, "You have to see the hands of a creator who set the parameters to be just so because the creator was interested in something a little more complicated than random particles."[33] While fine-turning does not prove God's existence—and certainly not the personal God of the Bible, the universe's fine-tuning remains a signpost for the existence of a fine-tuner and fits well with the Christian belief in God as the Creator.

The Beginning of the Universe

"Inside" their story. The question of whether the universe had a beginning or if it has existed eternally has been debated throughout history. Aristotle, for instance, believed in the eternality of the universe, while Christians and Jews have long believed that the universe was created. For much of Western history, the prevailing belief has been in the eternality of the universe. Then scientists discovered redshift in light from faraway galaxies, cosmic microwave background, and thermodynamics, which led to the majority of scientists today agreeing that the universe indeed had a beginning.

Those who disagree with this consensus sometimes argue for an "infinite regress" of causes with no ultimate beginning. But one must push beyond the empirical work of science to suggest this. Others have speculated that the universe was created in a quantum vacuum. But this only takes us back to an earlier form of the initial question. If this is the case, where did this quantum vacuum—a kind of universe-making machine—come from? Likewise, some will argue the laws of physics created the universe. But these laws merely describe what we see; they don't create. And their existence raises a more important question: Where did they come from?

"Out" to a better story. Our experience in this world points to the following line of reasoning: (1) "everything that begins to exist has a cause," and since the scientific evidence now supports that (2) "the universe began to exist," then a reasonable conclusion is (3) "therefore the universe has a cause."[34] Used in the wrong context, this argument can cause people's eyes to begin to glaze over. However, in certain contexts, this argument has served as a powerful signpost to God because the key second premise is supported by strong philosophical arguments and scientific evidence.

Yet if this second premise is challenged—and the person is willing to consider it more deeply and is capable of doing so—often the needed step is to discuss these arguments in more detail (see the sources suggested in the endnotes). Note that the first premise is not just that everything that exists has a cause, but that everything that *begins* to exist has a cause. This way of stating the issue sidesteps the question that skeptics will often raise: "Well, then, who or what caused God?" God, according to the Christian narrative, never began to exist. Again, to be clear, this argument does not demonstrate the personal, holy God of Christianity. Yet the current scientific evidence, which indicates the universe had a beginning, fits well with the ancient story found within the Hebrew and Christian Scriptures: the universe had a beginning because it was created by God.

THE ORIGINATING CLAIM OF CHRISTIANITY

The originating claim of Christianity is that Jesus of Nazareth died and rose again in human history. This claim, among other factors, also led to the early worshiping practices of the first generation of Christians. Because such claims lie at the very heart of Christianity and are historical in nature, it is valuable to have others consider the best explanation for how they arose. Given that many of the people you will talk with have not considered historical scholarship on this question, the best approach is often to begin "outside" of their story—to explain how Christianity makes sense of the evidence—and from there to periodically go "inside" the narratives that offer counter-explanations.

Outside In

When discussing any event in ancient history, 100 percent proof is impossible and there are no purely neutral observers. This is especially true when approaching high-stakes questions that bear profound implications. In conversation, we should avoid portraying ourselves as unbiased or calling on unbelievers to be impartial. We can, however, seek to be fair, and we can ask the unbeliever to try to approach the Christian claim with as much fairness as possible.

An Unexpected Death

Almost all historians today, even those who are not Christians, agree that Jesus died at the hands of the Romans by crucifixion.[35] In contrast, Jewish scholars before and during Jesus' time were not expecting the Messiah to die on a cross. Indeed, first-century Jews found it strange to hear the disciples continuing to proclaim Jesus as the messianic King after he had been shamefully crucified. This death was reserved for the most despised criminals. No Jews in their right minds, not even Jesus' own disciples, would have imagined that the long-awaited Jewish King would die on a cross.

The disciples' repeated failures to understand Jesus' statements concerning his death were due to their preconceived expectations—they, along with other first-century Jews, believed that Jesus would do the normal things expected of the coming Messiah. This would have included serving as a national deliverer, perhaps engaging in a military victory, and establishing a visible kingdom on earth. It certainly would not have included dying a dishonorable death on a cross. It can be assumed, then, that the disciples did not see Jesus' death coming. By extension, they would not have been expecting the resurrection either.

A Counterintuitive Claim: Resurrection

The work of scholars such as N. T. Wright has shown that the resurrection of Jesus was an unpopular notion with first-century Jews and Greeks—not the sort of thing one would make up if trying to start a movement. The dominant Greek view was that bodily resurrection was impossible and unwanted. The Greeks believed the soul was good but not the physical body.

Most Jews did look forward to a future bodily resurrection, but they viewed this as a corporate resurrection of *all the righteous* rather than for one particular person.[36] This future resurrection was thought to occur alongside the renewal of the entire world. The Jews were not looking for the resurrection of an individual in the middle of history, after which the problems of the world would continue unabated.

Thus, claiming that the disciples made up the story of Jesus' resurrection does not sit well with the fact that people were not expecting the Messiah to be killed or to rise from the dead. And if they would have had the wherewithal to come up with this radical idea out of seemingly nowhere, they would have likely kept it to themselves. For neither Jews nor Greeks were open to this idea.[37] We know from the historical record that Jesus was not the first would-be Messiah to garner a following before being executed. But only Jesus' followers claimed his resurrection. As N. T. Wright explains:

> In not one single case do we hear the slightest mention of the disappointed followers claiming that their hero had been raised from the dead. They knew better. "Resurrection" was not a private

> event. It involved human bodies. There would have to be an empty tomb somewhere. A Jewish revolutionary whose leader had been executed by the authorities, and who managed to escape arrest himself, had two options: give up the revolution or find another leader . . . Claiming that the original leader was alive again was simply not an option.

Unless, of course, he was.[38]

The First Counterintuitive Witnesses

It is also odd for a first-century context that in each of the four gospels, women were presented as the first eyewitnesses to the risen Jesus. At that time, women were not believed to give trustworthy testimony on important matters, which is why they were not allowed to testify in a court of law.[39] How would the public respond to an unpopular doctrine being propagated by people who did not culturally count as witnesses? It surely would not have helped. It would be counterintuitive to invent a story in this way, with the hope of it catching on, unless, of course, the various reports all agreed with this unhelpful detail because it was simply the way it happened.

More Counterintuitive Witnesses

Peter, James, Paul, and at one time more than five hundred people claimed to have seen the resurrected Jesus. Paul writes in 1 Corinthians 15 that the appearance to five hundred was just one of the many times when people saw Jesus and that many of these witnesses were still alive, which meant Paul's claim could have easily been refuted if he had been lying.

From the gospels, we learn that among those witnesses were Jesus' half brother James (1 Corinthians 15:7), who was an unbeliever during the time of Jesus' ministry (Mark 3:21, 31; 6:3–4; John 7:5). However, following Jesus' death and resurrection, James is reported as being not only a believer but a prominent Christian leader in Jerusalem (Acts 15; Galatians 1). Furthermore, he also, according to Josephus and other sources, became a martyr for the faith.

Paul himself had been an active persecutor of the church, who from his own testimony (and from Luke's in Acts) claimed to have had an encounter with the risen Jesus. Instantaneously, Paul went from an active persecutor to a bold proclaimer of the gospel. Paul was so convinced he had experienced the risen Jesus that for the rest of his life he suffered both spiritually and physically for the sake of the gospel.

While it has been argued that Jesus' followers were in such a state of grief that they hallucinated, this does not explain why so many people at different times had the same hallucination. As projections of the mind, hallucinations are singular and subjective events. Regarding mass hallucinations—in which people in a group hallucinate the same image—modern psychologists have provided little scientific evidence to substantiate such occurrences.[40] Nor does grief explain why Paul, a committed Jewish leader who was persecuting Christians and clearly not grieving, would have hallucinated. Nor does the hallucination theory explain why Jesus' body was not produced by the authorities, who had the power and motive to extract the body to end this new movement.

The Body

If the resurrection claim had been made-up, it would have been counterintuitive for the story to have begun where it did—in Jerusalem. The location where Jesus died and was buried would have been the easiest place to disprove the disciples' claim of resurrection. All the Jewish or Roman authorities had to do was produce the body.

Some have sought to explain the inability to produce the corpse by arguing that Roman policy didn't allow the crucified to be buried, and thus Jesus' body was likely eaten by animals or discarded after his death. In other words, there was no body left to produce. In some parts of the Roman Empire, and especially during wartime, the bodies of the executed were indeed regularly left on their crosses to rot or to be eaten by animals. But if this was normally how the Romans treated the Jews in and around Jerusalem, it seems the authorities would have offered an obvious reply to the Christian claim of an empty tomb: "*Of course* there is no body in the tomb because *he was never allowed to be buried*!" If it were a common practice at that time in Jerusalem, this would have been the obvious response to the claim of resurrection and an empty tomb.[41] Yet this is not how the authorities or Christian critics responded, apparently because it was common knowledge that the Romans normally allowed the Jews around Jerusalem to bury their dead. Instead, the story was circulated that the body had been stolen, which makes sense as a response only if the body was truly missing from the tomb.

Motive

If the disciples fabricated such a claim, why would they carry the deception so far? The apostles and early Christians were persecuted for their beliefs. Stephen was stoned (Acts 6–8); Herod Agrippa killed James the brother of John (Acts 12:1–2; supported by Josephus, *Antiquities* 20.200); and Nero sponsored the first statewide persecution in the early 60s (see Tacitus, *Annals* 15.37–41). Paul recounts how he experienced extreme persecution (2 Corinthians 6:4–9), and most scholars accept the tradition that he was martyred in the 60s (1 Clement 5:5–7; Eusebius, *Historia ecclesiastica* 2.25.5–8). According to Acts 5:17–42, Peter and John were sent to prison and flogged. John 21:18–19 implies that it was well known by the time John's gospel was written that Peter died as a martyr.[42]

It is difficult to see why Jesus' earliest followers would have been willing to endure such persecution if they knew themselves to be suffering for a hoax they invented. Thus, Gary Habermas emphasizes the long-standing and still incisive historical point:

> Virtually no one, friend or foe, believer or critic, denies that it was their convictions that they had seen the resurrected Jesus that caused the disciples' radical transformations. They were willing to die *specifically for their resurrection belief.* Down through the centuries many have been willing to give their lives for political or religious causes. But the crucial difference here is that while many have died for their *convictions,* Jesus' disciples were in the right place to know the truth or falsity of the event for which they were willing to die.[43]

The Transformation

To offer a historical explanation for these events surrounding the origins of Christianity, one must be able to explain, as Craig

Blomberg writes, "how a small band of defeated followers of Jesus were transformed almost overnight into bold witnesses, risking death by proclaiming his bodily resurrection before many of the same people who fifty days earlier had participated in his crucifixion."[44] Recall the prominent alternative narrative that says the early disciples made up the idea of Jesus' resurrection. Where would this novel idea have arisen? There was no precedent in Judaism for a raised Messiah. For those who believed in the resurrection, it was something that would happen for all the faithful at the end of history rather than for a single man in the middle of history. Thus, there was no clear context to formulate this idea—unless, of course, an actual event generated it.

WORSHIPING A MAN

The worship of a crucified and resurrected Messiah was scandalous in the first-century world and calls for an explanation. To Jews, it was blasphemy to worship a human. And as New Testament scholar Michael Bird has explained, "To Greeks, worshiping a man recently raised from the dead was like doing obeisance to the first zombie you met in a zombie apocalypse."[45]

While there could possibly be occasional exceptions in the Jewish community, devout first-century Jews—such as the very first disciples—were strict monotheists. In other words, they only worshiped one God, the Creator of all things.[46] These were not pagans who worshiped many gods; they were Jews who adhered strictly to one of the most central verses in the Hebrew Scriptures: "The LORD our God, the LORD is one" (Deuteronomy 6:4). And yet, quite remarkably, they worshiped Jesus!

It is important to note that Jesus was not worshiped as some kind of special angel. Angels do not create. This was a function of God in the Hebrew Scriptures. But it is clear that in some of the earliest biblical texts we have, Jesus *does* create (e.g., 1 Corinthians 8:4–6; Colossians 1:15–20). Angels are not to be worshiped (Revelation 19:10; 22:8–9), yet Jesus was worshiped in the early church because his followers viewed him as sharing in the divine identity with God the Father (e.g., Hebrews 1; Revelation 1:4–5).[47]

This devotion began almost immediately rather than growing over a long, gradual process. Historian Larry Hurtado emphasized that the early disciples "define and reverence Jesus with reference to the one God" and explained further that "we see the powerful effect of Jewish monotheism, combining with a strong impetus to reverence Jesus in unprecedented ways."[48]

How did such a dramatic paradigm shift happen so fast? What motivated this almost immediate shift? Such shifts in thinking normally come in gradual stages, but the evidence suggests that these conservative Jewish disciples made the shift rapidly. You should not make the mistake of thinking it was only one thing that caused this shift. Their reflection on Jesus' claims and actions, together with a close rereading of the Hebrew Scriptures, were part of the impetus behind this shift. But their rereading of the Scriptures, their reevaluating of their previous understanding of Jesus' teaching, and—most importantly—their worship of Jesus are difficult to imagine without a dramatic paradigm-shifting *event*.

So while unbelievers will offer various theories to counter the historical evidence surrounding the question of Christian origins, once combined, the strands of history weave together to present a powerful case for the resurrection, the pivotal event of the Christian story. And if someone believes that Jesus really rose from the dead, they have good reason to trust him and his story.

CONCLUSION

This chapter on reason(s) for faith closes part 2 instead of opening this section for two related reasons. First, we increasingly find ourselves in a post-Christian world where people believe Christianity is strange and undesirable. By opening with common experiences and the basic features of personhood (chapters 6–9), we open doors for engagement before we ask them to consider more traditional lines of evidence for Christianity. Second, because the heart often races in front of our head, convincing someone they should *want* to believe is often first necessary before they are open to the reasons they *can* believe. By asking them to examine their experiences and to reflect on their deepest aspirations and problems, this section of the book has modeled how to lead someone to try on the Christian story—to reimagine the world through gospel lenses. Of course, along the way, objections to the Christian story will come, and it is to some of the most popular we now turn.

NOTES

1. Paul Kalanithi, *When Breath Becomes Air* (New York: Random House, 2016), 168, emphasis in original.
2. See Charles Taylor, *A Secular Age* (Cambridge, MA: Harvard University Press, 2007), 362–66, 560–93.
3. Kalanithi, *When Breath Becomes Air*, 169, emphasis in original.
4. Kalanithi, *When Breath Becomes Air*, 170, emphasis mine.
5. Kalanithi, *When Breath Becomes Air*, 171. For another account of someone who once assumed this reductionistic story but then tells his own coming-of-age story—from childish scientism to growing into a mature faith in God—see Alister McGrath, *The Big Question: Why We Can't Stop Talking about Science, Faith, and God* (New York: St. Martins, 2015), 1–75.
6. Alister E. McGrath, *Re-Imagining Nature: The Promise of a Christian Natural Theology* (West Sussex, UK: Wiley Blackwell, 2017), 143.
7. McGrath, *Re-Imagining Nature*, 143.
8. Kalanithi, *When Breath Becomes Air*, 170.
9. See Alister E. McGrath, *The Territories of Human Reason: Science and Theology in an Age of Multiple Rationalities* (Oxford: Oxford University Press, 2019), 24–26.
10. See Alasdair MacIntyre, *Whose Justice? Which Rationality?* (Notre Dame, IN: University of Notre Dame Press, 1988).
11. Charles Taylor refers to this as a "'subtraction' story," the (false) narrative that secularism is the "neutral" position that is left over once all religious and "supernatural" beliefs have been canceled out (*A Secular Age*, 26–29).
12. See Albert Einstein, *The World as I See It* (1984; repr., New York: Citadel, 2006), 125.
13. Thomas S. Kuhn was instrumental in challenging the assumption that scientific theorizing was the straightforward accumulation of facts (*The Structure of Scientific Revolutions*, 50th anniv. ed. [Chicago: University of Chicago Press, 2012]).
14. In these discussions people sometimes assume there is a singular and static scientific story to be told about the world. Yet this just isn't the case. John Gray, who is far from accepting of any traditional religion view, admits that "science cannot replace a religious view of the world, since there is no such thing as 'the scientific worldview.' A method of inquiry rather than a settled body of theories, science yields different views of the world as knowledge advances" (*Seven Types of Atheism* [New York: Farrar, Straus and Giroux, 2018], 12).
15. Andrew Briggs, Hans Halvorson, and Andrew Steane, *It Keeps Me Seeking: The Invitation from Science, Philosophy and Religion* (Oxford: Oxford University Press, 2018), 175.

16. Briggs, Halvorson, and Steane, *It Keeps Me Seeking*, 178, emphasis in original.
17. See Rodney Stark, *For the Glory of God: How Monotheism Led to Reformations, Science, Witch-Hunts, and the End of Slavery* (Princeton, NJ: Princeton University Press, 2003), 150–58.
18. See McGrath, *The Big Question*, 37–38; for more on the third point, see Peter Harrison, *The Fall of Man and the Foundations of Science* (Cambridge: Cambridge University Press, 2009).
19. C. F. von Weizsäcker refers to modern science as "a legacy of Christianity" (*The Relevance of Science* [New York: Harper, 1964], 163).
20. John Polkinghorne, *Science and Creation: The Search for Understanding* (London: SPCK, 1988), 20.
21. John C. Lennox, *God's Undertaker: Has Science Buried God?* (Oxford: Lion Hudson, 2009), 61. For more on this, see Paul Davies, *The Mind of God* (London: Simon and Schuster, 1992).
22. See McGrath, *The Big Question*, 86–87.
23. Alvin Plantinga, *Where the Conflict Really Lies: Science, Religion, and Naturalism* (Oxford: Oxford University Press, 2011), 314. For earlier forms of this argument, see C. S. Lewis, *Miracles* (1947; repr., New York: Macmillan, 1978); Richard Taylor, *Metaphysics*, 4th ed. (Upper Saddle River, NJ: Prentice Hall, 1991).
24. See Friedrich Nietzsche, *Nietzsche: Writings from the Late Notebooks*, ed. Rüdiger Bittner (Cambridge: Cambridge University Press, 2003), 26; Thomas Nagel, *The View from Nowhere* (Oxford: Oxford University Press, 1989), 79; John Gray, *Straw Dogs: Thoughts on Humans and Other Animals* (London: Granta, 2002), 27.
25. John Gray, *Seven Types of Atheism* (New York: Farrar, Straus and Giroux, 2018), 13.
26. McGrath, *The Big Question*, 88, emphasis in original.
27. Plantinga, *Where the Conflict Really Lies*, 350.
28. These reasons are not "proofs" in the sense that they are rationally coercive. As C. Stephen Evans writes, "Arguments might well make their conclusions plausible or probable to some people without being convincing to everyone" (*A History of Western Philosophy* [Downers Grove, IL: InterVarsity, 2018], 427–28).
29. See Plantinga, *Where the Conflict Really Lies*, 198.
30. Plantinga, *Where the Conflict Really Lies*, 198–99.
31. Plantinga, *Where the Conflict Really Lies*, 213–14.
32. Plantinga, *Where the Conflict Really Lies*, 214, emphasis in original.
33. Francis Collins, "Reflections on the Current Tensions between Science and Faith," Christian Scholars Conference, Pepperdine University (2011), quoted in Alan Lightman, "The Accidental Universe: Science's Crisis of Faith," *Harper's Magazine* (December 2011), https://harpers.org/archive/2011/12/the-accidental-universe/3.
34. I am simply outlining the basic argument as given by its leading proponent; see William Lane Craig, "Classical Apologetics," in *Five Views on Apologetics*, ed. Stanley N. Gundry and Steven B. Cowan (Grand Rapids: Zondervan, 2000), 48–53; William Lane Craig and James D. Sinclair, "The Kalam Cosmological

Argument," in *The Blackwell Companion to Natural Theology, ed.* William Lane Craig and J. P. Moreland (New York: Wiley, 2009), 101–201.

35. Numerous Christian and non-Christian sources record the death of Jesus. See Tacitus, *Annals of Imperial Rome* 15.44 (AD 115); Flavius Josephus, *Antiquities of the Jews* 18.3 (AD 93); Mara bar Serapion in a letter to his son (likely late first century AD); possibly the Babylonian Talmud, Sanhedrin 43a (circa second century AD); Gospel of Matthew; Gospel of Mark; Luke's writings—Luke and Acts; Gospel of John; Paul's first letter to the Corinthians.
36. The examples of Lazarus being resuscitated from the dead and Herod Antipas thinking Jesus was John the Baptist "raised from the dead" are different from Jesus' resurrection. Jesus did not rise again only to one day grow old and die again. Instead, the claim was that Jesus was resurrected to an eternal glorified body.
37. For an extensive work on the Jewish and non-Jewish worldview concerning resurrection, see N. T. Wright, *The Resurrection of the Son of God* (Minneapolis: Fortress, 2003).
38. N. T. Wright, *Who Was Jesus?* (Grand Rapids: Eerdmans, 1993), 63.
39. See Richard Bauckham, *Gospel Women: Studies of the Named Women in the Gospels* (Grand Rapids: Eerdmans, 2002), 268–77; Wright, *Resurrection of the Son of God*, 607.
40. For modern research on hallucinations, see André Aleman and Frank Larøi, *Hallucinations: The Science of Idiosyncratic Perception* (Washington, DC: American Psychological Association, 2008).
41. For more on this discussion, see Craig A. Evans, "Getting the Burial Traditions and Evidences Right," in *How God Became Jesus: The Real Origins of Belief in Jesus' Divine Nature—A Response to Bart D. Ehrman*, ed. Michael F. Bird (Grand Rapids: Zondervan, 2014), 74–75.
42. Eckhard J. Schnabel documents some of the persecution the early Christians experienced (*Early Christian Mission* [Downers Grove, IL: InterVarsity, 2004], 2:1533–38).
43. Gary R. Habermas, "The Resurrection Appearances of Jesus," in *Evidence for God: 50 Arguments for Faith from the Bible, History, Philosophy, and Science*, ed. William A. Dembski and Michael R. Licona (Grand Rapids: Baker, 2010), 174–75, emphasis in original.
44. Craig L. Blomberg, "Jesus of Nazareth: How Historians Can Know Him and Why It Matters," Gospel Coalition, http://thinkingmatters.org.nz/wp-content/uploads/2011/07/JESUS-OF-NAZARETH.pdf.
45. Michael F. Bird, "Of Gods, Angels, and Men," in *How God Became Jesus*, 26–27.
46. See Deuteronomy 6:4; Isaiah 45:5–7; 2 Maccabees 1:24–25; Romans 11:36; 1 Corinthians 8:4–6.
47. See Richard Bauckham, *Jesus and the God of Israel:* God Crucified *and Other Studies on the New Testament's Christology of Divine Identity* (Grand Rapids: Eerdmans, 2008).
48. Larry Hurtado, *Lord Jesus Christ: Devotion to Jesus in Earliest Christianity* (Grand Rapids: Eerdmans, 2003), 151–52; see Bird, "Of Gods, Angels, and Men," 30.

PART

3

Objections to the Story

By wading into life's most foundational questions and our culture's social imaginaries, we've explored a way to invite others to try on a *better* story. We've used "inside out" as a guide rail to explore a collection of features of personhood and late modern aspirations—asking others to consider which meta-story these best fit within. Rather than pursuing an abstract, all-encompassing formula, our approach has been to map the Christian story onto prevailing assumptions, observations, and experiences of life to help others see how Christianity makes better experiential, social, and rational sense than its rival narratives.

Yet even if we succeed in this, reasons for unbelief often still remain. Often the more the Christian story persists to both haunt and stir something in them, the more their questions will arise. We need to learn to respond in a way that helps them take the gospel more seriously and humbly suggests how paradoxical ideas may actually fit together, while avoiding dealing out superficial answers that glibly undermine the deep mysteries at the heart of the faith. This requires great care and is even more challenging when time is limited.

The following section suggests ways to at least begin to respond, given that in most opportunities to engage others (conversations, public talks, sermons), you will be limited by time and attention spans. Though it is certainly not the final word on each topic, the last three chapters modestly hope to give you at least a first word in response.

Though you will often hear many of the same objections—such as ones that raise the question of evil or point to the restrictive nature of Christian morality—remember that everyone you speak with possesses a distinct, personal story. Be careful not to assume you know what is at the heart of their objection. Listening well is the first step in an apologetics of love.

Given that we often find ourselves in different contexts with different challenges, the purpose of this section isn't to supply an encyclopedic digest for answering all objections. A "dump truck of data" approach rarely proves to be winsome. Effective responses depend on wisdom to correctly apply knowledge, virtue to embody the truth, and a genuine love that bears with others.

chapter

11

An Oppressive Story?

A common sentiment today is that Christianity is oppressive. If a secular friend shares this opinion with you, it is important to avoid giving a hasty response that may not address the person's specific concern or may be interpreted as being insensitive to how they might have personally been harmed by Christians in the past. When someone objects on moral grounds, avoid becoming overly defensive, but rather be patient and ask questions to better understand where they're coming from. We would also do well to keep questions simple and nonaccusatory. Ask questions that, quite simply, give them an opportunity to expound generously. "Why do you say this?" "Have you experienced this yourself?" "Tell me more about what you mean."

When someone objects to Christianity because they believe it to be oppressive, they could mean any number of things, or a unique combination thereof. They may, for instance, understand Christianity as asking them to deny their most fundamental identity and desires, to instead live by what seems to them as outdated and oppressive rules. Thus, to them, Christianity oppresses their very self—what we might call *identity oppression*.

Others may have had bad experiences with Christians or the church. They may have been treated poorly by professing Christians, or may have witnessed Christians living selfish, immoral lives. We can call this *experiential oppression*. Still others may be deeply disturbed by the history of Christianity—by how Christians have often been purveyors of injustice and oppression. Let's call this *historical oppression*.

Regardless of the underlying reason—identity, experiential, historical, or something else—it is a serious thing to believe that Christianity is an oppressive force. We must treat it as such and ask questions to understand *why* our secular friend holds this belief.

PART 1: IDENTITY OPPRESSION

"Christianity is about oppressive rules and denying my most fundamental identity." Christianity is often misconstrued as being solely about rules—not just any rules, however, but outdated restrictions that tear down our truest human longings and self-expression. When we hear this objection, we should be gracious and, to an extent, empathetic, for we've all experienced false, legalistic versions of the faith that have inflicted damage on us or others by making rules and restrictions not just central but the sole standard of faith. Our task at this point is to explain and ask them to reconsider the actual message of Jesus.

Jesus announced that he came not to suppress people or steal their joy, but to free them from the shackles of the world, the flesh, and the devil. In short, he came so that people might truly flourish: "I have come that they may have life, and have it to the full" (John 10:10).[1] Yet, as already discussed, most people's "common sense" visions of the "good life" have been highjacked by cheap facades found in cultural stories about freedom, happiness, and individual identity. The challenge, then, in responding to this objection is that the false veneer cast over their imaginations must be stripped away before they can see the true flourishing that Christ offers.

To begin to do this, it's important to bring to the fore the cultural assumptions that lead to this objection. One such assumption is what we described earlier as "expressive individualism," the belief that everyone has within themselves an identity to be discovered—a "true self" just waiting to be actualized.[2] According to this belief, human flourishing occurs when we "follow our heart" and authorize our own norms for life (recall "Sheilaism").

Even as we point out the problems with expressive individualism, we can affirm some of the cultural developments that have accompanied it, such as the freedom to choose a spouse or a career path. Following "inside out" to respond to this objection, you will want to begin by offering an internal critique in order to help someone be open to seeing how the gospel is actually good news.

"Inside" their story. 1. Consider how the current self-actualizing, me-centered approach to life undermines their most vital and life-giving relationships. There are only thin reasons to dig in and do what it takes to maintain a long-term commitment to friends, romantic partners, and family when they are viewed as instruments to one's self-actualization. If, for instance, I feel my spouse is restricting my ability to pursue what my heart is telling me, why should I continue to devote myself to her? Similarly, according to this perspective, why should I put up with my friends if the benefits they provide me are outweighed by my obligations to them? If I find a relationship to be confining, why not find new relationships that don't demand self-denial and sacrifice?

Of course, most would agree that all healthy relationships require a measure of self-sacrifice. But how much? At what point does this self-sacrifice become too confining? If someone were to consistently hold to this "don't confine me" attitude, it's difficult to see how they would ever find anything but weak, malnourished relationships. As we saw in chapter 7, at this point in a conversation someone may reply, "I don't push away from all relationships that demand sacrifice. For example, I love my kids, and I'm willing to make great sacrifices for them." This is something worth exploring. Many who have rejected the Christian story as repressive do actually strive to live sacrificially in some of their most intimate relationships. In doing so, they affirm their desire to pursue meaningful relationships ahead of personal freedom, valuing others more than their own self-actualization and autonomy.

This is a signpost that is right at home within the Christian story. By recognizing that their most important relationships—especially with their children—require them to deny their own desires in order for genuine flourishing to occur, they are also conceding a key point at the center of Jesus' life and teaching. They are admitting that personal sacrifice is essential for deep, life-giving relationships.

2. Consider how impractical it is to flourish by looking only within yourself. In fact, this is not just impractical, it is impossible. We can't help but constantly look to those around us to learn what we should value and how we should legitimize our own significance. We are always defining our lives in dialogue with our community. Recall how we embrace and mimic "hero" narratives told to us by our communities and traditions. By embedding such stories into us, and in countless other ways, the communities we live in teach us what to worship, what to seek, and what to value above all else—whether it's money, beauty, power, intellect, or self. We all look to something or someone for our identity and sense of worth, which leads us to a third problem with denying Christianity in the name of freedom.

3. Consider how our modern pursuit of freedom is crushing. Jesus taught that everyone has a master—those things that we build our lives around, those things that become controlling forces. Our masters are often what we would consider to be "good things"—things like career, success, possessions, security. They are important to life, but once we begin to pursue them as ultimate, as if by attaining them we'll finally be free, they inevitably become our masters or gods. They control, restrict, and consume our time and wreak havoc on our emotions. When we make them ultimate, they will eventually let us down, even as they completely control us.

4. Consider our relationships with others, especially those we admire and hold most dear. If we consider our reputation to be the most important thing in the world, we will build our lives, happiness, and worth around what others think of us. If this is the case, their response to our efforts will often seem inadequate, and their responses will start to control our lives. Our lives will feel empty and incomplete when they reject us or let us down, or if they are taken from us. Knowing this, we will do anything to avoid losing them or putting them in any position in which they might think less of us or reject us.

One defensive tactic is to claim, "I don't care what anyone else thinks about me" and live our lives with a loose grip on all relationships. We've already discussed why this is not practical (we can't completely escape the need for approval). The pursuit of this ideal is also problematic because it leads to being chained to a life without deep, loving relationships.

Anyone who has ever been in a loving relationship knows that it confines you. It limits your freedom—as it should. You sacrifice for your newborn and find joy in seeing them grow and flourish, even as they make strenuous demands on your life. Seeking freedom *from* limitations is crushing because it prevents us from receiving and giving the love we were meant for. Instead, for true freedom, we need the right restrictions, which teach us to love the right things in the right order.

"Out" to a better story. In Western culture, we like to see ourselves as rugged individuals forging our own way through life. We desperately grasp for complete freedom and self-determination, not realizing that we do so at the expense of our own humanity. Jesus came to show us the way to be truly human, but this wasn't a life free from submission. That is impossible for us. We all submit to and are enslaved by something. Jesus, however, paradoxically promised true freedom (John 8:32–36) through submission. He promises us liberation by constraining us in love.

This raises perennial questions that permeate every generation and culture: What is it like to be true to our humanity? To flourish in life? To live the "good life"? Christianity teaches that the answers to these questions are not ultimately found in an abstract system or a list of rules. High moral standards, similar to the "twelve steps for life" genre of books, can inspire for a time, but if the rules are all there is, inevitably we will one day be faced with a confusing lack of meaning ("Why am I striving so hard to be moral?"), as well as a depressing lack of hope ("What do I do when I can't measure up to my highest moral aspirations?"). In contrast, in Christianity the answer to these questions is a person—a person we were meant *for* and a person we were meant to be *like*—who stands behind the rules.

The commands of the Bible don't simply point to themselves. They are pointing us to a greater reality—the person who is the way to true freedom and forgiveness. Unlike any other religious founder, Jesus didn't say that the key to life is to simply follow his moral code or teaching. He didn't say, "If you live a good life, then I will accept you." In essence, he called us to stop trying to *achieve* freedom or *merit* love, but rather to *receive* eternal life and his love as a gift—accomplished for us in his life, death, and resurrection. This frees us from the burden of trying to earn love and frees us to reflect the One we were made for.[3]

During his time on earth, Jesus lived a life that was and remains a breathtaking picture of the ideal human life. He combined power with humility. Innocence with courage. Truth with generosity. His compassion beckoned the most vulnerable and brokenhearted. He healed people of their physical and spiritual sickness. He taught with authority, like no other, in fact, and all those who hungered for truth flocked to him because of it. The corrupt leaders feared him because he could not be tamed. He stood for justice while offering forgiveness to all, even to those who killed him. In all this, Jesus is the picture of human flourishing through his perfect submission to the Father.

Consider what it costs to become an elite musician or athlete. Elite musicians and athletes have the freedom to play, create, and improvise in beautiful and exciting ways. However, in order to achieve this freedom, they must restrict themselves, giving up a lesser kind of freedom to do whatever it is they think or feel on a whim for a greater freedom. Carefully following the instructions and examples of experts, they make daily sacrifices of their natural desires—time, pleasure, money—to pursue the higher goal of the freedom that comes through expertise. Awe-inspiring improvisation on the soccer field or in the concert hall is only made possible by long hours of disciplined training and intentional sacrifice. True freedom comes through suppression.

This is also true in parenting. We give our children rules to teach them how to be free from bad habits that will control their lives; we give them rules so they can learn to be truly free. In the same way, the Bible doesn't give commandments to restrict people from flourishing—the opposite is true. God's rules lead us to learn his wisdom for a virtuous life, guiding us on the path to true flourishing. But this life begins with a command to receive, to place our ultimate faith in him, as a child trusts in a parent, in order to accept the love we were meant for.

Receiving God's love is the way to begin a life of freedom because it transforms us into people who love God in return. Loving God first and people second, followed by other things in life, is what it means to love in the right order. Loving God first allows us to begin loving other things without ultimately despairing when they let us down or crushing the people we love with the weight of our expectations. We can freely enjoy the gifts of this world, when we don't make them into gods. The key to true freedom isn't to exhaust ourselves on the impossible task of avoiding being mastered, but rather to submit ourselves to the One we were made to love and serve.

PART 2: EXPERIENTIAL OPPRESSION

"Christians claim to be about love and justice, but I actually find them to be callous and self-centered." It is entirely fair for non-Christians to call us to account for not living consistently with the story we claim to be true. We should expect this, and even welcome it. "Christians are hypocrites" is an objection we hear painfully often. To the degree that they are calling us to simply live out the story we confess, we should be prepared to listen, repent, and point to Christ. Jesus is the standard, and we should agree we fall short repeatedly and often in terrible ways.

This objection is the very reason we should never disconnect apologetics from discipleship and a strong doctrine of the church. Our lives should bear witness to the truth. What Anne Snyder has pointed out in the political arena rings true for us here: "Who persuades us that we don't already look up to? Very few successful arguments, however rational, can stand apart from tone or relationship."[4] A crisis for Christian witness is the crisis of Christian virtue. But in this conversation, how might you respond?

Just because someone who claims to be a Christian does something bad doesn't mean Christianity is bad. As the secular philosopher John Gray has written, it isn't just religion that can go bad; any human activity—including science—has the potential for evil.[5] In the same way it would be foolish to dismiss science because some scientists produce weapons for mass destruction and drugs that are used for torture, it would be foolish to dismiss Christianity just because some Christians do evil things. It must also be recognized that though genuine believers sometimes do evil things, there are pseudo-Christians—believers in name only—just like there are pseudo-scientists.

According to Christian theology, individual Christian growth takes place over time. Even when someone genuinely converts to the Christian faith, their life does not immediately conform to the teachings and ways of Jesus. And like all Christians, though the new believer will mature over time, they will never reach perfection in this life. While a new believer will likely begin to change in many positive ways, they may still act much less morally than someone else who has no religious belief but grew up in a wholesome and stable environment. No person reaches perfection, and the possibility for mistakes, even grave mistakes, never goes away. The church is a hospital for the morally sick, which includes all people, even those who seem irredeemable to the common person. Think about how little sense it would make for the church to admit only those who are perfectly well, for the entire purpose of a hospital is to bring healing to those who are in need of it—and all the more for those who are sick and broken.

PART 3: HISTORICAL OPPRESSION

"The church has constantly been on the wrong side of history." Unfortunately, it isn't just individual Christians who have failed. Skeptics often point out certain glaring failures of the church, such as slavery and segregation, to justify wholesale misgivings about the Christian faith. While the church often did fail in addressing these issues, there are certain false narratives that have accompanied these failures (we'll see some of these below). If someone brings up the issue of the church's failures, we should certainly be willing to admit these past wrongs. Avoid minimizing the church's sins, be willing to patiently listen, and lament the stains on the church, past and present. However, there is often more to the story than how popular accounts portray what happened. As we will see in two cases below, it is actually renewal movements *within* Christianity that served to correct injustices within the church and society.

Slavery

When seeking to understand what the Bible says about slavery, Christians have at different points throughout history allowed self-interest to cloud their interpretation. For example, in the nineteenth century, many southern Christians in the United States used the Bible to support race-based chattel slavery. We should be quick to condemn such behavior and to take a closer look at the Scriptures.

The Bible does not view slavery as "natural." As Old Testament scholar Christopher Wright explains, in the Bible slavery "was not regarded as a divinely ordered part of creation itself," and "the first mention of slaves and slavery is in the context of a *curse*" (Genesis 9:25–27), where it is "seen as something unnatural, fallen and accursed."[6]

Slavery was "accursed" because Genesis 1 and 2 had established humans as created in the image of God with inherent dignity. Yet in a historical and cultural context where slavery was the norm, the Israelites too had slaves, though slavery in the agricultural society of Israel was far different from how people often imagine. In ancient Israel, slaves were largely domestic workers, many of whom were working off debt and alongside the rest of the family, with legal rights and protections. And again, as Christopher Wright explains, the laws concerning treatment of slaves were more humane than the nations around them:

> Slavery in the Old Testament was not simply tolerated with a "rubber stamp" of uncritical approval. Aspects of Old Testament thought and practice in this area virtually "neutralized" slavery as an institution and sowed the seeds of its radical rejection in much later Christian thinking. Certainly, these aspects . . . made Israel unquestionably unique in the ancient world in its attitude to slavery. This is a fact unanimously acknowledged by ancient Near Eastern scholars.[7]

The biblical authors tolerated the institution and regulated it, without endorsing it as the ideal. This is an important distinction, which is clarified when we read the Bible along its redemptive arch. This is what Jesus makes clear concerning marriage when he is asked about the Old Testament divorce laws and directs his listeners to Genesis 2 (Matthew 19:1–11). Jesus explains that Moses permitted divorce due to the hardness of the people's heart, a concession because of sinful circumstances, but that this was not God's ideal. In essence, in his ministry Jesus proclaims he is pointing backward to creation and its ideals before the fall in order to point forward to the new creation he is ushering in.

Why, then, if Jesus is pointing back to creational ideals as he proclaims that a new creation is breaking into the world through the kingdom he is inaugurating, do we see the apostle Paul continue to give instructions for just regulating slavery without explicitly calling for abolition? Why not set out to burn down the entire institution of slavery? Keep in mind that Paul, as well as the other apostles, had to deal with the reality they were facing—a fallen world that in many ways was built around slavery. The New Testament scholar N. T. Wright explains Paul's situation:

> What alternatives were actually open to him? He was committed to the life, and the standards, of the new age over against the old (Col. 3). But a loud protest, at that moment in social history, would have functioned simply on the level of the old age: it would have been heard only as a criticism by one part of society (Paul, not himself a slave-owner, had nothing to lose) against another. It would, without a doubt, have done more harm than good, making life harder for Christian slaves, and drawing upon the young church exactly the wrong sort of attention from the authorities. If Paul is jailed for proclaiming "another king" (Acts 17:7), it must be clear that the kingdom in question is of a different order altogether from that of Caesar. In addition, inveighing against slavery *per se* would have been totally ineffective: one might as well, in modern Western society, protest against the mortgage system.[8]

Paul was not in a position to burn down the institution. For, as we might say, he didn't have a flamethrower available. But the apostle did light a spark. For instance, the logic in his letter to a slaveowner in the New Testament book of Philemon or in his insistence that in Christ there is "neither slave nor free" (Galatians 3:28)—fueled by the creation norms of Genesis 1 and 2—would eventually become a fire that set the institution ablaze. From our perspective, looking back on the horrors of slavery, we grieve that this didn't happen sooner. Yet as a matter of history, it is clear that the assumptions that led to the protest movements and eventual widespread moral repudiation of slavery in the Western world were in fact fueled by the Christian story.

Kyle Harper, a classical historian, gives one example by way of a Christian pastor in the fourth century, Gregory of Nyssa, whose sermon on slavery was an "extraordinary rupture" of the ancient world's widespread acceptance of slavery. In this homily we have the only surviving criticism "of slavery as an institution from the entire ancient world."[9] Gregory's argument was "entirely novel in the ancient world but would reverberate in later centuries with tremendous consequence."[10] Drawing on the creation normal of Genesis 1 and 2, his logic was rooted in the belief that humans were created in the image of God and were of incomparable worth. Humans, therefore, should not be sold or owned.[11]

Though Gregory was largely ignored in his day, eventually the theological reasoning he used would infiltrate the moral vision of the Western world. As historian Rodney Stark explains:

> Of all the world's religions, including the three great monotheisms, only in Christianity did the idea develop that slavery was sinful and must be abolished. Although it has been fashionable to deny it, antislavery doctrines began to appear in Christian theology soon after the decline of Rome and were accompanied by the eventual disappearance of slavery in all but the fringes of Christian Europe. When Europeans subsequently instituted slavery in the New World, they did so over strenuous papal opposition . . . Finally, the abolition of New World slavery was initiated and achieved by Christian activists.[12]

Unfortunately, the church too often misinterpreted the Bible and was sadly far too slow in getting this right. Slavery in the American South is a devastating case in point. The good news, however, is that in the end, the church applied the implications of the creational ideal to the issue of slavery. It was Christian men and women, who realized the implications of the Bible's teachings, that played a pivotal role in undermining and abolishing slavery. We see this illustrated in the untiring work of Thomas Clarkson (1760–1846) and William Wilberforce (1759–1833) in Great Britain and in the organized efforts of the Quakers in America.[13] And Christian theology—in particular, the doctrine of the image of God—was an essential, though often unacknowledged, historical foundation for the development of universal human dignity and rights as a modern moral ideal.[14]

Segregation

Because of weak biblical support for segregation, Christians often hid their prejudice behind political doctrines such as states' rights and the separation of church and state. Rather than advocating for the marginalized and working toward racial equality, as is explicitly and powerfully taught in the Scriptures, white Christians and white churches in the American South largely took a passive stance toward discrimination. Often they did worse, actively supporting the Jim Crow laws to the detriment of their Christian witness. Again, fear and self-interest worked against clearheaded theological reflection and moral action.

So again, it is important to show how the Christian story provided the resources to undermine segregation. In particular, through the leadership of Martin Luther King Jr., James Lawson, Fannie Lou Hamer, Fred Shuttlesworth, and Bob Moses, Scripture and the Christian faith were driving forces in the desegregation movement. This is seen in the following four biblical dynamics.

1. The desegregation movement's approach was shaped by the Old Testament prophets' fiery preaching against the sinfulness of humanity and for the pursuit of justice. Many black anti-segregationist leaders had no faith in the liberal doctrine of natural progressive development. Many of them saw it as impractical and ineffective because, like James Lawson and C. S. Lewis, they believed "the normal course of human society was corrupting [and] sinful."[15] Change would only come if Christians actively and vigorously pushed back on societal prejudice and selfishness. The framework for their perspective was informed by the biblical narrative, not a secular one.

2. Those opposing segregation were motivated by a belief in God's active presence in the world. Black anti-segregationist rallies, often permeated with a deep spirituality and belief in the miraculous power of God, had the feel of revival crusades. This is not to say that all anti-segregationist leaders were Christians, but most were sincerely driven by biblical revelation and Christian hope. As historian David Chappell asserts, "It is hard to imagine masses of people lining up for years of excruciating risk against southern sheriffs, fire hoses, and attack dogs without some transcendent or millennial faith to sustain them."[16] The example of the courageous and bold suffering of Jesus Christ in the face of injustice strengthened many amid the cruelty and heartache they were experiencing.

3. Perhaps most prominently of all, the nonviolent nature of the movement was shaped by the love ethos of the New Testament as taught and modeled by Jesus in the gospels. Martin Luther King Jr. continually emphasized the importance of the Christian doctrine of love to the anti-segregationist movement: "Our actions must be guided by the deepest principles of our Christian faith. Love must be our regulating ideal. Once again we must hear the words of Jesus echoing across the centuries: 'Love your enemies, bless them that curse you, and pray for them that despitefully use you.'"[17] The change brought about by King and his supporters was not achieved through violence and hate, but by the peace and love found in Jesus' teachings. The Christian story provided King the resources to pursue peace and reconciliation with hope. The Christian story, for those who follow its script, is unmatched by secular narratives in its ability to sow love for others, even those who hatefully spit on the one who comes in peace.

4. A hope in the coming kingdom of God—where there will be neither Jew nor Gentile, neither slave nor free—motivated the anti-segregationists to anticipate the kingdom in their lives together. As abolitionist leader James Lawson explained, Christians should desire to break down racial barriers because "the redeemed community of which [they are] already [citizens] recognizes no barriers dividing humanity."[18] One of the central goals of the Christian life is to be an outpost for the coming kingdom, and that includes seeking equality for all people in Christ. As famously presented in Martin Luther King's "I have a dream" speech, which was full of biblical quotes and illusions, the moral vision of a united America not segregated by race was grounded in the ideal picture of justice and inclusion presented in Scripture.

THE RESOURCES TO SELF-CORRECT

Because Jesus is now represented by imperfect disciples, there are plenty of examples where people bearing the name of Christ have not lived out its message. Slavery and segregation are just two examples of egregious moral failures, but these examples also show how Christianity has the internal resources to correct both its followers and societal injustices. As we saw in chapter 7, left to themselves (without sneaking in religious assumptions), secular stories stumble when trying to find a matrix of beliefs that provide rational reasons to morally obligate people to make inconvenient changes and sacrifices for the good of others. The Christian story, on display in the transformative power of the anti-slavery and desegregationist movements, offers powerful motivation and an enduring hope to stand as a corrective force against evil and injustice.

NOTES

1. For more on human flourishing and the Christian message, see Jonathan T. Pennington, *The Sermon on the Mount and Human Flourishing: A Theological Commentary* (Grand Rapids: Baker, 2017); N. T. Wright, *After You Believe: Why Christian Character Matters* (New York: HarperOne, 2010).
2. See Robert Bellah et al., *Habits of the Heart: Individualism and Commitment in American Life* (Berkeley: University of California Press, 1985), 333–34.
3. For more on how "virtue and grace are compatible, not opposites," see Pennington, *Sermon on the Mount and Human Flourishing*, 305–8. Pennington notes that he is articulating an essentially Augustinian perspective.
4. Anne Snyder, "Persuading in a Divided Age: The Christian's Privilege," *Comment* 27, no. 2 (March 1, 2013), www.cardus.ca/comment/article/persuading-in-a-divided-age-the-christians-privilege.
5. See John Gray, "What Scares the New Atheists?" *Guardian*, March 3, 2015, www.theguardian.com/world/2015/mar/03/what-scares-the-new-atheists.
6. Christopher J. H. Wright, *Old Testament Ethics for the People of God* (Downers Grove, IL: IVP Academic, 2004), 337.
7. Wright, *Old Testament Ethics for the People of God*, 333.
8. N. T. Wright, *Colossians and Philemon: An Introduction and Commentary* (Downers Grove, IL: InterVarsity, 1986), 173–74.
9. Kyle Harper, "Christianity and the Roots of Human Dignity in Late Antiquity," in *Christianity and Freedom*, vol. 1, ed. Timothy Samuel Shah and Allen D. Hertzke (Cambridge: Cambridge University Press, 2016), 132.

10. Harper, "Christianity and the Roots of Human Dignity,"133–134.
11. Harper, "Christianity and the Roots of Human Dignity," 134.
12. Rodney Stark, *For the Glory of God: How Monotheism Led to Reformations, Science, Witch-Hunts, and the End of Slavery* (Princeton, NJ: Princeton University Press, 2003), 291.
13. See Stark, *For the Glory of God,* 291–366.
14. See Harper, "Christianity and the Roots of Human Dignity," 123–48.
15. David L. Chappell, *A Stone of Hope: Prophetic Religion and the Death of Jim Crow* (Chapel Hill: University of North Carolina Press, 2004), 69.
16. Chappell, *Stone of Hope,* 102.
17. Martin Luther King Jr., *Stride toward Freedom: The Montgomery Story* (1958; repr., Boston: Beacon, 2010), 51.
18. Quoted in Chappell, *Stone of Hope,* 69.

chapter
12

An Unloving Story?

> *"Can you understand why a little creature, who can't even understand what's done to her, should beat her little aching heart with her tiny fist in the dark and the cold, and weep her meek unresentful tears to dear, kind God to protect her? Do you understand that, friend and brother, you pious and humble novice? Do you understand why this infamy must be and is permitted? Without it, I am told, man could not have existed on earth, for he could not have known good and evil. Why should he know that diabolical good and evil when it costs so much?"*[1]

These are the words of the fictional character Ivan Karamazov in Fyodor Dostoyevsky's classic, *The Brothers Karamazov*. Beyond literary merit, Dostoyevsky's scene between Ivan and Alyosha is uniquely relevant for us today, as it represents one of history's deepest Christian thinkers exploring the deepest crevices of the secular mind, wrestling with the question of evil, and offering a model for how one can respond. In a sense, Dostoyevsky was practicing "inside out" long before us. Ivan is the model rationalist in Dostoyevsky's story, who rejects God on the basis of the cruel suffering he sees in the world. In this quote, he is questioning his brother Alyosha as to why God would make a world where little children suffer. Ivan's collective protests in these chapters include both logical objections and gut-level anger, but this quote is representative of perhaps his most profound and visceral problem with the notion of a good God.

Even for the smartest or coldest rationalist today, their core problem often mirrors Ivan's earnest objection. It genuinely pains them to think of the suffering in this world, particularly for the defenseless, and the immediate reaction is to not want anything to do with God (whether or not he exists) or his justice (whether or not it exists). And yet Ivan, also mirroring the typical late modern person, is a complex character. His skepticism is accompanied by a profound longing. This is, after all, the same Ivan we saw earlier confess:

> "Though I may not believe in the order of the universe, yet I love the sticky little leaves as they open in spring. I love the blue sky. I love some people, whom one loves you know sometimes without knowing why. I love some great deeds done by men, though I've long ceased perhaps to have faith in them . . . It's not a matter of intellect or logic, it's loving with one's inside, with one's stomach."[2]

Don't imagine that most unbelievers can be neatly stereotyped by equating them with headlining atheists who simply mock belief in God on supposedly purely rational grounds. Suffering is an objection that feels weighty for extremely personal reasons, but the very fact that we humans are so disturbed by our sufferings—that there is really something good that is being harmed, and that this shouldn't be so!—will not let Ivan, or our secular friends, off so easily. Suffering can cause us *all* to doubt our story at times—even, surprisingly, the atheist.

Similar to previous issues we have discussed, a few thoughtful questions can help set the course for the conversation: *Would you mind telling me more about why you find suffering and evil such an obstacle to believing in God? Was there a particular time in your life when you remember coming to this conclusion?* Their responses will likely provide clues into whether they are struggling more with the abstract *logical problem of evil*, which is the perceived rational contradiction between the existence of suffering and a loving and powerful God, or the more concrete *experiential problem of evil*, which is related to how people grapple with bad things that happen in their own lives. Sometimes their response will dovetail with the question of why God himself would inflict judgment on his creatures, which we will call the *problem of judgment*.

PART 1: THE LOGICAL PROBLEM

"It is illogical to say that God is good and evil exists." The logical problem may sound something like this in conversation: "The problem I have with Christianity is that I don't see how a good and all-powerful God could allow suffering and evil in the world. If God was all-powerful, he could stop all the evil in the world. And if he was good, he would. Thus, if he allows suffering when he could do something about it, he is not really good, and if he allows suffering because he can't do anything about it, he is not really all-powerful."

In responding to this objection, recall that this probably shouldn't be happening at the beginning of the conversation. By now you should be building on a foundation of thoughtful questions and dialogue. From here, then, I recommend two things. *First*, level the playing field by helping the person see that evil is an intellectual problem for *both* Christian and secular accounts. *Second*, explain how the logical objection on the basis of evil and suffering is ultimately unsuccessful, while secular solutions have a foundational problem that cannot be fully resolved without borrowing from other stories.

Challenges for Both Stories

Christians create a problem for themselves when they suggest they can easily "solve" the logical problem of evil. For example, some will say the solution is that evil exists because God created human beings with the freedom to make their own choices. The quote we opened this chapter with from *The Brothers Karamazov* should, however, give us pause, lest by attempting to explain away the problem, we create more problems than we "solve."

While the free will defense can provide some solace—and it is vital that we affirm meaningful human agency as part of a response to this question—we need to consider how a thoughtful critic might strike back against this "tidy" answer: "That's fine, but why give beings (angels or humans) such freedom?" To this, many would say that a world with evil and free beings is better than a world void of evil but also void of the freedom to do bad things. However, many unbelievers will be skeptical that the latter is better than the former.

"After all," they reason, "I'm okay giving limited freedom to my son, but if he decides to use his freedom to run into a busy street to play, I will quickly curb it. So why did God allow the first humans to 'play in the road' so to speak? It seems like God should have curbed their freedom so as to prevent them from sinfully hurting themselves, while at the same time allowing them the freedom to pursue diverse interests. Isn't this the Christian conception of the afterlife, where, as I understand it, people will supposedly be 'free' and yet unable to sin?"

The person might add to this that the God of the Bible seems to perform miracles all the time. So why does this same God seem so powerless to stop the evils of history? For instance, couldn't God, in all his power, have allowed Hitler freedom, but then have done something minor, such as sent a minor gust of wind blowing in a slightly different direction, so that the bullet that struck Hitler during World War I would have actually killed him? Wouldn't this small 'miracle' have saved millions of lives in World War II and the Holocaust? Do Christians really have an answer for why things are better the way they actually happened?

Alvin Plantinga, former Notre Dame philosopher and recognized by both believing and secular philosophers to have successfully defended theism in response to the logical problem of evil, is right to give us caution when he says, "I'd also hesitate to say that the freewill defense . . . is a sort of conclusive solution to the argument from evil or the problem of evil, or a resolution of it . . . Christians don't, nor do other believers in God, as far as I know, really know why God permits evil."[3] In most conversations it will be worthwhile to return to Plantinga's point, and we will discuss it further later, but first we have more to do to level the playing field. While we should admit that a comprehensive reason for the "whys" of suffering is far beyond our ken, we should also ask the unbeliever to consider the most challenging part of the secular account of evil and suffering.

The secular story encounters a challenge within its own objection to the Christian story, namely, secularists have no clear basis on which to judge something as good or evil. The categories of good and evil are a serious problem for the skeptic. The false assumption that needs to be exposed is that one can just assume such categories. Secularists who try to argue for moral obligation rather than just subjective moral feelings, as we saw in chapter 7, lack a rational framework for doing so. And as we've seen in chapter 9, the very language of "real evil," something beyond personal or cultural subjective preference, is not coherent within purely secular accounts. In *The Brothers Karamazov*, this is on display when Ivan concludes that without God everything is permitted.[4] Though he admittedly can't live out this conclusion, he nonetheless holds it as the rational conclusion in a godless world. Christianity provides an obvious grounding for a real morality; nontheistic viewpoints do not.

Comparing the Two Challenges

The problem for the secular accounts is that they can't provide the moral categories that make sense of the problem. This is what C. S. Lewis famously pointed out in *Mere Christianity* concerning his own thinking as an atheist: "My argument against God was that the universe seemed so cruel and unjust. But how had I got this idea of *just* and *unjust*? A man does not call a line crooked unless he has some idea of a straight line. What was I comparing this universe with when I called it unjust?"[5] Lewis recognized that the categories of good and evil he was using to form his objection required some kind of absolute standard to measure against. We might say that if the Christian needs to answer the problem of evil, the atheist needs to answer the problem of good and evil.

In the course of a conversation, some may not want to discuss their own view but simply say that Christianity does not make sense on its own terms. They seek to sidestep their problem of not having a clear grounding for good and evil by trying to avoid making a judgment about whether good and evil actually exist. Don't let them off the hook so easily! Since people intuitively live as moral beings, and given the fact that through this conversation we are comparing competing metanarratives, it is reasonable to ask them quite directly, "Do you believe in real good and real evil? If so, how do you ground such categories? Have you ever considered that it might just be Christianity that best accounts for these moral instincts?"

As we've seen, Christians aren't in a position to give a comprehensive explanation of evil. The lesson is to avoid rushing in with glib responses, and be willing to admit that evil raises certain questions that remain a mystery within the Christian story. But does this mean the logical problem of evil is an insurmountable problem for Christians? No. Not unless you suggest that God has promised to tell us everything we'd like to know about everything. But the Bible never offers this. In fact, it promises the exact opposite. Many times, we will not know why.[6]

The Bible itself emphasizes that it is impossible to exhaust the reasons an infinite God permits evil to occur. It is common in our current culture to assume, as we first saw in chapter 3, what Charles Taylor refers to as the "immanent frame" that gives people the sense that the universe they live in—and all the social and ethical orders within it—"can be fully explained in their own terms and don't need to be conceived as dependent on anything outside, on the 'supernatural' or the 'transcendent.'"[7]

The typical person today has developed a heightened view of what they can understand about the world through their own reason. While previous societies wrestled with the experiences and questions of suffering, this did not normally lead to widespread disbelief in God until, as Taylor recounts, human confidence in our own ability to analyze and draw conclusions became dominant and our sense of mystery faded from the social imagination.[8] But it is exactly this confidence in our ability to understand the world comprehensively that the Bible challenges (e.g., Deuteronomy 29:29; book of Job; Romans 11:33–36). When Christians allow for God to be reduced to a larger version of ourselves, we are playing into the hands of those who base their objection to God on the existence of suffering.

An important part of our response to this objection is to help our secular friend recognize the problems that come from overstating their own reasoning and, after recognizing this, to then cast a grander vision of God:

> "You are right to say Christianity teaches that God is both all-powerful and perfectly good, but your picture of the Christian God is too simplistic and does not correspond well with what Christians have long believed about him. According to the Bible,

> God has revealed himself so that he can be known personally, but he has not revealed himself exhaustively (take Deuteronomy 29:29, for example). We can know him, but because he is the Creator and we are his creatures, we have creaturely limits. He is infinite, and we are finite; we cannot see or understand all the reasons he has for what he does and what he allows. So while you are correct to say that God is omnipotent and good, it is important that you also include *his infinite knowledge and wisdom* as you consider the evil and suffering in the world."

In other words, this objection only stands if you accept the principle, "If God had a good reason for allowing evil, I would know what that reason is."[9] Yet this principle fails to convince. Why should we think it is so?

We might also compare our ability to understand God with an infant's ability to fully understand its parent.[10] I can remember when my wife and I took our young daughter in for her first vaccination shots. Had she been able to articulate her feelings, she would have likely questioned, *Why are these two people who have doted on and diligently cared for me all my life allowing this stranger to cause me so much pain?* At that point in her maturity, the gap between our reasons for allowing her to experience pain and her capacity to understand was too great. As she grew up, there were many similar situations in which we asked her to trust our wisdom and judgment, even when she couldn't fully understand.

Others may object, "But the analogy of a parent and child breaks down. Over time, an ideal father would give his daughter more reason to trust him through the evident care he shows for her. That's not how it is with us and God. He doesn't show us that sort of evident care." However, this is exactly what Christianity claims that God *has* shown us and *does* show us. God publicly entered the world in the person of his Son Jesus Christ and suffered with us and for us. He bears the marks of pain. When looking at the cross, no believer can wonder, *Does God care?* He cared so much that he sent his Son to hang on a cross and die to make things right. The incarnation and death of God's Son—the centerpiece of the Christian story—give us reason to trust that God cares. It is when we look at the crucified Jesus that "we come to understand what it means that God is compassionate, that God is a God who suffers with us."[11]

Today even most secular philosophers admit that the logical problem of evil does not amount to a rational defeat of Christianity. Simply because we do not know why God allows evil does not mean that such a Being would not have good reasons for permitting it. Demonstrating that an omniscient and eternal God cannot have such reasons simply has not been done. This means that arguably the most significant rational problem regarding suffering does not need to be a barrier for belief. In contrast, the problem of grounding real good and evil without transcendence is an abiding problem for secular narratives. But unlike secularism, the Christian story provides a clear framework for making sense of the human experience of real good and real evil and provides an existentially powerful response to the problem—God has entered our story and taken our suffering upon himself.

PART 2: THE EXISTENTIAL PROBLEM

"Whether I believe in God or not, this belief will not help me escape suffering." Thus far, this chapter has dealt primarily with the logical problem, but our last point—that God entered our story to suffer for us—begins to address the experiential problem of suffering. Suffering is not just a Christian problem; it is a human problem, perhaps *the* human problem. Suffering and death are experiences that cast a shadow over everyone's lives. They are no respecters of persons or worldviews. It is true that no one escapes suffering. The question is, "Which story has the resources to enable us to flourish in a world where suffering and loss are unavoidable?"

Traditional versus Secular Stories

Secular stories of suffering differ from traditional views. Most major traditional views claim that, in some way, suffering has real meaning—it is something we should learn from, grow through, or even be transformed by. Traditional religious views also typically emphasize that this current life is not the end of the story.[12] For instance,

Buddhism admits there is suffering in the world but claims that evil is based in a broader illusion. The reason people suffer is that they have unfulfilled desires, so the solution is to subjugate all desire and, in doing so, achieve enlightenment. Only when we rid ourselves of desire and detach ourselves from the material world will we achieve self-transcendence and peace.

A common view in ancient Greek and Roman cultures, and one still prevalent today, is that a person cannot outrun fate, so they must endure whatever evil befalls them in stoic resolution. This acceptance, or stoic resolution, in the face of suffering and death is the path to achieving a legacy of glory and honor. According to religious accounts that include something like karma, whenever someone suffers, it is because they have committed a corresponding evil action. A person's lot in life is directly related to the actions they have taken in this or previous lives, and they receive exactly what they deserve. Thus, according to this view, the way to avoid suffering is to do good.

These traditional beliefs assume stories about the world that don't line up with crucial elements of Christianity. If you are talking to someone who adopts a traditional story but rejects Christianity, you would want to spend more time interacting with how the Christian story contrasts and at times overlaps with theirs. But when talking to someone who has adopted a secular account, as is our focus in this book, these general examples can be helpful starting points because they allow you to make high-level distinctions between traditional and secular views before moving into the unique story of Christianity and how it provides depth and grounding where a secular one falters.

In contrast with traditional accounts, secular narratives admit that suffering is ultimately meaningless and there is no life after we die. From a secular perspective, then, *if* there is such a thing as "meaning" or a "meaningful life," it can only be found in this life and must be rooted in the happiness and fulfillment we create for ourselves.[13] Because suffering has no transcendent meaning or purpose, it should be avoided and eradicated at all costs. There are two general secular responses for how to live in the face of the common human problem of suffering: the *secular pessimistic story* and the *secular optimistic story*.

The secular pessimistic story. There is no ultimate meaning, purpose, or morality in the universe. God is dead, and so is transcendent meaning. One day we will all cease to exist. We are the accidental by-product of a mechanistic universe that is generally hostile toward life. While no one in their right mind wants to suffer, at the end of the day, we must admit that we live in a cruel world where suffering is both meaningless and ultimately inescapable.

As bleak as this is, we would be right to acknowledge that this view has a certain unflinching consistency to it. Indeed, if the universe will eventually suffer heat death, in the end nothing will be remembered, and our lives won't matter. However unpleasant, we can affirm the sober, experiential realism this view holds: this world can be cruel, and no human achievement will ever be able to eliminate suffering or prevent a future extinction.

The consistency of this pessimistic view is also its downfall, for no one can live this story on a daily basis. We all live as if there is meaning in the world. Even a hardened and pessimistic secularist like John Gray admits that although "other animals do not need a purpose in life," humans "cannot do without one."[14] Humans will assign meaning, purpose, and morality in the day-to-day trials of life; it is simply what we do and how we live. Of course some may respond, "In our weakness, we humans assign meaning to our actions to cope, but those of us who are strong enough will just resign ourselves to the absolute meaninglessness and absurdity of all of life." But can they really shrug off their despair so easily?

In response, the best approach is often to continue to ask them questions about how this plays out in their life. In order to be consistent, they would need to deny the universal features of personhood we addressed in part 2. But this would place an overwhelming existential weight on their shoulders. Sometimes people who start with this pessimistic take, in the course of the conversation, will suggest that the best approach is simply not to think about the implications of living in a meaningless universe: "Indeed, there is no ultimate meaning and nothing in our life will amount to anything significant, but it's best if we just don't think about that." The irony here is that their rejection of the Christian story as anti-intellectual, wishful thinking has led them to defend an anti-intellectual refusal to think. They suggest that the best approach to life is to *not think* about what they believe is true about the world. In contrast, as we will see, Christianity says the best way to live is to actually *think more* about the deepest truths of the universe, not less.[15]

The secular optimistic story. This view affirms that because there is no transcendent meaning in the world—at least one that we can discover—we are left to create our own meaning. We have been liberated from having to conform to some external source of truth or meaning and are free to determine what is good and meaningful for ourselves. As Jerry Coyne in *The New Republic* explains, "Secularists see a universe without apparent purpose and realize that we must forge our own purposes and ethics . . . But although the universe is purposeless, our lives aren't . . . We make our own purposes, and they're real."[16] Often, this perspective is accompanied by an idealism regarding humans' ability to overcome suffering. Rather than waiting for any benevolent deity to act on our behalf or placing our hope in an afterlife in which all will be made right, we must, as the "Humanist Manifesto" states, "save ourselves."[17]

Christians do not believe people can save themselves or create their own meaning, but we must be careful not to imply that our secular optimist friend has no meaning in his life. If we were to do so, he could easily reply, "I have a caring relationship with my wife. I am raising my kids to be kind and moral people. I create jobs with my business, and I volunteer every Saturday morning. I sacrifice, and in some sense suffer, for all of these things because each has great meaning and value." These are all good commitments that we should affirm rather than denigrate. We can take our affirmation a step further and commend our friend for his sincere commitment to not just live rightly but to actively combat evils in this world. Many religions remain passive in the face of evil, so we may applaud his desire to right various wrongs. This is an important piece of common ground between Christians and optimistic secularists, and something we should pursue together. Yet despite this common ground, there are issues.

There are at least two significant problems with the optimist secularist perspective. First, this view lacks a cogent rationality. If we create our own webs of meaning and significance, what happens when we are all gone? If our meaning and significance will disappear with humanity's destruction, how can we conclude that these efforts bear any significance, either now or in the long run? Some will say, again, that we simply must not ask these questions. There is no need to think about them, and certainly no good comes from asking them. Just live your life right now the best you can. But if one's understanding of the world demands them to *not* think about certain inescapable aspects of life—namely, death and suffering—then what are the rational merits, really, of this view? Any view that asks its followers to simply forget or ignore hard questions deserves to be questioned.

Second, this view is awfully thin, experientially speaking. If meaning is assigned only within the confines of this life, then what happens when the sources of that meaning—family, career, friends—fail to live up to expectations? What happens when, in the inevitability of life, the delicate filaments that compose the web of meaning we've constructed for ourselves are torn? When this happens, as Tim Keller explains, our very concept of meaning and significance itself will be threatened, undermined, or destroyed.[18] And then one can't help but despair of life itself, for it's not suffering by itself that is unbearable, but rather meaningless suffering that we humans can't endure. In fact, this is why many cultural anthropologists recognize that a secular story, absent of any ultimate meaning for suffering, is the worst possible account for handling the experiential problem of suffering, because "only secular culture sees suffering as accidental and meaningless, just an interruption or destruction of what we are living for. And so our society makes it difficult to fully affirm the goodness of *all* life, even life in the midst of affliction."[19] As Keller goes on to say, "Western societies are perhaps the worst societies in the history of the world at preparing people for suffering and death, because created meaning is not only less rational, but also less durable."[20]

The Christian Story

For Christians, suffering and death should be neither sought after nor avoided at all costs. Instead, living well requires us not to attempt to ignore the universal experiences of suffering and death, but rather to think deeply about them. Unlike what is believed in various forms of secularism, Christians believe that suffering is not only meaningful, but it can also teach and transform us into something magnificent (2 Corinthians 4:17). As C. S. Lewis famously put it, for Christians, "God whispers to us in our pleasures, speaks in our conscience, but shouts in our pains."[21] Through suffering, God mysteriously works to refine us, stripping us of idols and teaching us to not look for our true home in the wrong place. But God does not shout to us in our pain from the sidelines, aloof and unconcerned. Instead, he enters into our agony and cries out to us from within our human story. As the entertainer Stephen Colbert shared in a remarkably unguarded interview with CNN's Anderson Cooper, referencing J. R. R. Tolkien's stories as a formative influence, "The great gift of the sacrifice of Christ is that God does it too, that you're really not alone. God does it too."[22] Colbert's point is that the Christian story provides not a way to escape the plight of suffering, but a way to walk through the pain with a God who cares. With a God who gives us grace amid our suffering.

Christianity understands pain and suffering not as a sign that the world is meaningless and arbitrary, but rather that it is not the way it was originally intended to be. Because humans turned away from God, the giver of life, the result was a distorted creation and the invasion of death. Evil is not an illusion; it is very real. It cannot simply be defined by relative personal or cultural preference. Evil is anything that stands against God and his plan for creation.

While Christians can agree with secularists that we should fight for justice and peace, we must be sure to assert that these categories are not just a matter of our own cultural preferences. Christians have a much more stable basis for philanthropic causes than shifting cultural ideals. In other words, while we can agree with our secular friends that we should fight to end things like sex trafficking and injustices against women, we ought to ask them, "How can these things be considered anything more than mere cultural preferences?" The justification that Christianity provides for activism is far stronger, because it is based on the inherent worth of humans made in God's image, the divinely given vocational calling to care for people and creation, and the moral obligation all humans have to their Creator.

The Christian story also provides a powerful motivation, absent in secular views, for making sacrifices and enduring pain for the sake of justice and goodness. For in Christianity, justice and goodness have transcendent meaning; they matter to God and will matter for eternity.

The Christian message is that God, in the person of Jesus, is redeeming this fallen world and will one day usher in justice and eternal peace. In his poignant work *Lament for a Son*, former Yale philosopher Nicholas Wolterstorff reflects on Jesus' words, "Blessed are those who mourn," and then asks, "Who then are the mourners?" He concludes that the mourners are "those who have caught a glimpse of God's new day, who ache with all their being for that day's coming, and who break out into tears when confronted with its absence . . . The mourners are aching visionaries."[23]

Secular visions of justice struggle to kindle such deep commitment to this world alongside such hope for the future. Consider, for example, the Stoics, who said that in facing life's challenges, we should steel ourselves and seek to empty ourselves of emotion: "Be calm. Disengage yourself. Neither laugh nor weep."[24] And the Epicureans: "Watching calmly as others drowned in misery, the Epicureans were content in the tranquil retreat of their secluded gardens."[25] For those like the philosopher Lucretius, "'Humanity' could do what it pleased. It was no concern of theirs."[26] Wolterstorff sums up how Jesus, in stark contrast, tells us, "Be open to the wounds of the world. Mourn humanity's mourning, weep over humanity's mourning, be wounded by humanity's wounds, be in agony over humanity's agony. But do so in good cheer that a day of peace is coming."[27]

A Day of Peace and Justice

According to the Christian story, God will one day right every wrong—even though it is a mystery to us how exactly he will make this come true. Fundamental to our problem of coping with evil, both rationally and experientially, is the failure to imagine there is some way, though unimaginable to us now, for an infinite God to vindicate himself on the last day. The failure, as Dostoyevsky put on the lips of Ivan, is to:

> believe like a child that suffering will be healed and made up for, that all the humiliating absurdity of human contradictions will vanish like a pitiful mirage, like the despicable fabrication of the impotent and infinitely small Euclidian mind of man, that in the world's finale, at the moment of eternal harmony, something so precious will come to pass that it will suffice for all hearts, for the comforting of all resentments, for the atonement of all the crimes of humanity, of all the blood they've shed; that it will make it not only possible to forgive but to justify all that has happened with men.[28]

To dare to imagine a God who has purposes and plans that are beyond our present ability to imagine is not only in line with the biblical story, but it also gives the hope to persevere in the face of tragedy and evil. Luc Ferry refers to this as the "seductive promise" of Christianity.[29] Not only does the God of this story enter into our suffering, taking our wounds on himself, but because Christians know they are saved by and into an eternal love, they can rest in the assurance that "the life of [their] loves will not come to an end with earthly death."[30] Life after death, grounded in the resurrection of Jesus, offers a powerful vision that guards against both a passive quietism and an overwhelming despair in the face of evil. Instead it provides a compelling reason to actively love and dare to hope.

Even at this point, if someone dares to begin to imagine a day when, as J. R. R. Tolkien put it, "everything sad [is] going to come untrue,"[31] they may object, "But doesn't a day of justice and peace mean that certain people will be judged? Why wouldn't a loving God simply forgive all people?" To this question, we turn in our final section of this chapter.

PART 3: THE PROBLEM OF JUDGMENT

"I can't believe in a God who is angry and will judge." If the conversation turns this way, one approach to helping someone reflect more deeply about their own question is to ask them to consider the nature of "love," "judgment," and "forgiveness."

Love

Love, even at a human level, causes us to oppose what we see as evil. We love our kids. If one of them were to become a dreadful person, ruining their life and their family's future with reckless living and destructive behavior, we would not be indifferent. We would be angry. Deep love, in this case, is necessarily connected to a capacity for deep anger. Indifference toward destructive behavior in someone you claim to love would call into question the sincerity of that love.

Analogies have their limits, of course, and human love is quite different from God's love. Still, the illustration is a good place to start in that it helps debunk the notion that love is the opposite of anger. Not so, for even in our finite experiences, love and anger are deeply connected. Because God is loving, he is not indifferent toward the corruption of the world he loves. God's judgment flows out of both his holiness and his love. It is part of his settled and active opposition against anything that opposes the good.[32]

Judgment

Another perspective on divine judgment is the New Testament's claim that God, in his judgment, is giving people over to their desires (Romans 1:18–32). In other words, God punishes people who want freedom from him by permitting men and women to have that very freedom in spades. The apostle Paul paints a verbal picture of how humans, once detached from God's authority, spiral deeper and deeper into narcissistic idolatry and destructive behavior. Like a drug addict who refuses help and continues binging on the drug that is destroying him, our insistence on idolatry turns us deeper into our own self-absorption, despair, and ultimately ruin. From this perspective, through judgment God says, "Okay, have what you desire."

This perspective of course is not the only way in which the Bible describes God's judgment, but it is a very stark one. Here, the Western individualist need only shake her fist at God to be given what she desires above all else—freedom and space to choose her own path. God permits this choice, but also promises that this path leads to destruction. This understanding of God's judgment begs us to think deeply about human culpability.

Forgiveness

Forgiveness is a popular sentiment in late modernism. Many people long for worldwide peace and reconciliation. This yearning is beautiful, and it's something we should share and affirm. Too often, however, one's desire for peace amounts to nothing more than cheap sentiment—"Why can't we all just forgive each other and get along?" But this desire by itself lacks substance and realism. In a culture that promotes individualism, personal rights, and self-actualization, the sacrifice that forgiveness requires is difficult and often unbearable.

Take, for instance, the powerful executive who takes advantage of his employees and investors to the tune of a rich pension. Or the officer who purposefully misuses evidence, resulting in an unjust sentencing. Or, perhaps closer to home, the coworker who slanders and abuses to get ahead. Not only do we instinctually sense that these actions are wrong, but we also recognize that they are difficult to forgive. And this is only intensified if we assume, as do many late moderns, that our lives are fundamentally about pursuing our own interests. Doesn't a strong sense of justice dictate that we seek justice for grievances committed against us? Indeed, while the desire for justice should be affirmed, an important question is how we can pursue it without unleashing an escalating cycle of violence. How can we become people who are able to forgive without undermining the human desire for justice?

The Christian story enables us to move beyond merely coping with evil. The gospel enables us to live peaceably with others, even those who act despicably, because it provides a substantive foundation for forgiveness and assures us that justice will be done in the end. Theologian Miroslav Volf, a Croatian who experienced cruel violence in the Balkan civil wars, has famously argued that forgiveness is only possible because of God's justice. Our hearts desperately want justice to be served. We want the guilty to be punished. We desire for things to be made right. Volf asserts that if God does not bring people to justice, if he does not, one day, make a final end to evil, then he is not only a God who is unworthy of our worship, but our capacity to forgive will be undermined by a quest for vigilante justice.[33]

Volf asks us to consider how much of our discomfort with a God who judges is due to our own parochial cultural perspective: "It takes the quiet of a suburban home for the birth of the thesis that human nonviolence corresponds to God's refusal to judge. In a scorched land, soaked in the blood of the innocent, [that thesis] will invariably die. And as one watches it die, one will do well to reflect about many other pleasant captivities of the liberal mind."[34]

The Christian story provides reasons to seek a just legal system where crimes are prosecuted, so believing in a future judgment is in no way suggesting that governments should ignore evils. But the Scriptures also recognize the realities of injustice that still plague a fallen world. Many times it appears that evil escapes those in authority or, worse, that those in authority are the evil ones! The Christian story recognizes what human experience teaches us far too often—those who lie, cheat, and kill often seem to get ahead. If there is no God to bring a final judgment, then why shouldn't we each pursue vigilante justice and attempt to settle our own scores against those who have wronged us? If this world is all that exists, "now" is the only time to get even. And it is up to us to "play God."

The paradigm changes dramatically for the Christian, for God sees all and will one day make all things right. Thus, the Christian story offers two powerful reasons to forgive others. First, the belief in divine justice serves as a restraint. We are not to seek vengeance, because ultimate judgment is God's prerogative, not ours. God will see that justice—perfect justice—is done in the end. Second, the belief in human sinfulness calls us to recognize that we are all guilty. We are all accountable before God for our sins.

And yet, God not only promises that justice will be served, but he secured forgiveness by paying the debt of our guilt through Jesus' sacrifice. When we trust in Jesus, God declares we are entirely forgiven. He has removed all our objective guilt and thereby enables us to be free from the stranglehold of bitterness we feel toward those who have wronged us. Forgiven by God, we are empowered to offer true forgiveness to others, mirroring the forgiveness we have received.

God promises to render a just verdict against any being who refuses to turn from evil. Though much remains mysterious about the coming day of reckoning, it fits within the story that makes sense of our desire for justice, our problems with forgiveness, and our anger toward that which destroys what we love. Beneath our expressions of these desires for perfect justice, true forgiveness, and eternal love is a heart yearning for the One in whom each of these is found.

The Kiss

This brings us back to Ivan Karamazov. In perhaps Dostoyevsky's most famous chapter, "The Grand Inquisitor," Ivan shares a story with his younger, devoutly Christian brother, Alyosha. It's a story Ivan himself created as a clever articulation of his own rationale for rejecting God. In the story, Jesus appears in sixteenth-century Spain and is immediately arrested by the Grand Inquisitor—an old, powerful church leader overseeing the burnings of heretics and the daily lives of commoners. After taking Jesus to prison, the Inquisitor unleashes a sophisticated yet venomous condemnation of Christ, accusing Jesus of forcing freedom on mankind and thus also forcing evil and suffering on a helpless and defenseless world. Amid his spiteful harangue, the Inquisitor invites Jesus to speak and respond to the accusations being levied against him, yet Jesus remains silent.

After a triumphant finish, Ivan shares how the Inquisitor looked at Jesus and "saw that the Prisoner had listened intently all the time, looking gently in his face and evidently not wishing to reply. The old man longed for Him to say something, however bitter and terrible. But He suddenly approached the old man in silence and softly kissed him on his bloodless aged lips. That was all His answer."[35]

Dostoyevsky's entire novel is a multifaceted and storied response to the question of evil. Yet the kiss is the most poignant answer. Jesus' kiss was no ironclad justification of evil. It was an act of forgiveness and love, emblematic of God's love for the world revealed on the cross, a love so powerful that it can penetrate even the hardest heart. After finishing his story, Ivan shares that the Inquisitor, while maintaining his rejection of God, "shuddered" at Jesus' act, and that the kiss of Christ "glows in his heart." The Inquisitor, clothed in an armor of rationality and cleverness, was disarmed, at least for a moment, not by logic but by love. Interestingly, Ivan, much like the Inquisitor, was holding fast to his rejection of God as he finished his story and asked for his brother's thoughts. Alyosha, never able to keep pace with his older brother's brilliant intellect, responds by kissing Ivan, loving him despite his rebellion. As time passes, it is Alyosha's commitment to a livable story—the Christian story—that forces Ivan to shudder at his own rationalist, unlivable story.

This chapter has outlined how to respond to the objection that the Christian story is unloving, not by definitively "solving" the question of evil or comprehensively explaining how justice will one day finally be served, but by telling a story of a God who in Jesus kissed the world by taking upon himself its evil and pain. "Inside out" served to guide our response as we stepped inside our secular friends' perspectives to understand the sincerity and complexity of their objection and then asked them to try on the Christian story's resources to live a life of hope, faith, and love amid evil and suffering. We now turn from responding to moral objections against the story to exploring the objection that the story of Jesus is simply not true.

NOTES

1. Fyodor Dostoyevsky, *The Brothers Karamazov*, trans. Constance Garnett (New York: Macmillan, 1922), 254.
2. Dostoyevsky, *The Brothers Karamazov*, 242.
3. "Afterword: Trent Dougherty and Alvin Plantinga: An Interview on Faith and Reason," in *Two Dozen (Or So) Arguments for God: The Plantinga Project*, ed. Jerry L. Walls and Trent Dougherty (Oxford: Oxford University Press, 2018), 457.
4. See Dostoyevsky, *The Brothers Karamazov*, 278.
5. C. S. Lewis, *Mere Christianity* (1943; repr., New York: Macmillan, 1960), 45, emphasis in original.
6. This is why Plantinga adds that even though we may not fully know why God permits evil, "I guess that's all right . . . There are lots of things we don't know, and I think that is one of them" ("Afterword: Trent Dougherty and Alvin Plantinga," 457).
7. Charles Taylor, "Afterword: *Apologia pro Libro suo*," in *Varieties of Secularism in a Secular Age*, ed. Michael Warner, Jonathan VanAntwerpen, and Craig Calhoun (Cambridge, MA: Harvard University Press, 2010), 307.
8. See Charles Taylor, *A Secular Age* (Cambridge, MA: Harvard University Press, 2007), 223, 306–7, 317–19.
9. See C. Stephen Evans, *Faith beyond Reason: A Kierkegaardian Account* (Grand Rapids: Eerdmans, 1998), 134.
10. See Stephen John Wykstra, "Rowe's Noseeum Arguments from Evil," in *The Evidential Argument from Evil*, ed. Daniel Howard-Snyder (Bloomington: Indiana University Press, 1996), 139–42.

11. Henri J. M. Nouwen, *Love, Henri: Letters on the Spiritual Life* (New York: Convergent, 2016), 127.
12. For an important resource and a deeper look at how various worldviews understand suffering and evil, see Timothy Keller, *Walking with God through Pain and Suffering* (New York: Dutton, 2013).
13. Some will say that meaning in life is found in the utilitarian idea of serving the greater good. Accordingly, suffering might serve the "greater good." However, several problems exist with this view. It lacks the clear resources to motivate one to sacrifice personal happiness for the happiness of others. Moreover, the "greater good" still has no ultimate meaning. The significance of a selfless act will die with humanity. And "the greater good" or "happiness," as Alasdair MacIntyre observes, has various forms, and thus it is not a useful guide. A framework that provides a transcendent *telos* for humanity is needed to ground the "good" (see *After Virtue*, 3rd ed. [Notre Dame, IN: University of Notre Dame Press, 2008], 51–78).
14. John Gray, *Straw Dogs: Thoughts on Humans and Other Animals* (London: Granta, 2002), 199.
15. For more on this point, see Timothy Keller, *Making Sense of God: An Invitation to the Skeptical* (New York: Viking, 2016), 65–69.
16. Jerry A. Coyne, "Ross Douthat Is on Another Erroneous Rampage against Secularism," *New Republic*, December 26, 2013, https://newrepublic.com/article/116047/ross-douthat-wrong-about-secularism-and-ethics; see Keller, *Making Sense of God*, 63.
17. "Humanist Manifesto II," American Humanist Association, 1973, https://americanhumanist.org/what-is-humanism/manifesto2.
18. Keller, *Making Sense of God*, 73–74.
19. Keller, *Making Sense of God*, 73, emphasis in original.
20. Keller, *Making Sense of God*, 74.
21. C. S. Lewis, *The Problem of Pain* (New York: Macmillan, 1962), 93.
22. "Anderson Cooper Interviews Stephen Colbert," *Anderson Cooper 360 Degrees*, August 18, 2019, www.cnn.com/TRANSCRIPTS/1908/18/acd.01.html.
23. Nicholas Wolterstorff, *Lament for a Son* (Grand Rapids: Eerdmans, 1987), 85–86.
24. Wolterstorff, *Lament for a Son*, 86.
25. John Gray, *Seven Types of Atheism* (New York: Farrar, Straus and Giroux, 2018), 52.
26. Gray, *Seven Types of Atheism*, 52.
27. Wolterstorff, *Lament for a Son*, 86.
28. Dostoyevsky, *The Brothers Karamazov*, 247–48. Though in the novel Ivan calls this into question. Ivan's attitude is difficult because he longs for ultimate harmony and justice, but at the same time he believes the suffering of the defenseless can never be made right because the very fact that the suffering occurred is irredeemable. While he does not want the "tormenters" to go to Hell, he also does not want the tormenters to be forgiven because that would trample on the sufferer. He basically puts himself in an impossible situation, but this is a tension that resonates with many late moderns—they often want nothing to do with the idea of divine

wrath, but they also long for an ultimate justice and have a deep hatred toward what they perceive to be evil.

29. Luc Ferry, *Learning to Live: A User's Manual* (Edinburgh: Canongate, 2010), 86.
30. Ferry, *Learning to Live*, 87.
31. J. R. R. Tolkien, *The Return of the King: Being the Third Part of The Lord of the Rings* (New York: Ballantine, 1965), 246.
32. See Timothy Keller, *Reason for God: Belief in an Age of Skepticism* (New York: Dutton, 2008), 73. Keller cites Becky Pippert: "Anger isn't the opposite of love. Hate is, and the final form of hate is indifference . . . God's wrath is not a cranky explosion, but his settled opposition to the cancer of sin which is eating out the insides of the human race he loves with his whole being."
33. See Miroslav Volf, *Exclusion and Embrace: A Theological Exploration of Identity, Otherness, and Reconciliation* (Nashville: Abingdon, 1996), 303.
34. Volf, *Exclusion and Embrace*, 304.
35. Dostoyevsky, *The Brothers Karamazov*, 277.

chapter
13

An Untrue Story?

Even if someone begins to see the Christian story as good rather than oppressive, and beautiful rather than unloving, they might still conclude, along the lines of Julian Barnes, that it is only a "beautiful lie" or a "supreme fiction."[1] Could it really be a true story?

PART 1: THE PROBLEM OF MIRACLES

"We now know better than to accept the veracity of a story filled with miracles." Despite a growing openness to the miraculous within late modernism, still many write off the biblical story as a "fiction" due to its miracles. Some will likely echo the influential view of the eighteenth-century Scottish skeptic David Hume, who claimed that one could never be confident in the actual occurrence of a miracle because a miracle would violate the laws of nature. Any alleged miracle is, therefore, not to be believed, since it defies the most obvious and universal observations regarding nature, making its occurrence highly improbable. A major problem with this argument is its circularity. It reasons deductively, excluding in advance any evidence for miracles. Thus, it simply employs one set of generally observed experiences (natural laws) to disallow other attested experiences and the physical evidence that supports these claims.[2]

Others simply assert that since miracles cannot be proven empirically, that is, they are not repeatable and testable, they cannot be accepted as true. Theoretically, even if a miracle happened, it could not be believed since it could not be scientifically confirmed. Of course, the problem here is that science, as discussed earlier, is only one way to confirm truth, and a limited one at that.

Testimony, direct experience, and physical evidence are all valid means to evaluate miraculous claims. People throughout history and across the world have testified to the reality of miracles. Many of these eyewitnesses to miracles are well educated and reputable people who, in many cases, were at one time skeptical of miracles. Still, it is common for people to deny these accounts wholesale. What, then, do we make of those people claiming to have witnessed or experienced miracles? What is the best explanation for the countless eyewitness accounts?

For those who are skeptical, it seems that any naturalistic explanation for such phenomena is more credible than accepting an actual miracle. How then does the skeptic explain the testimonies of miracles in so many different locations and eras? There are several proposed explanations. One explanation is *fraud*. People are simply lying. For whatever reason—perhaps fame, power, or money—they make up stories about miracles. A second explanation is *hallucinations*. People under great stresses and mental pressures sometimes think they see things that are not truly there. A third involves *psychosomatic healings*. The mind has an incredible power to heal, or at least convince itself that the person's body has been miraculously healed. A fourth explanation is *wish fulfillment*. People deeply desire to experience a miracle. They want to live in a world in which God invades the normal processes of life to fantastically deliver them or their loved ones. Belief in miracles offers hope for a difficult world.

But are these the best explanations for the many firsthand accounts of miracles? They are certainly valid in some cases. Miracles are not normal events. If they were normal, no one would consider the event a miracle. Miracles by nature are not repeatable. They cannot be placed in a test tube, so to speak, and proven empirically. Fraud, hallucinations, psychosomatic healings, and wish fulfillment undoubtedly account for some so-called miracles. Not every claimed miracle is true.

These naturalistic explanations, however, do not adequately

account for all of the incalculable number of miracles that have been professed. One might explain away some miracles, but explaining away the eyewitness testimony of so many miracles requires a *faith* in one's own limited experiences over *faith* in the firsthand accounts of witnesses. Hence, doubting the possibility of miracles is rooted in belief. Why not be open to doubting your faith in your limited personal sample size to consider the testimony of so many throughout history and still today?

Academic works, such Craig Keener's two-volume tome *Miracles*, provide a vast catalog of apparent credible claims of the miraculous. Not all of these claims need be factual to undermine naturalistic accounts of the world; just the veracity of one would poke a damaging hole in the "this material world is all there is" story.

A better story for these occurrences is that at least some of them are pointers to a reality beyond this world. "Natural laws" is simply a way to describe what normally happens, but we go too far when we insist that what normally happens is what always happens.

In the end, however, we should grant that if someone denies a reality beyond the physical world, then they have a sufficient reason to deny the reality of miracles. But it is important to stress that this is *not* a valid argument against miracles unless you accept the initial assumption. As we said earlier, this is ultimately a narrowly circular argument. The logic is built on the leap of faith that there is no God who both transcends and cares for this world. But if this leap of faith is called into question, the logic leads to the opposite conclusion. To return to the question of probability, what are the chances of genuine miracles if there is a God? If someone is willing to grant that there *might* be a God, then she has good reason to at least be open to the many accounts of mysterious and unexplained occurrences—and also open to the Christian story.

PART 2: THE PROBLEMS WITH THE BIBLE

"The Bible is unreliable, so the story it tells can't be taken seriously." In some sense, this entire book is focused on answering the question of why one should take the story the Bible tells seriously. In this vein,

the historian John Dickson has argued that the truth of the Bible is supported by the way the story it tells fits with what we already intuit about the world. As a historian himself, Dickson is not minimizing the importance of historical questions, but rather emphasizing the power of Christianity's story.

> I believe the Bible is so popular and influential because it tells a story we recognize as true. I don't just mean it tells an accurate story . . . What I mean is that its account of humanity and the world we live in *rings true*. Reading the Bible can be like meeting someone you don't know who, oddly, somehow seems to know *you* deeply. It is uncanny. Sometimes when you read the Bible, you find yourself asking, "How does this book know that about me? How does it know that about our world—especially when it was written so long ago?"[3]

One of the most powerful things you can do with an unbeliever, if they are willing, is to open the Bible, read it with them, and discuss what it is actually saying. Ask them to see if it fits with what they see and experience in their everyday life. They might just realize, to their surprise, that the Bible is reading *them* more than they are reading *it*.

Still, for many, prior to being willing to consider the explanatory power of the Christian story, let alone reading the story, they will want to know whether any good historical reasons exist to take such a story seriously. If not, why spend any time in it?

When giving a short response to this objection, it is typically best to focus on the New Testament gospels, since they provide the earliest accounts of Jesus' ministry. This helps keep things succinct. As particular questions come up, you can explore those together. But stay focused. You don't want to get lost in the periphery. Focusing on the gospel accounts necessarily keeps the focus on Jesus, who stands at the center of the Bible and the heart of the gospel story.

It's also worth noting that these accounts of Jesus can be a strategic place to start, since Jesus vouched for the legitimacy of both the Old and New Testaments. He held the Hebrew Scriptures in high regard and personally commissioned the apostles, who were central in the formation of the other New Testament writings. If we trust Jesus as Lord, then we will certainly wish to agree with his high view of the rest of Scripture.

It can be easy for Christians to take harsh criticism of the Bible and its story personally. It is this story, in fact, and the truth it tells, in which Christians source their identity, so for someone to dismiss or attack it can elicit real discomfort or pain. We must do our best to remember that our identities are firmly secure in the living person of Christ, not in our conversation, nor in our ability to defend anything in that conversation. Listen, then, to your secular friend with patience, graciousness, and interest. Understand their specific concerns, ask specific questions, and be prepared to ask them to consider some of the historical reasons to take the gospels seriously.

The Gospel Writers Relied on Eyewitness Testimony and Careful Research.

It is popular today for the media to report sensational and skeptical claims about other discovered "gospels" that offer new facts about who Jesus was. Occasionally, you will meet someone who parrots such reports. The reality is that even most nonbelieving scholars still affirm that the four traditional gospels are the best historical sources for studying Jesus. Bart Ehrman, the well-known critic of Christianity, emphasizes today's mainstream scholarly consensus concerning the New Testament gospels:

> The oldest and best sources we have for knowing about the life of Jesus . . . are the four Gospels of the New Testament, Matthew, Mark, Luke, and John. This is not simply the view of Christian historians who have a high opinion of the New Testament and its historical worth; it is the view of all serious historians of antiquity of every kind, from committed evangelical Christian to hardcore atheists.[4]

One of the reasons for increasing skepticism concerning the four gospels is that in the early part of the twentieth century, a group of scholars made critical mistakes that slanted many people's view of the gospels. These scholars believed the gospels to be folk literature, analogous to old German fairy tales. They asserted that stories of Jesus were passed down orally by way of anonymous community traditions, and that, over time, the stories took on a life of their own, independent of the historical events from which they originated. Though it was Jesus' disciples and other eyewitnesses to his ministry who communicated the original gospel traditions, these traditions were altered when the eyewitnesses died, so the critics said.

This theory is comparable to the telephone game. In telephone, someone begins by sharing a secret with another person. The one receiving the secret then passes it on to another person, and so the game continues down through a chain of participants. By the time the secret reaches the last person, who then utters it aloud, the secret has been horribly mangled and only vaguely resembles the original words spoken. Likewise, late modern scholars argue that by the time the gospel traditions were written down, they only vaguely resembled the original accounts of what had happened.

A major problem with this theory is that many of the eyewitnesses to the events in Jesus' life were alive and active in the early church until well after the gospels were written. In *Jesus and the Eyewitnesses*, New Testament scholar Richard Bauckham argues that these eyewitnesses would have functioned as authoritative sources and guardians for the oral gospel tradition. It was common in oral societies for people to serve in such roles. Returning to the telephone game analogy, it would be as if the person who began by telling the secret proceeded to listen each time the secret was passed on from person to person, making sure it was passed down correctly.

Skilled historians who lived in the period when the gospels were written relied as much as they could on eyewitness testimony. We see this in the opening of Luke's gospel, where he purposefully appealed to eyewitness testimony and used the historiographical language of the day (1:1–4). Far from a haphazard attempt to patch together oral traditions, Luke specifically assured his readers that great care had been taken in the book's composition.[5]

A second-century pastor by the name of Papias provides further helpful information concerning the eyewitness nature of the gospels. Papias identified three generations of people: (1) the eyewitnesses themselves, (2) the elders who sat at their feet, and (3) the disciples of the elders. Papias writes that when he was younger, in the 80s at the latest, many members of the three generations were still alive, including the eyewitnesses. By that time, the gospel of Mark had been completed, and Matthew and Luke had either been written or were in the process of being written. This evidence suggests that the gospels were not oral traditions passed down only to be mistakenly altered during transmission; rather, they were oral history that had been guarded carefully by the eyewitnesses themselves.

In another important point, Bauckham argues that the names present within the gospels are meant to assure the readers of their accuracy.[6] Throughout the gospels, figures are distinguished by use of their proper names; these people were meant to serve as living guarantors of the tradition. For instance, Mark, whose gospel account was likely the earliest to be written, specifically named not only Simon of Cyrene, but also his two sons Alexander and Rufus (Mark 15:21). None of the other gospels keep the names of the sons; they only mention Simon. It appears that Mark expected his readers to know both sons. But even so, why reference them by name? The best explanation is that Mark is referencing Simon's testimony by way of his sons, who were known figures in early Christianity.[7] Matthew and Luke, who wrote their gospels later, might not have had reason to include Alexander's and Rufus's names, because they would no longer have been well known. This suggests that Mark mentioned Simon's two sons in order to point out living eyewitnesses who could corroborate his account.

Consider also the identification of the primary witness at the beginning and the end of the gospels of John and Mark (sometimes called an "*inclusio* of eyewitness testimony"). In the gospel of John, the beloved disciple, traditionally understood as the author, appears at bookends to the narrative (John 1:40; 21:24).[8] In Mark, Peter's presence in the opening and closing of the gospel (1:16; 16:7) corresponds with the early tradition that Mark was dependent on Peter's eyewitness experience.[9] Peter's name also occurs with remarkable frequency throughout Mark's gospel. All this suggests that the gospels were written too soon after the gospel events happened—eyewitnesses to Jesus' life were still alive and prominent in the church—to be myths.

The Gospels Are Too Counterintuitive to Be a Hoax.

The negative portrayal of the disciples. In the gospels, when Jesus tells his disciples that he will be killed, they don't understand. In fact, the gospels regularly portray the disciples as misunderstanding Jesus. As Jesus attempts to teach them humility and the importance of serving others, they argue over which of them is the greatest. Some of the disciples fall asleep when Jesus needs them most. At one point, Peter so misjudges Jesus' mission that Jesus refers to him as "Satan" (Matthew 16:23).

This is an odd way to portray the leaders of a movement whose message you are promoting. Can you imagine a PR campaign that intentionally portrays its leadership as dim-witted and "satanic"? What advantage could the gospel authors have to write like this, apart from the goal of faithfully presenting what actually happened?

The role of women. In the first century, women were not allowed to testify in a court of law because it was believed they could not give trustworthy testimony on important matters.[10] It is remarkable, then, that all gospel traditions not only depict women as playing an important role in Jesus' ministry, but also as being the first eyewitnesses to Jesus' resurrection.[11] It would be counterintuitive to invent a story in this way. Were the "myth" model for gospel formation true, it would have been easy for early Christians to change details of the story to fit first-century norms, including refashioning the account so that women were not featured so prominently, especially at the resurrection. This, of course, is not what happened, as women were and remain central to the resurrection story. The prominent role of women in the gospels is best explained by the commitment of the early church to be faithful to the eyewitness accounts of Jesus' life.

The differences. If the gospel writers all sounded exactly the same, it would be natural to conclude they were only using one source or that they had colluded to smooth out anything that could be perceived as contradictory. But this isn't what we find in the gospels. While the basic story is the same across all four gospel accounts, the details vary from one to another. This is in part because they were writing according to the literary conventions of their day, some of which we are familiar with today, like when we compress the week's events into a short explanation or summarize a long conversation with our boss down to a few minutes for the sake of our listeners. However, at other times, the gospels appear to be telling aspects of the story differently because multiple witnesses are testifying to the same events, without depending on each other. We see this, for instance, in the different resurrection traditions found in the gospels. This is the legitimate diversity that should be expected among multiple credible sources. Take, for example, a family vacation for which, after returning home, each family member recounts the events of their time together. Though each person would give many overlapping details (location, transportation, major occurrences), we would expect each to tell the story of their vacation with legitimate differences in perspective, such as the events they choose to describe, how they summarize those events and accompanying conversations, and the order in which they arrange the events. We see and even expect this kind of legitimate diversity when multiple credible sources recount historical events today, and it can help explain what we find in the accounts of Jesus in the New Testament.[12]

Corroborating Ancient Sources

Another way to interact with someone who is suspicious of the gospels' reliability is to compare the basic stories of the four gospels with what we know from the earliest non-Christian sources. To this end, the biblical scholar Peter Williams has examined the writings of Cornelius Tacitus (writings circa AD 98–117), Pliny the Younger (writings circa AD 98–113), and Flavius Josephus (circa AD 79–95).[13] You may use Williams's book (which includes the relevant portion of the source material) as a guide or go to the sources directly to show how the story of the gospels corresponds with the stories found in these accounts. Williams summarizes his major findings:

> We have seen
>
> - the confirmation of basic facts from the New Testament, such as Christ's death under Pontius Pilate in Judaea between AD 26 and AD 36,
> - that Christ was worshiped as God early on,

- that Christ's followers often experienced persecution,
- that Christians spread far and fast,
- that some early Christian leaders would have known of Christ's family origins.[14]

The relevance of the first item, the confirmation of the basic facts of the New Testament, is obvious. With respect to the other points, Williams explains that since Christian beliefs traveled "far and fast" (as the multiple non-Christian accounts confirm), it would have been extremely difficult for its core message and practices to be changed, especially when Christians were willing to suffer and even die for these convictions. Those who argue that the central features of the Christian story were fictional ideas that seeped into Christian teaching as later innovations have the historical problem of explaining when and how this happened. Williams writes:

> The idea that core beliefs arose decades after Christianity began to spread does not explain why Christianity proved popular in the first place or how people who adhered to a version of Christianity without these beliefs came to adopt them later. The later agreement of Christians that Jesus Christ was God's Son, prophesied by Jewish Scriptures, crucified for sinners, and raised from the dead by God is best explained by supposing that these and other central beliefs were established *before* Christianity began to spread.[15]

With no institution able to enforce such consensus, the best explanation for this widespread agreement is that the core plotline of the gospels was the message being spread by witnesses from the beginning.

These fundamental elements of the gospel story line can also be seen in Paul's letters and in early creedal statements, such as in 1 Corinthians 15:3–5, which even unbelieving historians date to just a few years after Jesus' death: "For I delivered to you as of first importance what I also received: that Christ died for our sins in accordance with the Scriptures, that he was buried, that he was raised on the third day in accordance with the Scriptures, and that he appeared to Cephas, then to the twelve."

Notice how this chapter, as well as the summarized arguments from Williams and Bauckham, avoids attempting to do too much. It is normally ineffective to set out in conversations to "prove" the Bible. Instead, our goal is to have others see they can't easily write off the gospels as invented legends, so that they might be willing to step into the story and encounter Jesus within its pages. The Spirit works through the gospel to change hearts. Our aim is to give reasons why they should take the story serious enough to try it on and see for themselves how it fits.

This short chapter only provides a few highlights from the breadth of high-level scholarship published in support of the reliability of the gospels.[16] If someone rejects Christianity because they believe the Bible is unreliable, we should ask them to consider this careful scholarship that supports the credibility of the gospel authors and the story they tell. A warning: should you become well acquainted with this literature, it's still important to avoid taking a "dump truck" approach to conversations. Learning to be concise and contextualize this information for others is essential to constructive conversations. And in the midst of all the details that can come up in such discussions, don't lose sight of the core facts: Christ has died. Christ is risen. Christ will come again.

NOTES

1. Julian Barnes, *Nothing to Be Frightened Of* (New York: Vintage, 2009), 53, 58.
2. See Craig S. Keener, *Miracles: The Credibility of the New Testament Accounts*, vols. 1–2 (Grand Rapids: Baker Academic, 2011), 1:161–62.
3. John Dickson, *A Doubter's Guide to the Bible: Inside History's Bestseller for Believers and Skeptics* (Grand Rapids: Zondervan, 2014), 10, emphasis in original.
4. Bart D. Ehrman, *Truth and Fiction in the Da Vinci Code* (Oxford: Oxford University Press, 2004), 102.
5. See Richard Bauckham, *Jesus and the Eyewitnesses: The Gospels as Eyewitness Testimony*, 2nd ed. (Grand Rapids: Eerdmans, 2017), 1–11, 116–24.
6. See Bauckham, *Jesus and the Eyewitnesses*, 39–239.
7. See Bauckham, *Jesus and the Eyewitnesses*, 51–52.
8. See Bauckham, *Jesus and the Eyewitnesses*, 127–29.
9. See Bauckham, *Jesus and the Eyewitnesses*, 124–27.
10. See Richard Bauckham, *Gospel Women: Studies of the Named Women in the Gospels* (Grand Rapids: Eerdmans, 2002), 268–77; see also N.T. Wright, *Resurrection of the Son of God* (Minneapolis: Fortress, 2003), 607.

11. Bauckham also argues that the variations in the lists of women in the gospels further indicate each Evangelist's care in naming the women who served as eyewitnesses (*Jesus and the Eyewitnesses*, 51).
12. For a response to critiques on the reliability of the New Testament documents, see Andreas J. Köstenberger, Darrell L. Bock, and Josh D. Chatraw, *Truth in a Culture of Doubt: Engaging Skeptical Challenges to the Bible* (Nashville: B&H, 2014), 79–106.
13. Peter J. Williams, *Can We Trust the Gospels?* (Wheaton, IL: Crossway, 2018), 17–35.
14. Williams, *Can We Trust the Gospels?*, 35.
15. Williams, *Can We Trust the Gospels?*, 24, emphasis in original.
16. For an example of some of this scholarship, see N. T. Wright, *Jesus and the Victory of God* (London: SPCK, 1996); Craig Keener, *Christobiography: Memory, History, and the Reliability of the Gospels* (Grand Rapids: Eerdmans, 2019); C. E. Hill, *Who Chose the Gospels? Probing the Great Gospel Conspiracy* (Oxford: Oxford University Press, 2012); C. Stephen Evans, *The Historical Christ and the Jesus of Faith: The Incarnational Narrative as History* (Oxford: Oxford University Press, 1996).

Conclusion

I'm a sucker for Disney movies. Besides just the happy endings, I've become captivated by Disney's ability to tap into the cultural narratives of our day and then sing, illustrate, and story their way into our imaginations. As I was finishing this book, my family went to see *Frozen 2*, which is just another case in point of what we have come to expect from Disney. The writers creatively layered the movie for different audiences. So while my six-year-old was spellbound by the magical worlds and giggling at the slapstick humor, I was taken by the film's charm and intrigued by its exploration into the vicissitudes of life. (Okay, I'll confess. I liked the songs too!)

One of the quotes that piqued my interest early in the movie, and ended up becoming a repeated mantra throughout, was introduced by the sage troll Grand Pabbie, who counsels Elsa and Anna, "When one can see no future, all one can do is the next right thing." This line takes on a deeper significance later in the film as the characters have to face their own fears and insecurities. Perhaps most surprising is the existential crisis experienced by Olaf, who has gone from the comical, optimistic snowman in the first movie to an insecure and at times despondent wayfarer, asking questions about the meaning of life and dropping philosophical one-liners. Olaf has come to realize the more he learns about life, the more he feels disoriented. He's coming of age, but this has not left him as a triumphant know-it-all. In fact, he knows he hasn't arrived. At one point, he expresses (in song, of course) the hope that when he gets older, "*absolutely*" everything will make sense, but the adults watching the film are clearly supposed to pick up on his naivete. The irony as Olaf sings is that the older characters in the film are plainly wrestling with their own fragility and doubts. Aging will not, by itself, solve his problems. Adding to Olaf's malaise is that he realizes that while he longs to capture his idyllic childhood experiences and for things to stay the same, life doesn't work like that. Things change. And in the movie, Olaf even has to face the greatest change and uncertainty of all—his own death.

Olaf serves as picture of our fragile existence in a late modern world, a time when there are multiple rival meta-stories swirling in the cultural air that often leave people with more questions than answers. Grasping for a foundation, people are increasingly looking internally to get their bearings, hoping to find a way to navigate life by way of their emotions. As one of the lines in the movie expresses, "You feel what you feel, and your feelings are real." Certainly, feelings are real. This, however, should lead us to important questions: *How should I interpret what I feel? What's behind my feelings? Which of my feelings can be trusted?*

Today people at least know they feel certain things, but they, like Olaf, can't help but at times feel disoriented. They long to capture the idyllic experiences of their past, the pleasures of the present, and the fulfillment of the yet to be. Yet the harder they grasp, the more they sense it slipping through their fingers. They feel the death of each passing experience and the loss of dreams that will never be fulfilled, while at the same time longing for something more—all with the uneasy awareness that a final death casts a dark shadow over their lives.

This book has been about stepping into the stories forming their imaginations and shaping their desires to offer a Christian reading on their anxieties, fears, hopes, and joys. It has also been about asking unbelievers to try on the Christian story to see how it actually makes sense of their experiences and how it speaks to their deepest aspirations and longings. But as we do this, we also need to admit that all their uncertainties will not evaporate when they try on and, Lord willing, eventually embrace the gospel story.

In light of these uncertainties, our tendency can be to timidly avoid actually inviting people to step out over the threshold of doubt to believe. After all, there remains so much that is unknown. In response, of course, we should ensure them that they are not alone in their wondering. We should encourage people to continue exploring the mysteries of faith with the aid of two thousand years of Christian reflection. But we also need to make clear that God doesn't promise to answer every question they will have (Deuteronomy 29:29). So they shouldn't wait too long; they will need to make a choice. This means *we* shouldn't wait too long either; we will need to call for them to decide—even when they haven't figured it *all* out yet. Because we won't ever have it *all* figured out.

Absolute proof isn't our lot in life, at least not for the biggest questions we humans ask. We make our biggest decisions in life—who to marry, what job to pursue, who to trust our children with, and, yes, what to believe about God—without absolute proof. We make such decisions based on our experiences, history, and the testimony of others, while living with certain nagging questions unanswered. This is what it means to grow up. As Alister McGrath has written, "A willingness to live with unresolvable questions is a mark of intellectual maturity, not a matter of logical nonsense as some unwisely regard it."[1] Being able to make such decisions wisely is the mark that a person has finally come of age.

Our advice to others in the midst of our cross-pressured existence in late modernism should be to not wait until they solve all the mysteries before deciding what they will believe about Jesus. Being stuck in limbo, refusing to step out and make a choice—one way or the other—is itself a mark of immaturity. Calling for a decision about the most important person in human history is, thus, a call to maturity. Jesus stands unrivaled in history as the only human who both claimed to be God and who—starting with his own family and friends—has had billions of people over the last two thousand years believe him. Though mysteries remain, we can boldly invite others to follow the long line of "doubting while believing" sojourners (Mark 9:24) who have gone before us, trusting in Christ as "the next right thing."

MORE THAN A STRATEGY

This book has been about navigating the challenges and opportunities to speak into this post-Christian context with a humble confidence in the power of the Spirit. Yet the shift in the primary story of our culture has not just changed the dynamics of our evangelism, discipleship, and teaching; it has also changed our imaginations.

Identifying false cultural narratives is not just about conversations with unbelievers; we need to do this to see clearly what is happening to *us. What story is actually forming our imaginations?* We best pay close attention to this question, lest we forfeit our imaginations. The "Disneys" of our age are happy to take this, along with our money. For they know stories unlock our imaginations, opening a path into our hearts (as well as our wallets!).

To navigate the challenges of being a Christian witness in a post-Christian context, we must become "the right sort of person, a person of apologetic virtue."[2] This book has attempted to model a way to engage by applying an "inside out" apologetics. This approach is dependent on gospelized imaginations, not primarily on technique. Rather than brute memorization of facts and figures, which are a Google search away, apologetics wisdom is gained as we plant our lives within the community of faith, following exemplars and by faith living the day in, day out story of the cross and resurrection.

When our imaginations have been formed by the gospel story, we retain not only our strategy but something even more powerful for our witness—our very lives. As the theologian Søren Kierkegaard once wrote, "Christ is the truth in the sense that to *be* the truth is the only true explanation of what truth is."[3] The gospel should not only shape our apologetics, but as we step into the story—singing, reading, fasting, praying, and confessing the gospel—it will shape how we spontaneously imagine each moment of our lives. As this happens, we will not only speak the truth; we will embody the truth—for which there is no greater apologetic.

NOTES

1. Alister E. McGrath, *Mere Apologetics: How to Help Seekers and Skeptics Find Faith* (Grand Rapids: Baker, 2012), 167.
2. This quote from Kevin Vanhoozer came from a prepublished paper, a version of which later appeared in his *Pictures at a Theological Exhibition: Scenes of the Church's Worship, Witness and Wisdom* (Downers Grove, IL: InterVarsity, 2016).
3. Søren Kierkegaard, *Practice in Christianity*, vol. 20 in *Kierkegaard's Writings*, ed. Howard V. Hong and Edna H. Hong (Princeton, NJ: Princeton University Press, 2013), 205; see Kevin J. Vanhoozer, *First Theology: God, Scripture and Hermeneutics* (Downers Grove, IL: IVP Academic, 2002), 365.

Acknowledgments

The idea for this book came while coauthoring *Apologetics at the Cross* with my friend Mark Allen. *Apologetics at the Cross* was written primarily as an introductory textbook, and I quickly saw the need for a shorter book written for those outside the classroom. Mark graciously blessed my effort to develop some of our key ideas and offered some helpful feedback on the manuscript.

A host of others also read at least a portion of early drafts, including Jack Carson, Micailyn Geyer, Connor Schonta, John Alsdorf, and Michael Wittmer. Each offered helpful suggestions, and I'm thankful for their advice. I am also grateful that Madison Trammel, Ryan Pazdur, and Dirk Buursma joined forces as part of Zondervan's keen editorial team to guide this project to publication. Zondervan took a chance several years ago on me as a young author, and it is a privilege to continue to work with them. Thank you to Holy Trinity Anglican Church for granting me time to complete this book and for your vision to serve the kingdom well beyond our community.

Three contemporary authors also deserve mention, for they've each discipled me through their writings and have kindly offered personal encouragement in unexpected ways. The Oxford historian and theologian Alister McGrath's work has inspired me to incorporate wisdom from the history of Christian thought to meet contemporary apologetic challenges, and it was an honor to work with him as a coeditor on the newly published *History of Apologetics.* Though Alister is certainly known in the United States, my hope is that his creative retrieval of the past and his winsome approach to engagement increasingly become a model for North American apologists.

Tim Keller, the pastor-apologist par excellence, has modeled an approach that has inspired a rising generation of ministers for a post-Christian age. As Mark and I were working on *Apologetics at the Cross*, Tim published his remarkable book *Making Sense of God*, which we were delighted to see corresponded to the "inside out" approach we were developing at the time. I'm grateful that despite the demands on his schedule, Tim has taken time on several occasions to meet with me to discuss our mutual interest in apologetics.

James K. A. Smith, the Calvin University philosopher, continues to point me back to Augustine, challenging me to think more deeply about how love and story are central to who we are as humans and to how persuasion works. As I finished this manuscript, he published *On the Road with Augustine*, which is, among other things, a kind of post-Christian apologetic that uses example and story to open the doors to Christianity. My hope is that more apologists will follow in Jamie and Augustine's footsteps on that score.

Finally, a thank you to my family. My wife, Tracy, and my children, Addison and Hudson, are a constant reminder of God's love. You are gifts that bring my life such joy.